BANANA COWBOYS

Banana Cowboys

The United Fruit Company
and the Culture of Corporate Colonialism

JAMES W. MARTIN

University of New Mexico Press · Albuquerque

First Paperback Edition, 2022
Paperback ISBN: 978-0-8263-6390-9

Library of Congress Cataloging-in-Publication Data

Names: Martin, James W., 1972– author.
Title: Banana cowboys: the United Fruit Company and the
    culture of corporate colonialism / James W. Martin.
Description: Albuquerque: University of New Mexico Press,
    [2018] | Includes bibliographical references and index. |
Identifiers: LCCN 2017019123 (print) | LCCN 2017035240
    (e-book) | ISBN 9780826359438 (e-book) | ISBN
    9780826359421 (printed case: alk. paper)
Subjects: LCSH: United Fruit Company. | Banana trade–Polit-
    ical aspects–Latin America. | Banana trade–Political
    aspects–Caribbean Area. | Corporations–Political
    aspects–United States. | Imperialism–Economic aspects. |
    United States–Foreign relations–Latin America.
Classification: LCC HD9259.B3 (e-book) | LCC HD9259.B3
    U547 2018 (print) | DDC 338.7/664804772098–dc23
LC record available at https://lccn.loc.gov/2017019123

Cover photograph: "Bringing fruit to loading platform,"
    UF54.051, Box 54, United Fruit Company Photograph
    Collection, Mss: 1 (1891–1962), U860, Baker Library.
Frontispiece: "Men Playing Billiards, ca. 1920s," UF54.004,
    Box 54, United Fruit Company Photograph Collection,
    Mss: 1 (1891–1962), U860, Baker Library.
Designed by Lisa Tremaine
Composed in Basic Sans and ITC Cushing

CONTENTS

ACKNOWLEDGMENTS

I have accrued many debts related to this book. They begin with my education at three land-grant universities in the West. Dale T. Graden and Dennis West, my Latin American studies mentors at the University of Idaho, provided the bedrock. These passionate, brilliant scholars showed a kid from small-town northern Idaho the joys of diving into a much wider world. But for their fabulous teaching, my journey would have been very different. They remain the touchstone of my scholarly commitment. At Washington State University, Eloy González, Ana María Rodríguez-Vivaldi, Bonnie Frederick, and the late John Kicza all fed my interests in history and Spanish and inspired me to go deeper. At the University of New Mexico, I encountered a bigger world and many scholars who helped me. First and foremost, this project would not have come to be without the encouragement and inspiration of Linda B. Hall, my advisor and dissertation chair. I started working on the United Fruit Company in her US–Latin American relations seminar at the University of New Mexico. It was there that I found my direction in graduate school. With her encouragement, a paper on the company's tourist marketing grew into a farther-reaching interest in the company's role in Latin America. From her I learned to appreciate that the cultural bonds of US–Latin American relations matter a great deal, and that those stories are worth telling. Several others at the University of New Mexico welcomed me warmly and influenced me in decisive ways: Judy Bieber, Elizabeth Hutchinson, Kimberly Gauderman, Patricia Risso, Jonathan Porter, Charlie Steen, Richard Robbins, and Fritz Cocron stand out in the faculty. All helped me think about empire in ways new to me. Walter Putnam and Andrew Sandoval-Strauss graciously served on my dissertation committee and offered valuable comments that helped me carry the dissertation forward. I owe Sam Truett much for his wonderful borderlands seminar and his invaluable advice as a historian of industrial frontiers. The *New Mexico Historical Review*, the state history journal housed in the UNM History Department, was my home away from home for most of my time in Albuquerque. To editor Durwood Ball, I extend my thanks for many hours in his office poring over manuscripts and learning about writing and the work of publishing history. The staff of the UNM

History Department, in particular Tony Goodrich, Helen Ferguson, Yolanda Martínez, Cindy Tyson, and Dana Ellison ran the place very well and made it warm and inviting. At the University of New Mexico, the Department of History, the Center for the Southwest, and the Latin American and Iberian Institute provided vital funding for my initial research into United Fruit.

My deep thanks go to my peers at the University of New Mexico. There are too many to list who made the journey intellectually and personally rich. Jeff Roche, John Herron, Jonathan Ablard, Gary VanValen, Adam Kane, Colin Snyder, Erik Loomis, Lincoln Bramwell, and Joseph Lenti helped me find a sense of community. At the *New Mexico Historical Review*, Jennifer Norden, Ev Schlatter, Sarah Payne, Jimmy Scholz, Kim Suina, Kyle VanHorne, Courtney Collie, and Susan Schuurman filled my days with hard work and the most intellectual fun I've ever had. My *NMHR* friend Javier Marion and his wife, Julie, graciously hosted me while I researched in New England. Blair Woodard has proved a committed friend and colleague who has helped me understand this profession much better than I would have otherwise. He is a fellow traveler through the thickets of US–Latin American relations. Jeffrey Sanders, my first office mate at the University of New Mexico, helped make hard times easy and suggested unexpected avenues of inquiry when they were most needed. I am indebted to Blair and Jeff for their in-depth readings of my work at crucial junctures.

This project came to fruition in Bozeman. I owe much to Montana State University and the community of scholars I have found here. The Department of Modern Languages and Literatures, the Dean's office of the College of Letters and Science, and the Office of Research and Economic Development have provided funding toward the completion of *Banana Cowboys*. Besides their friendship and support, Galen Brokaw, Rob Campbell, James Meyer, and Michael Reidy gave valuable comments on parts of the manuscript. Michael in particular helped me navigate the sections dealing with medicine and science, areas new to me. I am indebted to several treasured colleagues for their kindness, support, and camaraderie over the years: Bridget Kevane, Ada Giusti, Patricia Catoira, Chris Pinet, Michael Myers, Peter Tillack, Hua Li, Yanna Yannakakis, Brett Walker, Molly Todd, Billy Smith, Tim LeCain, Mary Murphy, Dale Martin, Bob Rydell, Jack Brookshire, and Omar Shehryar stand out. Outside of the university, the friendship of Erik Szemes and Nick Leib has brightened many moments. To office administrator Tracy Knudsen, thanks for ironing out a thousand logistical wrinkles related to this project with such good cheer over the years.

A broader community of scholars has also made this book possible. For their encouragement at different stages of this project, I am grateful to Sterling Evans, John Soluri, Atalia Shragai, Thomas F. O'Brien, and Marcelo Bucheli. UFCO vet and historian Clyde Stevens graciously offered pointers about the Bocas del Toro area in Panama. Jason Colby is my most kindred spirit in the little world of United Fruit scholars. Our long conversations about the nooks and crannies of our shared archival journeys in the United States and Central America have been great fun. His comments on the final manuscript were essential.

Without archivists and reference librarians, historians would be hamstrung. A multiarchival project such as this one needed lots of help in this department. Interlibrary loan offices at the University of New Mexico and Montana State University worked myriad small miracles for me, bringing troves of fundamental sources to my hands. The staff at several facilities deserve deep thanks—everywhere I worked I experienced deep professionalism and knowledge: the Bentley Historical Library in Ann Arbor, Michigan; the Baker Historical Library in Cambridge, Massachusetts; the Smathers Library in Gainesville, Florida; the Cape Cod Community College Library in Wellfleet, Massachusetts; the Francis Countway Library of Medicine in Boston; the Rauner Special Collections Library in Hanover, New Hampshire; the Library of Congress; the Archivo Nacional de Panamá; and the Archivo Nacional de Costa Rica.

I also wish to extend my thanks to the staff at the University of New Mexico Press. Editor Clark Whitehorn has been joy to work with since his prompt overnight reading of a chapter years ago at a conference. Copyeditor Jessica Knauss's excellent work has made this book a smoother read than it would have been otherwise. The peer reviewers of the manuscript, with their deep knowledge of the UFCO, played a decisive role in guiding the project to completion. Of course, what mistakes the reader may find are mine alone.

I have found a deep well of love and sustenance in my family. My parents, Jim and Jean, always stood behind me in the strange, long journey of becoming an academic. Both taught me from an early age to value and think about the past, and how we came to be where we are. Being around my mom at Fox Creek has grounded me and provided a place where I can recharge. I miss my dad and wish he could hold this book in his hands. My favorite characters in these pages remind me of him a bit. My sisters Marta, Julie, and Lorna have been a font of love all along. In Bozeman, Jack and Jane Jelinski have had my back through thick and thin since 2004. The warmth of their home has been my touchstone, and their friendship—even closer now as my in-laws—has made my life a brighter place. My many days with Jack fishing on Montana rivers and streams, talking about everything from a trout's spawning colors to Golden-Age Spanish literature, have enriched my life immensely. My brother-in-law, Adam Jelinski, graces my skies with blazing passion and creativity. My kids Alex, Max, Maya, and Sam have filled my life with love, laughter, and fun: thank you.

My wife and best friend, Kristina, grounds my life in unwavering love, kindness, curiosity, and passion. May we walk many rivers together. Thank you, Kris, for everything.

Ways of Living, Ways of Knowing

Figure I.1. Hunting expedition near Tela, Honduras, 1923. R. B. Nutter to
R. P. Strong, 12 August 1923, p. 1, United Fruit–Nutter Folder, Folder 71, Box 13,
Richard Pearson Strong Papers.

In August 1923, a United Fruit Company doctor in Tela, Honduras, wrote
to a colleague and friend in the United States who had recently visited,
and attached a photograph to the letter. In it, the author, the bespectacled
Dr. R. B. Nutter, the division's medical superintendent, poses on the left with
several dressed and hung deer, along with eight unnamed men and a pack of
hunting dogs. Four of the men appear with rifles; another four stand casually
to the right. Their serious, tired, countenances speak to the afterglow of a
good hunt and the shared rigors of such an undertaking. Besides Nutter, it is
unclear exactly who is who—although we can be sure the scene included
both Americans and Hondurans back from "another ten days [*sic*] glorious
hunt in the interior." Nutter was writing to Dr. Richard Strong, his yearly
fishing companion and, as it happened, a luminary in the field of tropical
medicine, founder of Harvard University's School of Tropical Medicine, and a

consulting head of laboratories for the company's Medical Department. In warm tones, Nutter thanked Strong for a box of gifts for his Tela hospital staff, updated him on cases both had worked on, wished his wife well, and urged him to bring the "heavy tackle" for fishing on an upcoming visit. The photo speaks to the kind of relationship the two men shared, a professional collaboration spanning a decade that had evolved into a personal friendship and a camaraderie of outdoorsmanship that linked Boston to Honduras.

This image also captures an intersection of the imperial themes and places covered in this book. The very space that allowed such an image to exist forms the foundation: the world of the US corporate colony in early twentieth-century Latin America. By the early 1920s, the United Fruit Company (UFCO) was in the midst of its most dramatic expansion around the Caribbean Basin, a moment most famously narrated in *One Hundred Years of Solitude*, where the casual visit of an innocent American butterfly collector to the sleepy, war-ravaged village of Macondo precipitates a series of stunning transformations. Life behind the *gallinero electrificado*—the company's electrified chicken-fence separating the breezy verandahs, swimming pools, and wide avenues of the American zone from the town—moves along aloof from its surroundings, a placid gloss over the company's biblical powers of transformation and destruction and its brutalization of laborers.[1] Like the inhabitants of Macondo or of the other literary and real Latin American places invaded by US banana companies, those who engineered the UFCO's expansion and those who witnessed it—critics and apologists alike—marveled at these precipitous changes.[2] Incorporated in 1899 out of several parent companies, United Fruit soon established tropical divisions around the region. The UFCO's twin business strategies at the time, vertical integration and horizontal expansion, led it to capture as much of the production and distribution chain as possible and to expand its holdings over a wide geographic area.[3] These guiding principles reduced the company's vulnerability to a number of threats: tropical weather, plant disease, political difficulties with host nations, and business competition. By the 1920s, the UFCO was the largest agricultural enterprise in the world. Its nine major divisions around the region (Cuba, Guatemala, Honduras, Costa Rica, Panama, Colombia, and Jamaica) boasted company towns complete with hospitals, laboratories, ice and power plants, commissaries, social clubs, athletic facilities, bungalows, and swimming pools. Segregated from these amenities in the "white" or later

"American" zones and fanning out into thousands of acres of hinterland were much more rudimentary accommodations provided to the black West Indians and local Hispanic mestizos who did the heavy work on plantations, railroads, and wharves. Tying all of these nodes together were hundreds of miles of railway, more than one hundred steamships of the company's "Great White Fleet," and a state-of-the-art wireless telegraphy network.

This book focuses our attention on an underappreciated linchpin of this vast empire, the skilled laborers and white-collar men who worked on the "banana frontier." Prevailing attitudes during the first three decades of the century held that such positions could only be competently held by white, Anglo-Saxon males. What makes their story remarkable is that the UFCO had to build its sprawling empire at time when medical and popular perception harbored serious doubts about whether whites could healthily inhabit the tropics at all. Much of the story that follows examines various ways that the company—and often its employees themselves—fostered a sense of personal connection with challenging tropical surroundings and thereby sought to reconcile white bodies and minds to tropical life. In one sense, it is the story of how management attempted to channel those encounters and delineate the boundaries between white American men and "tropical" peoples and landscapes. At its heart, however, I focus on how those individuals experienced these "close encounters of empire" and enacted scientific and cultural imperatives over their surroundings.[4] Creating a sense of tropical Americanness was the beating heart of US corporate expansion in the Caribbean Basin. In the pages that follow, I track several ways this cultural process played out on the ground. These company men were in a curious position: often invested with power, but also vulnerable in fundamental ways. They existed in between the corporation and its domination of tropical peoples and places, at once subjects and agents. In the pages that follow, I attempt to capture that in-betweenness.

Historical scholarship on the United Fruit Company itself has done much to illuminate its crucial role in US–Latin American relations. Several works provide valuable insight into how the corporation transformed landscapes and social relations in Ecuador, Honduras, Costa Rica, Guatemala, Cuba, Panama, and Colombia, both within the period of this study and beyond.[5] Historians have established the close relationship between shifting productive geographies and the creation of consumer markets and cultural currents in the United States.[6] Other work has situated the growth of banana enclaves within a broader context of US economic, political, and cultural involvement in the region.[7] Most of these works and others have also emphasized the often contentious relations between the company and its nonwhite laborers.[8] Several of these works detail some aspect of the company's influence on the region's political processes, with others covering the best-known of these instances, the CIA- and UFCO-backed Guatemalan coup d'état of 1954.[9] The robust literature on United Fruit has largely sidestepped the culture of UFCO expatriate communities, with the exceptions of historians Jason Colby, Ronald Harpelle, and Atalia Shragai, who have undertaken important research on this topic.[10] These scholars provide valuable insight into the lived experience and cultural dynamics of US–Latin American relations, and relate those dynamics to a wider context of Western colonialism. *Banana Cowboys* amends this valuable work by delving into several underappreciated themes.

First, this study places a corporate-driven colonial project at its core rather than one driven by the state.[11] State-driven projects that involved thousands of US expatriates living in the tropics during that period have received well-deserved scholarly attention, covering in particular insular military occupations and the work of the Isthmian Canal Commission, charged with constructing the Panama Canal from 1904 until 1914. These works offer vital insight into the problems of governing white Americans living abroad, and reveal that keeping such colonies healthy, productive, and dedicated to imperial projects could prove vexatious, to say the least.[12] United Fruit's colonial project was similarly fraught, and the story of its rise and decline before the 1930s reveals that the power of US capital, as it operated on the ground and in the minds of its thousands of American employees, was riven with internal tensions and contradictions.[13] United Fruit was not alone among US corporations in the region, nor was it alone as an agent in a broader field of imperial encounters. But the size, scale, and duration of its enterprise and the colonies built around it set it apart from all of its contemporaries, even a state project as massive as the Panama Canal. This corporation's massive foray into progressive-era colonial government offers an opportunity to broaden our understanding of the scale and scope of US intervention in Latin America in the decades following 1898.

Like many images from colonial contexts, Nutter's photograph is powerful in its loaded silences, elisions, and obscured hierarchies. Who did the heavy lifting? Who hauled, dressed, and hung the deer? Who cooked the food, pitched tents, and carried provisions? Perhaps the gentlemanly Dr. Nutter and his friends enjoyed some immersion in "working at play," as one historian of leisure in the United States has put it, but it is far more likely that the white-collar expedition involved the labor of servants.[14] The image reminds us of the preponderant fact of United Fruit's banana- and sugar-producing enterprise in these decades: a racialized division of labor, where a cadre of white managers and technicians oversaw a much larger body of "tropical" workers, usually black West Indians and Hispanic mestizos. Scholarship on United Fruit has done much to document shifts in the company's labor recruitment strategies, but very little of this work has focused on the role of white employees in that hierarchy, except in passing.[15] A deeper understanding of the situation of subordinate white employees within that system is a central contribution of this study. In most narratives, the company's white cadres emerge in one dimension, as unthinking agents of the corporation's will, assumed to be defending its interests and enacting their own superiority over nonwhite Others. Undoubtedly there were many who did just that. An ideology of white supremacy undergirded the racial stratification of the enterprise, and explicitly restricted supervisory and most technical functions to white Anglo-Saxons, who were measured to some extent by how well they could manage "colored" labor. Colby's work has done the most to undermine the misperception that this white/nonwhite color bar represented a transplantation of Jim Crow segregation or a Southern culture of race relations to overseas plantation enclaves. In fact, the necessity of white supervision over peoples of color enjoyed broad support among white Americans, North and South, and United Fruit itself was dominated by New Englanders, not Southerners, as one recent book on the company claims.[16] *Banana Cowboys* focuses on various ways the "custom" of such a color bar had to be invented, constructed, and shored up continually, in settings as disparate as camps deep in the bush, plantation fields, company towns, and company laboratories and hospitals.[17] One of my arguments is that this process was essential to United Fruit's effort to "culturally conscript" its white employees to a broader imperial project of regional transformation.[18] The experience of men who worked for the company in these years suggests that their allegiance to this project was uneven.

Despite their privileged place within United's division of labor and the racial ideology that made them indispensable to company operations,

subordinate whites often found themselves at odds with company management. *Banana Cowboys* offers a crucial new dimension to a well-established
literature on labor relations in fruit enclaves by focusing on this largely overlooked set of actors. One of its principal arguments is that tensions between
management and "first-class" employees played a central role in the genesis
of its corporate-welfare campaign. As corporate power burgeoned in the early
twentieth-century United States, many concerns invested in shaping their
workers' lives outside of the workplace, usually by providing social and recreational opportunities designed to boost morale and loyalty and to burnish
a company's public image.[19] As such a corporate sensibility traveled south, it
amounted to what Colby fittingly terms "corporate colonialism."[20] Histories
of United Fruit and of early twentieth-century plantation regimes more
broadly have provided much insight into the strategies of working peoples to
negotiate with US enterprises, from informal negotiation, labor organization,
strikes, political mobilization, cultural resistance, and mobility.[21] But the
predicament of white expatriates has, perhaps understandably, remained
marginal to these narratives. Even in a colonial context in which management bolstered its cultural and racial affinity with upper-tier employees, the
latter were keenly aware of bread-and-butter issues and fought for their interests either bureaucratically or by deploying those strategies familiar to any
labor historian. Taking the Costa Rica division as a lens, this book begins by
showing that throughout this period, company men organized into committees, aggressively petitioned management, negotiated for improvements in
working and living conditions and better pay, demanded vacations, and pro-
tested retrenchments. Some North American railway engineers even organized a strike in 1907. Through it all the correspondence of company men
working in this and other tropical divisions sheds light on a persistently poor
climate within the company's ranks. White employees bent on organizing
could count on being summarily dismissed from their jobs and hounded out
of the host country by the authorities. The tension between management and
white labor might not have risen to the level of brutality experienced by nonwhite laborers, but as a matter of managerial attention, it most certainly
carried much weight. It was that tension within the white Anglo-Saxon ranks
that exercised the most decisive influence on the shape of United Fruit's foray
into corporate colonialism.

    More than a generation of scholarship has documented the intimate ties between Western colonial ventures and the creation of knowledge and systems of meaning, whether it be artistic or scientific.[22] This salient vein of imperial practice runs through the heart of Nutter's hunting picture. The personal bond between Dr. Nutter and Dr. Strong represented one of many linkages between the banana company and a much wider culture of scientific inquiry—in this case, in the field of tropical medicine. Nutter himself formed a key part of United Fruit's Medical Department, instituted in 1912 with the mission of mobilizing tropical medicine in the service of the corporation's interests in the region. Soon the company's tropical divisions formed essential nodes in a rapidly expanding network of tropical research stations and laboratories thoroughly enmeshed with the US government, the administration of other tropical possessions and protectorates, and the North American academic community, itself ever more tied to the service of US interests abroad. Strong himself embodies these intricate relationships: a veteran of the US administration of the Philippines earlier in the century, he was instrumental in forming Harvard's School of Tropical Medicine in 1913–1914. His relationship with United Fruit men cemented the school's feasibility, for the company's network of hospitals and laboratories provided a vast field of study for Strong, his colleagues, and their students.[23] Scholarly attention to the company's medical work has been scant—though valuable—either correctly noting that the system was designed to service primarily its expatriate colonies or as an instance of the company's paternalistic discourse.[24] The overarching medical project of company doctors revolved around what one scholar of American tropical medicine has termed "the exoneration of the tropics," that is, establishing that tropical environments were not deleterious to the health of Caucasian bodies—a fundamental revision of previous medical thought. Company enclaves were one place where doctors engineered this paradigm shift, and their work had a profound impact on the shape of fruit-company colonialism. For one matter, the way medicine was practiced and medical knowledge developed in the company's tropics played a key role in constituting and justifying its color bar. Much more than just as public discourse, corporate tropical medicine functioned as a series of constitutive practices that made social realities rather than merely "discovered" them. One of this book's contributions, then, is to relate the creation of knowledge to the practice of corporate empire on the ground, a largely unexplored terrain in the field of US–Latin American relations.

Nutter's hunting picture reminds us of another theme in this book: that
employees often mediated their relationship with their surroundings through
leisure and exploration. They often ranged far afield and avidly delved into
their surroundings. I explore this theme by focusing on a particular form of
leisure that drew in several expatriates from the company's sphere: the amateur pursuit of knowledge—in particular relating to natural science—
ethnography, and archaeology. Historians of science have generated a significant literature on the key relationship of such activities to Western expansion in various contexts, and I add to that literature by examining amateur
science in the context of corporate colonialism.[25] Ranging about the hinterland around enclaves in pursuit of biological specimens, archaeological artifacts, and ethnographic experiences did more than feed the personal interest
of individual hobbyists. No mere tourists, these individuals formed a key set
of linkages between the UFCO and the world of professional knowledge production in the United States. Often their activities intertwined seamlessly
with the company's interests; sometimes they led in directions not necessarily friendly to the positions of management. *Banana Cowboys* offers fresh
insight into the importance of amateur intellectual inquiry to colonial projects. How company men (and a few women) generated knowledge about their
milieus tells an overlooked tale of US empire in Latin America.

And then there are the men who inhabit Nutter's hunting photo and the
heart of *Banana Cowboys*. A world of gendered expectations and norms shaped
their experiences in fundamental ways. A certain culture of white masculinity on a corporate frontier undergirds this photograph. At a time when medical science was far from unanimous on the question of whether whites could
healthily inhabit the tropics for any length of time, gender ideology acquired
great currency in the company's sphere, as it did on many a frontier of empire.
This study adds a fresh insight into an ongoing discussion on the centrality
of gender ideology in US expansion more broadly.[26] The racial stratification
in company colonies required that white overseers and managers perform
their superiority in gendered ways. In other words, how one showed he was
a man at work and in off hours defined his place in these curious social environments. In the early twentieth century, then, a racialized cult of male vitality grounded in physical activity and the domination of tropical nature and
peoples took shape at the heart of workplace culture in the fruit company's
tropical sphere. North Americans of all professional stripes crafted various
gendered armatures for confronting anxieties about the climate and for

making sense of their relationship with the vast nonwhite workforce, itself usually viewed with no small apprehension. Company management worked hard to foster such a gendered culture in specific ways, and as such being the "right sort of man" functioned as a mechanism of what Mary Renda, in her recent history of the US occupation of Haiti, has termed "cultural conscription."[27] As in Haiti under the aegis of the US military, subordinate white men in United Fruit's sphere became the object of a concerted effort to reconcile them to a United States–driven colonial project infused with an ethos of uplift and governance. In United Fruit's sphere, a metaphor of frontier conquest, with antecedents in the western United States and Rooseveltian overtones, came to pervade workplace culture and define the norms of proper masculinity. Like the amateur explorers and collectors who understood their work as a benevolent expansion of the frontiers of knowledge, many of these men found meaning for their work and leisure within a frontier metaphor.

A word on the central term, *banana cowboy*, is in order. In the UFCO world, *cowboy* was shorn of its associations with reckless behavior. A banana cowboy was a tough, efficient herder of fruit. He was a white-collar employee, by the 1920s usually college-educated, who worked on the land, wore a Stetson, rode a horse or mule, often carried a pistol, and managed nonwhite laborers. The moniker was usually applied to those white Anglo-Saxons who worked in the UFCO's agricultural division, but it could also apply to those working in other areas. Marston Bates, an entomologist who figures in this story, later recalled his days as a banana cowboy in the late 1920s, although he never worked a farm. His use of the term years later suggests that it enjoyed broad currency in the company's world, even among technical professionals. One need not call himself such to embody the ideal. Everett Brown, a draftsman, never wrote of himself as such, but thoroughly embraced the company's frontier-flavored masculine culture. This urban northeasterner's embrace of rugged fieldwork on the company's far-flung frontiers will have much to tell us about the UFCO's corporate culture. Surely there were many employees who never described themselves as banana cowboys. The term is useful, however, because it captures an essential part of the UFCO ethos in the early twentieth century, the zenith of an Anglo-Saxon–headed division of labor. The racial and gender associations swirling around the term *cowboy* provide a useful encapsulation of what tropical work meant for many white American men who worked for United Fruit.

Finally, *Banana Cowboys* contributes to an ongoing transnational, cultural turn in historical scholarship on US–Latin American relations and on US expansion more broadly. A series of works that examine "contact zones" and "close encounters of empire" has deeply influenced this book.[28] Casting such a gaze on the charged colonial spaces of the export enclave, the tourist frontier, the research station, or the military occupation has done much to show how processes of empire—both within and independent of powerful institutions—formed a vital part in the formation of American identity. United Fruit's early twentieth-century colonies were important nodes in this suite of encounters, and being immersed in their social realities led company men to construct their own particular tropical Americanness. This book emphasizes that the creation of such systems of meaning was of a vital part of corporate colonialism. Another compelling thrust of contact-zone scholarship has been to bring a rigorous consideration of microhistory and the lived experience of empire to the fore. These perspectives illustrate the many cultural conduits through which places "out there"—whether in the US West, Alaska, the Pacific Rim, or Latin America—became constituted as vital spheres of US interest.[29] The cases that I take up here suggest some of the ways that the thousands of Americans who worked for the company in these years carried their tropical experiences home with them. One implication of this attention to subjectivities in contact zones is to complicate and variegate "dichotomous political-economic models that see only domination and resistance, exploiters and exploited."[30] This study does not lose track of the overarching fact that United Fruit did indeed dominate and exploit landscapes and people to the end of extracting profit; it adds to this picture that even those white North Americans charged with being "the exploiters" were subjected to a colonial regime that attempted—not always successfully—to mold and discipline them. The relationship of white Anglo-Saxons to the company's colonial projects thus provides a lens into the fractures and vexations running through those efforts all along, despite their significant success from a business standpoint. The business of US empire did not need to be monolithic in order to succeed.

Sources and Organization

Banana Cowboys weaves these imperial themes through its five chapters. It does not focus on one particular enclave, but touches on several. It is also concerned with the first three decades of the century, a period characterized by Anglo-Saxon dominance in the practice and rhetoric of the UFCO. By the early 1930s, this bar had begun to break down around the company's sphere for a series of reasons I encapsulate in the conclusion. It is this heyday of the *bananera* (banana company), its "Conquest of the Tropics," that I take as my focus. Those researching the UFCO must work around a daunting obstacle: the lack of a central company archive. United Fruit has assiduously shielded itself from the prying eyes of scholars, a point best evidenced by Philippe Bourgois's chilling tale of the disappearance of a trove of company records from the Bocas del Toro division he witnessed in the 1980s.[31] The Lorenzo Dow Baker collection held at Cape Cod Community College contains correspondence essential to understanding the Boston Fruit Company and the advent of the UFCO. A large collection of company letterbooks in the Archivo Nacional de Costa Rica in San José offers the best glimpse we have into the internal workings of a tropical division over the course of decades. The UFCO's own publications—especially the *Annual Reports to Stockholders*, the employee magazine *Unifruitco* (published between 1925 and 1931 and again from 1948 to 1958), and the *Annual Reports of the Medical Department*—form another important source base. I have also drawn from collections of personal papers of employees and scientists who were in some way affiliated with the UFCO, including two previously untapped correspondence collections housed in US archives. These different bodies of documentation at once limit the geographical and chronological scope of this study, but they have also enabled me to tell stories suggestive of broader dynamics. Wherever possible, I have tried to let the experience of individuals carry the narrative; a colonial project such as this one, it seems to me, acquires clearer focus and richer hues of nuance when seen through the eyes of those in the midst of it.

Chapter 1, "From Scramblers for Fruit to Banana Empire, 1870–1930," provides background for the analysis at the heart of *Banana Cowboys*. It narrates the rise of the UFCO's main parent branches, Minor Cooper Keith's Central American interests and, primarily, the Boston Fruit Company (BFC). The challenges the BFC faced in the 1880s and 1890s led its leadership to embrace the twin strategies of vertical integration and horizontal expansion. Even with limited scope and capital, the UFCO's progenitors sought to hedge their business by capturing as many links in the banana trade as possible, from cultivation through distribution in the United States. Technological and organizational innovations during those years collapsed physical distance between tropical production zones and US consumers, and set the stage for a vast investment in company colonies abroad.

Chapter 2, "Tropical Vexations," focuses on the genesis of that colonial project: the company's always fraught effort to uphold a division of labor in the tropics governed by an ideology of white supremacy. The chapter begins with the rationale behind that racialized division of labor, and echoes Jason Colby's argument that it was more than a custom imported from other recent American plantation experiences or from the Jim Crow South. Racial stratification rested on a series of essentialist constructions of "negro" and "native" labor and Anglo-Saxon leadership that had to be continually reconstituted. At a time when the only acceptable supervisors and technicians were white Anglo-Saxons, however, managers on the ground in the tropics confronted stubborn difficulties with this class of labor. Far from comprising a uniformly loyal, passive workforce aligned with management, these so-called first-class employees chronically frustrated the company's leadership with demands for better living and working conditions, widespread complaining about low pay, clumsy or domineering management, and lack of vacation time. Tropical diseases, on-the-job alcohol abuse and, occasionally, left-leaning labor organizing soured workplace culture or disrupted operations altogether. Disease, for one, posed serious difficulties for whites in the tropics and spurred a significant company investment in medical infrastructure. Medical constructions of temperateness played an important role in fixing the special status of whites in the tropics. Aside from illness, many Americans working for the company in these years found building a tropical career deeply frustrating. Years of struggling to recruit and retain the "right sort" of men in this environment led managers to become the chief advocates for a greater investment in corporate welfare, and it was only after Victor Cutter, a longtime tropical veteran, rose to the company's presidency in 1924 that "divisional betterment" hit high gear. The impetus behind this instance of corporate colonialism, then, grew out of circumstances and negotiations on the ground rather than as a template to be imposed from afar, like that of Henry Ford's failed rubber colony in Brazil in the 1920s.[32]

The next chapter, "Corporate Welfarism Meets the Tropics," turns to the landscape and lifestyle that resulted from this contentious relationship: the company towns and expatriate communities that were so striking to contemporary observers. Here I consider the role of company towns in combating the problems of maintaining large cadres of US employees in the lowland tropics. The built environment of these places functioned as one part of the company's effort to project "spectacles of corporate modernity," to borrow historian Ricardo Salvatore's term.[33] Those spectacles confronted the problem of cultural and social isolation among expatriate employees, personnel issues that posed difficulties for the company. Retention efforts rested on creating townscapes that appealed to the sensibilities of North American employees and rooted them in the company's broader mission. Town layouts, public spaces, and landscaping choices in tropical divisions projected American sensibilities onto the physical environment. Transplanting a template of small-town US life into an untamed environment provided United Fruit a chance to sell tropical life to its domestic employees and others. The company's landscape and town designs projected an image of nature made orderly, sanitary, productive, and visually appealing by US enterprise. The built environment also laid down a spatial template in which racial and social hierarchies were to be enacted, displayed, and reinforced. These spaces functioned as points of contact between US inhabitants and their surroundings. On the one hand, US colonies were insular, like García Márquez's Macondo chicken coop. Employees and the company together attempted to fashion patterns of community and family life that shrank the conceptual distance between distant tropical divisions and the United States and maintained racialized boundaries, as Ronald Harpelle has documented.[34] On the other hand, Atalia Shragai has shown that at the heart of life in these enclaves lay an intense, daily engagement with foreign surroundings and peoples, particularly after the 1920s.[35] Beyond providing living spaces and services, corporate colonialism in the UFCO's sphere involved a concerted effort to shape the attitudes and perceptions of its expatriates, in part by enlisting them in the projection of a spectacle of American modernity to workers and neighboring populations.

As United Fruit set about building colonies around the Caribbean Basin, the question of human health in tropical lowland colonies became of prime importance to its effort to control laborers and employees. Chapter 4, "Wandering Foci of Infection," takes up this instance of corporate medical colonialism. The company formed a medical department (the UFCOMD) in 1912 and soon thereafter hired a cadre of tropical-medicine experts who had cut their teeth on the Panama Canal project. In the following decades, these doctors made the company's burgeoning network of hospitals, laboratories, and field dispensaries a vital node in a wider field of inquiry into tropical health. Researchers and doctors from the US government and academic community took advantage of a massive population subject to the company's will, and kept a steady traffic through company divisions. Their collaboration with company doctors served a vital disciplinary function by opening workers' lives and bodies to examination and surveillance. Their work, which tended to pathologize racial differences, also gave medical imprimatur to the company's racialized division of labor and society. The medical distinction between tropical and temperate was thoroughly enmeshed in the colonial context of company enclaves. As doctors came to better understand the etiology of diseases in the early twentieth century, they began to identify "economic diseases" (those with an impact on business) and to construct a series of causes, mostly based on arguments about the link between behavior, morality, and health. The company's medical project played a vital role in cementing the racial differences within the company's labor structure. It also tied the company to a wider network of scientific influence in the region.

Chapter 5, "Becoming Banana Cowboys," takes up the company's effort to reconcile Caucasian "temperate" employees to extended life in these problematic tropical environments and enlist their loyalty to a broader mission of uplift and modernization. The disciplinary bent of the UFCO's medical colonialism wrapped up all in its midst, including white employees, although in far different degree than laborers of color. The company's field of operations lay within climates that many Western doctors considered insalubrious for whites—not exactly "white men's graveyards" since recent advances in parasitology, but still the object of older climatological worries and the moralistic bent of early twentieth-century tropical medicine. White American men, especially, ran the risk of falling into laziness and vice—character failings more typical of so-called tropical races I discuss in the previous chapter. Preoccupations about the potentially debilitating or emasculating effects of the tropics rippled into the company's culture and lingered there—anxieties evidenced by the company's continual assurances that American employees could live healthy lives and raise robust families in tropical divisions. Avoiding the dangers of tropical residence involved much more than doctors and laboratories—gender identity mattered a great deal, and the company exploited it. An ethos of strenuous masculinity, lived by employees and fostered in various ways by the company, could offset the potentially emasculating and alienating effects of routine office work—fears exaggerated by the presence of black and mestizo laborers. That masculine identity, often structured around frontier imagery from the US West, presented white-collar employees with a way to navigate their place in the labor hierarchy and offered transformative possibilities to some. Behind its empowering dimension, however, the manly culture of the banana cowboy served an important disciplinary function as a mechanism of cultural conscription, bracketing white failure as well as success in its idiom.

Banana Cowboys continues its consideration of the cultural dimension of corporate colonialism with "Serving Science on the Side." This final chapter examines certain forms of employee interaction with the tropical milieu that existed at a sometimes blurry confluence of personal leisure, knowledge generation and circulation, and forwarding the company's interest. Here I focus on the amateur work of several individuals whose private interests in archaeology, ethnology, and natural sciences helped cement the UFCO's relationship with the world of institutional knowledge production in the United States. The chapter begins by discussing the archaeological hobby in the company's sphere, from the famed ruins of Quiriguá, Guatemala, to the Ulua Valley of Honduras and the area around the company's sugar divisions in Cuba. For some adventuresome Anglo-American employees, work for United Fruit afforded the opportunity to take in their surroundings through particular forms of exploration akin to colonial expeditions to parts of far-off undiscovered lands. Such travels danced in the shadow of a long tradition of Victorian-era exploration of "darkest Africa," Asia, Latin America, and the polar regions, and the more recent and highly publicized expeditions of Theodore Roosevelt and Percy Fawcett in Amazonia. The expeditions of F. H. Baron, company agent at large, provide a window into pseudoscientific amateur exploration. Baron's travels along the Western littoral of Central America helped determine where United Fruit would open new divisions in the 1920s. On one voyage, Baron retraced the steps and mission of Richard Ogelsby Marsh, a flamboyant figure whose attempt to find the "white Indians of the Darién" had graced US popular culture in the middle part of the decade. Baron's interaction with landscapes and peoples and his status as a minor company hero shows that the masculine ethos of the colonial explorer enjoyed cultural currency, at least in the eyes of Baron himself and management, which publicized his exploits to American employees at large. The chapter also examines the travels and hobbies of Marston Bates, a company entomologist in Honduras and Guatemala, who later became renowned in US scientific circles and a successful popular author on all matters tropical. An avid insect collector since childhood, the intensely curious Bates maintained both for his own interest and that of the company a steady stream of written communication and taxonomic submissions with entomologists working for the United States Department of Agriculture. He was also an amateur historian, and fused his travels as a company agent with exploration and writing about historical sites in Guatemala. These cases offer insight into corporate colonialism as a cultural project that transcended the boundaries of the enclave and bound the company's presence in Latin America to a broader idiom and practice of empire.

In the end, the fractures and costs of corporate colonialism proved too much for the early twentieth-century model of an exclusively Anglo-Saxon–led fruit empire. A conclusion brackets this study, discussing the transformation of United Fruit's racial division of labor, a process that had roots in the 1920s. Labor historians, in particular Philippe Bourgois and Jason Colby, have described the shifting racial terrain of the company's Central American divisions, with conclusions suggestive of broader dynamics at play in all of its holdings.[36] In its mainland divisions, managers initially favored black West Indians, but over the course of the 1910s and 1920s, steadily Hispanized its ranks. The rationale behind this shift was twofold: racial segmentation of the workforce was meant to stifle labor's ability to organize, and the hiring and promotion of locals rather than black West Indians answered a frequent demand of political leaders in countries where United Fruit operated. Global economic crisis, plant disease, labor militancy, and the rise of nationalism around the Caribbean Basin have been well documented as factors that compelled the company to retreat from its high public profile, divest from direct production, seek new accommodations with local governments, and shift its locus of production away from the Caribbean littoral to the Pacific lowlands.[37] This book contributes to this picture by taking into account the role of corporate welfare and white employees in this terrain. By the 1930s, the company's fraught relationship with its subordinate whites and the sheer cost of recruiting, retaining, and disciplining so many of them contributed in no small measure to a significant alteration of its personnel policies. In short, economic necessity eroded what had once been a formidable color bar. Starting in the 1920s, Hispanic nationals began to gain access to technical and supervisory positions, and by the 1940s and beyond, the company's ranks looked far different than they had during the first decades of United Fruit's existence. The shape of company enclaves as zones of intercultural contact also shifted in the 1940s and 1950s, becoming less insular, as Atalia Shragai's work on UFCO colonies has shown.[38] This shift should not be seen as a triumph of racial equality, however, since the limits and blinders of the company's white North American managers continued to exercise a decisive influence on United Fruit's relationships with Latin America.[39]

This study of the cultural dimensions of Anglo-Saxon corporate colonialism illuminates how US empire worked on the ground and in the minds of those who at once implemented it and were shaped by it. It demonstrates concretely how ways of knowing, living in, and enjoying the tropics informed the culture of white-collar work in the racially stratified world of the early twentieth-century banana enclave. Whenever possible, *Banana Cowboys* pauses to consider the ambivalences and fissures in what has most often been portrayed as a unified edifice of US power abroad. The famed banana company's early twentieth-century colonial experiment provides a rich territory for exploring the anxieties and fractures that scholars have found at the heart such projects in several colonial contexts.[40] This study reveals that the spaces of that experiment were arenas in which the boundaries between white "temperate" Americanness and nonwhite "tropical" otherness were at once constituted and challenged. Establishing a US corporation as a part of this wider cultural history of empire is the underlying objective of this book. Although its political meddling, repressive labor practices, heavy-handed relationships with independent farmers, and ecological fallout have been explored, it is in the realm of the day-to-day practices of empire that the company's nature attains a fuller focus.

CHAPTER ONE

From Scramblers for Fruit to Banana Empire, 1870–1930

The tropical world of the banana company town has generated many fictionalized accounts.[1] O. Henry's *Cabbages and Kings* (1904) sets a series of tales in Coralio, a sleepy coastal town in the first literary "banana republic," Anchuria. Political intrigues occasionally visit Coralio, and the American presence, besides a few purchasing agents for the Vesuvius Company, is confined to a coterie of ne'er-do-wells and intriguers, some of them given in to the indolent charms of the "lotus"—the languid allure of the tropics.[2] The most famous literary banana town, Macondo, serves as a central motif in Colombian Nobel laureate Gabriel García Márquez's *One Hundred Years of Solitude* (1967), where the casual visit of an innocent American butterfly collector to the sleepy, war-ravaged village precipitates a series of stunning transformations. The ostensible lepidopterist, Mr. Herbert, invited to dine with the Buendía family, tries a curiously delicious fruit. Cloaked in his scientific innocence, the family pays the odd outsider little mind. Soon after his departure, the banana company arrives like a force of nature and Macondo becomes an overnight export-driven boomtown. Life behind the bananera's gallinero electrificado—the electrified chicken-fence separating the breezy verandahs, swimming pools, and wide avenues of the American zone from the old town—moves along aloof from its surroundings, a placid gloss over the company's biblical powers of transformation and destruction and its brutalization of laborers.[3] These literary prototypes, Coralio and Macondo, could bracket this study of United Fruit: on one end, the backwater with one toe in the international fruit trade; on the other end, the maximum expression of US corporate penetration in early twentieth-century Latin America, the full-blown banana enclave, its fate intricately intertwined with markets and decisions made across the sea. The brackets surround the last two decades of the nineteenth century (the United Fruit Company was incorporated in 1899) and the early 1930s, when global economic depression forced a series of transformations in the UFCO's enterprise. Over the course

of those years, the banana trade went from an ad hoc, windfall-based trade
to the province of highly capitalized, vertically integrated corporations with
vast reach and technological capabilities exceeding those of most nations.
The UFCO stood at the apex of this remade world. *Banana Cowboys*'s stories
focus on this period, and the current chapter lays the groundwork by surveying the origin and rise of United Fruit's empire.

The motives and forces that drove the UFCO's creation and expansion
start in the 1870s and 1880s, when its parent companies made their first
forays into the tropical commodity trade. United Fruit was a part of a larger
wave of mergers around the turn of the century that arose from the introduction, in 1899, of the New Jersey–based holding company, a revolutionary corporate mechanism that allowed for more highly capitalized, farther-reaching
combinations than ever before. The UFCO was initially formed as the combination of the two largest banana traders of the time, the Boston Fruit Company (BFC), owned and managed by Andrew Preston and Lorenzo Dow
Baker, and the railroad and banana empire of Minor Cooper Keith. The former had spent fifteen years expanding its reach in Jamaica, building a significant banana fleet of its own, and consolidating its hold over fruit distribution
in the US Northeast. Keith had been building railroads in Central America
since the 1870s and had amassed a series of agricultural properties in Costa
Rica and Colombia, which then included present-day Panama.

Looking back on the company's origins in its prosperous 1910s and 1920s,
United Fruit publicists and apologists described the company's rise in heady
terms, as a manifestation of the US mission to modernize and uplift a backward region, complete with the racial overtones common to expansionist
rhetoric of the time. Frederick Upham Adams, writing a classic study of the
UFCO in 1914, prognosticated that the future inhabitants of the lowland tropics would bow with gratitude before the company's achievements, and "will
realize that all this was made possible by the American citizens who were
the pioneers in this Conquest of the Tropics." Adams emphasized "the quick-
ening spirit of Yankee enterprise" as the driving force behind the company's
expansion.[4] United Fruit emerged not from the racially or culturally construed energies of its founders, but from a concrete set of circumstances
those hard-nosed Yankee businessmen faced in the banana trade of the late
nineteenth century. The difficulties these smaller enterprises faced, in particular how they learned to grow and move millions of tons of perishable

cargo over long distances, decisively shaped the first true US corporate empire in Latin America. By the mid-1880s, the future founders of United Fruit realized that the profitable movement of bananas into US markets from an enormous tropical hinterland depended on steady, measurable supplies of fruit and a tightly coordinated transportation system. To their eye the only acceptable way to organize such a system rested on a white, Anglo-Saxon–managed division of labor. Documentation on the internal operations of Keith's enterprises is scanty, but the BFC has left a significant collection of internal correspondence going back to the 1880s. A glimpse into the origins and expansion of the UFCO and a principle parent company provides vital background to the stories to come and offers insight into different dimensions of the transition from family-operated firm to transnational corporation in the Caribbean Basin.

The Roots of the Tropical Fruit Trade

Bananas, an Old-World cultivar with long roots in the New World, began arriving in US ports in the mid-nineteenth century as ancillary cargoes to more reliable commodities such as sugar. In the age of sail, the fruit's perishability ensured its sporadic arrival to US consumers and its status as a rare luxury. The parent companies of the UFCO moved into banana production from their roots in transportation. In 1871, New York–born Minor Cooper Keith, who cut his teeth raising cattle along the Texas coast, arrived in Costa Rica under contract to build a railroad linking the central valley to the Caribbean coast, a titanic engineering achievement that was only completed in 1890.[5] With a strong foothold in Puerto Limón, the country's Atlantic port, Keith sought to make his railroad pay by shipping bananas north. In 1872, he sent his first consignments from Costa Rica to New Orleans. By the late 1880s, the basic features of the banana enclave were in place under his purview. Keith had acquired several large parcels of land around Limón, which he dedicated mostly to bananas. He introduced the Gros Michel, the first commercially viable banana, a first step toward standardization in the trade. Although he purchased much fruit from independent growers, Jamaican workers, managed by white overseers, formed the heart of the labor force. Keith formed separate companies to handle banana cultivation in Colombia, which would later form the UFCO's Santa Marta and Bocas del Toro divisions. His various enterprises made up the western axis of the banana trade, one running between Central America and Colombia to New Orleans.

The eastern axis, based primarily in Jamaica, would be dominated by Boston-area interests. In 1870, Cape Cod–based merchant sea captain Lorenzo Dow Baker became one of the first who realized that the tasty, nourishing fruit could fetch a fair price on northern wharves. Baker acquired lands in Jamaica, but like Keith, he depended on independent growers to establish the trade.[6] With greater supplies reaching US markets in the 1880s and 1890s, fruit became cheaper and more popular with the consuming public, thereby intensifying the trade. To take advantage of the growing commodities trade of the 1880s, future United Fruit cofounders Andrew Preston and Baker—Baker a shipper/grower and Preston a Boston fruit salesman—joined forces. Preston's and Baker's business relationship united two geographies and three areas of expertise: banana cultivation, an understanding of transoceanic shipping, and access to North American markets. By the late 1880s, the Bakers (by then son Lorenzo Jr., known as "Loren," had joined the business as a fruit broker and plantation supervisor in Port Morant, Jamaica) had a solid foothold in tropical fruit cultivation. Unlike Keith, the Bakers and Preston maintained a lively written correspondence from these years, which provides insight into the internal decisions behind the creation of what would become the largest agricultural business in the world.

The first set of decisions concerned fruit supplies. Relationships with those independent growers in Jamaica brought much anxiety to the Bakers, for they represented an unstable link in the supply chain. One of the junior Baker's main responsibilities in the 1880s and 1890s lay in smoothing relations with these growers, large and small. Boston Fruit faced a contentious array of planters who naturally sought to better the terms of their contracts with competing shippers. Competing on this distressingly open market required continual face-to-face contact. The senior Baker frequently prodded his son to keep up these contacts with planters. "We want to keep hold of the large producers as much as possible," he wrote in 1885, and advised that Loren "occasionally see those people and see that they are not getting dissatisfied." Apparently, the cantankerous elder delegated a good portion of these diplomatic duties to his son, who knew how "to massage the little growers much better than I can."[7] Cementing relationships with one big planter could stabilize the company's fruit supplies in a locality, but maintaining the arrangement in the face of cutthroat competition required constant vigilance of other buyers. "If we can govern Noyes," wrote Baker Sr. of one large grower, "we can in measure govern Port Morant . . . [and] keep out that great opposition or competition."[8]

From the perspective of Boston Fruit's leadership, independent growers large and small often mistimed harvests, despite written instructions from company headquarters at Port Antonio, orders themselves received by telegraph from Boston. The company effectively moved information across space, but what planters chose to do with that information was another matter. Baffled, company leadership railed against the failure of these suppliers to appreciate the functioning of a transoceanic productive system. The only means by which Boston Fruit's buyers could shape the timing of harvests was to persuade independent planters to leave fruit on trees until as late as possible. Judging from the frequent complaints, many growers refused to make such fine distinctions. Baker Sr. routinely admonished his son to have growers "keep the fruit on the trees until it comes to perfection," a moment that differed depending on the fruit in question.[9] Poorly timed harvests produced low-grade fruit. Preston communicated the difficulties of making grade while depending on independent planters to Baker Jr. in the early 1890s: "I hope you may be able to secure it [fruit] in some way as we shall need it badly here IF it is full clean and bright which fact I pressume [sic] you can establish if you have control of the cutting. The time is past when importers can make a profit on thin and ordinary fruit."[10] (Emphasis in original.)

By the 1890s, the novelty of tropical fruits, at least for East-Coast consumers, had worn off. Sellers had developed grading standards for tropical fruits, and the increased trade reduced the market for overripe and irregular bananas, a mainstay of earlier days. In the face of consistent consumer demand, maintaining a profitable market depended on predictable, steady flows of high-quality fruit.[11]

Errors in harvest timing, usually brought about by the vagaries of wrangling multiple independent suppliers, resulted in snarled transportation. Ships could sail to the United States overloaded or wait days at port for cargoes. Either logistical mistake could destroy the profitability of highly perishable bananas. Before the advent of refrigerated maritime transport, holds overpacked with bananas reached high temperatures and hastened spoilage. Ripening bananas chemically generate heat, a process accelerated by cramped, underventilated spaces. Cargoes that exceeded orders from vendors also produced wastage. In the 1890s, Andrew Preston repeatedly sent bitter complaints from Boston to agents in Jamaica about hundreds of surplus banana bunches rotting on US piers.[12] Some of the company's own agents still misunderstood the workings of the increasingly regularized fruit trade.

Problematic relations with fruit suppliers, along with sheer distance to market, constrained the BFC's ability to expand its reach beyond Jamaica. The company's ships occasionally plied the northern coast of Panama in the 1880s and purchased bananas in the Bocas del Toro area, Minor Cooper Keith's territory in those years. Accounts of this route reveal that for Boston Fruit's capacities, at least, distance from market troubled the Bocas trade. The lack of refrigeration made the route from Panama too long for some cargoes of bananas. From the Bakers' perspective, a smooth coordination of harvests and loading operations might have made the Bocas trade work, but supply and loading lay beyond the company's reach. In 1887 the senior Baker added that the Central American trade was unprofitable on these grounds and because of the energy required to maintain good relations with growers.[13] A few months later, he wrote that the company had dropped the Bocas trade in order to focus on Jamaica, where "everything will be done to insure a steady regular service."[14] It is unclear whether the BFC resumed its Panama contacts in the 1890s, but by the time the company united with Minor Cooper Keith's interests to form the United Fruit Company in 1899, improvements in shipping technology had made the western Caribbean a far more important banana-producing area than the Antilles. For the time being, Central America represented enticing, unfulfilled promise.

Given these obstacles to geographical expansion, Preston and Baker Sr. believed that the key to stabilizing fruit supplies and qualities would be to expand their direct control over cultivation in Jamaica, a move toward "vertical integration," the acquisition of more links in the commodity-production chain.[15] The defensive nature of this strategy is borne out in the BFC's decisions. In the mid-1880s, Capt. Baker remarked to his son that "a large cultivation at hand" could fill occasional shortages in fruit orders from independent growers.[16] By the 1890s the company had acquired several properties around Port Morant and Port Antonio, Jamaica. From his vantage point in Boston, Preston came to consider the expansion of company-controlled cultivation vital to the future of the business. Elaborating on his vision to his confidant,

the junior Baker, he wrote in 1890, "I am in hopes if all turns out as it prom-
ises that some way can be devised to lead us out of the position of scramblers
for fruit."[17] His priority over the course of the next decade lay in transforming
the banana trade from "precarious" to "one of fair business risk."[18] The risk-
iness of the business rested on the dangers of what Preston termed the "open
market," where the company had to compete with other fruit buyers for the
product of independent growers. What had been the foundation of the BFC's
supply in the 1880s had become a dead end for the company. "I do not think,"
he stated in 1890, "that the time will soon come that such fruit as is now
demanded by the trade can be bought on an open market[. W]hen money can
be made under that system there is a fortune under the 'Control of Cutting
System.'"[19] Forging that system spurred the company's first moves at direct
investment in production, a process that eventually brought Preston relief
from "an immense amount of worry and care."[20]

Positioning Boston Fruit increasingly above the workings of the open market helped stabilize the company's banana supplies and smooth their transportation to the United States. This strategy entailed undermining competing
fruit buyers in Jamaica, a cutthroat approach to competition that would char-
acterize United Fruit's business practices for decades.[21] Boston Fruit, operating on a smaller scale, pioneered this bare-knuckled approach. While the
company's leadership sought to discipline an unruly market and geography
in order to ensure a smooth flow of well-sorted, high-grade fruit, they sought
to create the inverse for competitors. In one of many complaints about a
recent batch of thin bananas, Preston recommended that Baker Jr. facilitate
the sale of poor inventory to other buyers. "[T]he more you give them of it the
sooner they will cease to exist as such [competitors]."[22] United Fruit's future
founders felt that competition forced on them the practices of maximizing
company control of productive space and standardizing commodities. This
perspective laid the basis for United Fruit's later effort to equate the entire
productive geography of bananas with its own enterprise.

The difficulties of tropical weather also spurred direct investment in fruit
production. As heads of the BFC, Baker and Preston were keenly aware of
their vulnerability to heavy seasonal rains and winds, and consequently
began to hedge their investments by obtaining properties in different areas
of Jamaica—a process known as "horizontal expansion," a close adjunct of
vertical integration. Communications with BFC plantation managers in the

1890s reveal the company's effort to mitigate weather risk by owning dispersed properties.[23] Wind, in particular, damaged banana plants. A succession of hurricanes tore through company properties in the late 1890s, according to one company history destroying more bananas than Boston Fruit exported to the United States in those years.[24] The rash of rough weather continued to affect Jamaica during United Fruit's early years. A hurricane in August 1899 passed by some company plantations, but hit others hard. One manager, Stephen Hislop, detailed the damage to the junior Baker, who was in Boston at the time:

> The wind blew very strong from the north and did an immense amount of
> damage to our Banana plantations, we suffered very much worse than
> what I wrote you two weeks ago, of course then we had no time to see
> the damage; I went round with Mr. Watson the day after the blow and he
> considered 50000 trees a low estimate. Suffolk Park suffered most. . . .
> We are now feeling the effects of it not being able to get more than
> 10000 to 12000 [bunches] a week and very poor fruit. . . . [I]t is very
> hard work to make a good selection, and I am sure they can easily see
> the difference on the Boston end.[25]

The hurricane's impact on banana cultivations rippled across the rest of that year, and Hislop estimated that the effects would linger for months longer.[26]

From the wide-angle perspective of executives in Boston, hurricane damage drove home the benefits of the company's expansion across a much larger geography. Although Boston Fruit had bought fruit around the Caribbean littoral since at least the 1880s, the company's merger with Minor Cooper Keith's Costa Rican and Colombian interests in 1899 cemented the process of horizontal expansion. The rough weather of the late 1890s, in part, motivated Baker and Preston to form United Fruit. In the new company's first report to stockholders in 1900, Preston assured investors that tropical divisions were "sufficiently separated to insure the business of your Company against serious interruption by any one or more local climatic disturbances."[27] Minimizing risk by expanding across the region soon paid off. In 1903, a hurricane caused almost $170,000 in damage to company cultivations in Jamaica.[28] Over the next year, this division's shortfall amounted to some six million bunches. In 1904, the company claimed that Central American production had made up for 60 percent of this deficit.[29]

The leadership of Boston Fruit recognized geographical expansion as the key to minimizing the risks of climate and environment. In the 1880s and 1890s, they lacked the capital to pursue the strategy beyond Jamaica. With access to greater capital, the old BFC leadership led United Fruit to maintain geographically dispersed divisions and hold vast tracts of uncultivated land, a pillar of the company's business strategy for decades to come. Competitors and political opponents would maintain that *el pulpo* (the octopus) locked up potentially productive lands to stifle the functioning of a free market.[30] The appearance of fungal pathogens in the early twentieth century obligated United Fruit to shift production to uninfected areas by the late 1920s, including the Pacific Coast of Central America. The company attempted to stave off the serious problem of plant disease by increasing chemical inputs and geographically dispersing tropical divisions even more. John Soluri argues persuasively that the success of the company's transportation network probably played an important role in accelerating the spread of plant pathogens.[31]

Technology, Integration, and Expansion

The UFCO emerged in the midst of a wave of technological innovations that were then dramatically expanding the scale and scope of capitalist enterprise.[32] As it concerned the movement of commodities, this transformation entailed the eclipse of wind and muscle power and the advent of steam propulsion, and soon thereafter internal combustion. The introduction of wireless telegraphy and refrigeration also smoothed wrinkles in the commodity chain. The company's history offers a case study in the impact of such innovations. Along with technological changes came the development of logistical capacities to match the expanding banana trade. The UFCO's roots in transportation made that the basis from which it would expand along the commodity chain. Capt. Baker's maritime background shaped United Fruit's embrace of a company-owned steamship fleet. The company grew from Baker's origins in shipping, and he remained intensely interested in the workings of the ships and ports even as he managed all tropical divisions into the early 1900s. His technical expertise in this area refined the company's port operations and fostered the creation of a thoroughly professional United Fruit steamship fleet. That proprietary fleet formed a crucial element in United Fruit's rapid movement toward vertical integration in the early twentieth century.[33] By 1930, the "Great White Fleet" reached its peak capacity. Beyond moving cargo, the company's ships were to become the centerpiece of its tropical tourist trade. In the late nineteenth century, a number of factors moved the Boston Fruit Company toward developing a state-of-the-art steamship fleet that would bind together its geographically dispersed operations.

Difficulties in shipping coordination weighed on the BFC's leadership in the 1880s and 1890s. Failures in communication and coordination produced an accordion effect in Boston Fruit's movement of commodities. A hodge-podge of maritime propulsion technologies born of the transition from wind to steam power brought on some of this irregularity, as did a shortage of cargo space. The company's highest ranks experienced this kind of logistical stumble personally. The elder Baker himself occasionally worked days and nights to clear queued ships from port with adequate cargoes. Mistimed, multiple arrivals not only stressed Baker, they placed the company at the mercy of suppliers and dock labor. "We can make no money," he grumbled from Jamaica in 1887,

> when we are compeled [sic] to buy and ship so much in so short a time. We are obliged to keep a large stable of help and then we cannot buy without more orders overrun which takes away all the profit. There is any quantity of fruit if we could have another steamer to keep all at work steadily.[34]

By the late 1880s, Boston Fruit's scale had grown beyond its small fleet and the tramp steamers it chartered to make up the difference.

Along with the coordination of shipping traffic, Boston Fruit's leadership keenly felt the technological shortcomings of cargo vessels. Moving a perishable commodity across great distances made speed a top priority. Reducing the number of days between tropical divisions and North American ports through improved propulsion technologies annihilated the vast physical space between points of production and consumption. Slow vessels such as the sail-powered *Freeman* required quick turnarounds in port and special attention to their cargo. Capt. Baker cautioned his son to oversee personally its loading at Morant Bay in 1886.[35] The latest developments in wind propulsion barely made the grade for the Jamaica banana trade. Quick passages were possible, but irregularities in the weather could leave cargoes becalmed and rotting at sea. The chief improvement brought by steam propulsion in the 1880s and 1890s was a reduced dependence on weather as an energy source. When Andrew Preston marveled at the swift passage of the new sail/steam hybrid *Ethelred* in 1890—Jamaica to Boston in five and a half days—the promise lay in making that route as regular as railway service.[36] The introduction of steam engines, and soon thereafter in-line screw propellers, flattened the wrinkles that slack winds introduced into the BFC's transportation network. It was not that steam vessels were much faster than the best sailing ships of the time; their advantage lay in consistency. On an output-per-calorie basis, steam power was not necessarily more efficient than wind or muscle forms of transportation, but steam engines were able to convert fossil fuels into energy on a far greater scale.[37] In the case of shipping, wind-powered vessels or wind/steam hybrids had the advantage of low or no fuel costs, but the greater energy output of steam engines brought a dramatic increase in ship tonnage and some improvement over the speed of the best sailing ships. The annihilation of space through propulsion advances also laid the foundation for United Fruit's later expansion into Central America and Colombia. Steam power revolutionized the transformative power of capital.

A brief consideration of the company vessels from the 1880s to the 1930s illustrates technological transformations that helped shape the business's expansion.[38] The first generation of Boston Fruit banana ships dated from the 1860s through the early 1880s. Sails were the primary means of propulsion, with steam engines to supplement in case of slack winds. These vessels—the *Jesse H. Freeman*, the *Telegraph*, the *Lorenzo Dow Baker*, and the *Eunice P. Newcomb* among them—represented the best clipper-type ship design of the time, characterized by streamlined hulls that reduced the drag of the vessel in the water. These technologies could carry between five hundred and eight hundred gross tons of ship and between ten and twenty thousand stems of bananas through the water at ten knots or so. Passenger traffic was a small ancillary to this generation of company ships, which could carry around a dozen people besides crew.[39]

After the formation of United Fruit, ships purchased by the company steadily increased in tonnage and speed, keeping pace with the growing

Figure 1.1. The UFCO's four admirals, Spanish-American War surplus vessels adapted to banana and tourist duty. Postcard in the author's possession, ca. 1900.

scope and scale of operations. The company fleet was always a patchwork of overlapping vessel classes, but subsequent generations of ship design reveal the changing capacities of steamships. The four ships of the admiral class purchased from the US government in 1898 more than doubled the tonnage of the previous generation of steam/sail hybrids (to around 2,100 gross tons), and with stronger engines, they could reliably steam at more than fourteen knots. Typical banana cargoes on these ships ran at around 35,000 stems. Their greater capacity allowed accommodations for around sixty passengers. These were the first company vessels designed to foster the nascent Caribbean tourist trade, boasting well-decorated cabins and public areas. Refurbishing this class to burn oil rather than coal in the 1920s boosted the output of engines by 25 percent and prolonged the productive life of the vessels into the 1930s.[40]

Between 1904 and 1932 the company's ship purchases grew from between three thousand and five thousand tons to more than seven thousand, the top of the range before the advent of containerized shipping in the 1960s. These screw steamers could move at least as fast as the admirals and carry much more cargo and passenger traffic. Like their predecessors, they were combination vessels, which fused the functions of fruit/cargo shipment and tourist accommodations. The biggest and fastest ships in the company line, purchased in the early 1930s, far outshone the company's earlier vessels. With new twin-screw turboelectric engines, they could carry nearly seven thousand gross tons at almost eighteen knots. Built after the transition to oil-burning engines in the 1920s, this class of "mail boats" obviated the need to carry tons of coal and to house bulkier steam engines. More space on these ships could be devoted to passenger service and cargo than ever before.[41]

The UFC took up the strategy of acquiring a proprietary fleet after 1899, a move that departed from Boston Fruit's policy of relying mostly on chartered shipping. After the merger, the company sought to exercise greater control over a more far-flung shipping operation than that of Boston Fruit.[42] Within the BFC, however, the move toward owning a high proportion of ships had begun earlier. In the 1890s Baker and Preston probably could not afford to invest more in shipping, even though they wanted to. Over the course of the UFCO's first thirty years, its leadership steadily consolidated its possession of ships, although title over some part of the fleet always remained in the hands of other companies. Maintaining a tier of chartered ships, usually on leases that ran from three months to five years, brought a measure of flexibility to United Fruit's enterprise. These vessels absorbed short-term fluctuations in harvests and reduced the possibility of the highly capitalized proprietary fleet sitting idle.

The expansion of the company's shipping capacities drove its most dynamic period of geographical expansion. The fleet's rapidly increasing carrying capacity made possible continual expansion of cultivations. This dynamic characterized the company in the decades before World War II. By the end of this period, the same number of ships could carry far more tonnage than just twenty years earlier.[43] Feeding into these economies of scale were improvements in engine technology and conversion from coal to fuel oil, which increased the efficiency of the fleet. The superintending engineer of the Marine Department claimed that, from 1925 to 1927, consumption of fuel oil fell from between 12 to 28 percent per vessel.[44] Investing heavily in maritime transport enabled expansion around the Caribbean littoral and, in turn, depended on that expanded geographical scale to pay for such expensive fixed capital.

Refrigeration systems on vessels reinforced the benefits of faster propulsion technologies and communications systems. The chemical heating process of closely packed bananas, exacerbated by hot tropical weather, at first limited Boston Fruit's geographical reach. To some extent, the worst mistakes of overloading vessels became less common in the 1890s due to better coordination between market and production and to more careful oversight of loading in Jamaica. Company leaders, observing the longer life of fruit during cool passages, sought to discover and replicate those conditions. Experiments in forced-air ventilation were underway on the company's new steamers by the late 1890s. Blowers installed during 1898 on the *Dewey*—one of the four admiral-class vessels that formed the heart of the company's turn-of-the-century fleet—were not of themselves sufficient to cool bananas. In 1898 a Boston Fruit agent wrote Baker Jr. from Boston, "I don't think the [*Dewey*'s] blowers a success." He continued, "had it not been that they were able to keep the side ports open until Sunday and all the hatches open, I am afraid there would have been a repetition of her previous voyage"—a heavy loss in spoiled fruit.[45]

During United Fruit's early years, air circulation and refrigeration experiments produced positive results. From 1901 to 1902, company leadership boasted that efforts to improve air circulation brought a 3 percent reduction in the costs of transporting fruit from tropical to domestic ports, due to fewer overripe stems.[46] Looking to recent successes in refrigerated transatlantic banana shipment, Andrew Preston recognized that chemical refrigeration systems "could offer . . . customers a more stable product and widen the field of [the company's] activities."[47] Preston began communicating with refrigeration companies in 1903, and soon settled on the design provided by the American Linde Refrigeration Company. The *Venus*, an iron steamship built in 1877 and chartered to United Fruit, became the test case. In Philadelphia, workers insulated the *Venus*'s cargo hold with pine boards and some seventy thousand pounds of cow hair, and installed the refrigeration appliance. After some initial setbacks, engineers soon found the right combination of humidity and temperature. These efforts reduced the rate of overripe fruit arriving in US ports from around 12 percent to 2 percent.[48]

By 1904, Preston could write to stockholders that "the largest steamers of the United Fruit Company's fleet have been fitted with a cooling equipment which permits the delivery to the trade in the interior of the choicest fruit in the best of condition."[49] Here Preston referred to the *San José*, the *Limón*, and the *Esparta*, the first banana carriers built to the company's specifications, all introduced to the service in 1904. Refitting many company vessels to burn oil rather than coal in the 1920s reduced the amount of space required for coal storage, which in turn could be dedicated to housing refrigeration equipment. Like the company's other technological innovations, the ability of refrigerated vessels to shrink the physical distance between banana plantation and US consumers assumed a prominent place in company propaganda. Tourists on the company fleet could experience bodily this triumph over hot climates as refrigerated air from cargo holds entered passenger cabins through special air ducts.[50]

Ground transport of bananas presented problems similar to those of maritime transport, and United Fruit likewise leveraged technology to overcome the difficulties of distance, terrain, and climate. Like screw-propeller steamships, steel rails and locomotives expanded the company's reach into Caribbean lowlands. Ancillary modes of transportation, all depending in whole or part on imported steel components and steam power, formed the "capillaries" of the company's ground transportation infrastructure. These technologies laid the basis for incorporation of those "wastelands" into an agribusiness serving consumer markets in North America and Western Europe.

In the 1880s and 1890s, Boston Fruit relied mostly on animal power, and its managers considered the movement of harvested fruit the province of independent producers. The vulnerability of animal power and dirt wagon roads became especially clear when heavy rains turned roads into impassible quagmires. In October 1891, Boston Fruit agent Cecil Langlois complained that the weather was taking a toll on the fruit harvest in Jamaica. Where even empty carriages sank up to their axles, loaded wagons fared even worse. The roads were so bad that pickers could not reach banana cultivations.[51] While Boston Fruit operated on a relatively small scale, it made sense to keep most of this transportation expense and risk in the hands of growers, but as the business grew in the 1890s the company saw the benefit of minimizing the use of mules and oxen. Boston Fruit built its own rail line from fruit properties in Jamaica by 1898. After the line's construction, company agent Stephen Hislop happily wrote Baker Jr. that the run from plantation to port took only thirty minutes.[52] In Minor Cooper Keith's Costa Rican properties, the process worked in reverse—railroad construction preceded large-scale banana cultivation. In any event, banana men understood the

Figure 1.2. The capillaries of the UFCO's transportation network, where rails made muscle power more efficient. "Bringing fruit to loading platform," UF54.051, Box 54, United Fruit Company Photograph Collection, Mss: 1 (1891–1962), U860, Baker Library.

crucial, intimate relationship between the fruit's commercial viability and railroads.

Within a few years after the UFCO's incorporation, the construction of railroads in tropical divisions almost totally displaced mule- or ox-driven transport of fruit. Like trains in the Chicago hinterland a few decades before, railroads in the company's tropical divisions transformed the "age-old restrictive relationship between biological energy and movement." No longer would the transportation of bananas be beholden to the biological limits of humans and animals to convert food calories into movement.[53] After the completion of rail networks, animal power continued to serve United Fruit where it made sense—as the smallest capillaries of the transportation system. Mules and oxen could bridge economically the relatively small distances between cultivations and rail sidings. Where it could, United Fruit built extra-small-gauge rail networks to link farms to main railways. These "trams" brought some of the economies of railroad technology without heavy investments in ballast and other road infrastructure. In the late 1920s, the company operated more than seven hundred miles of tramway. In some cases, small steam engines pulled tram cars. Mules also pulled banana wagons over tram lines. Joining animal power to steel rails multiplied several times the amount of weight each mule could carry per calorie burned. Mules hauling without rails typically carried two to four stems of bananas on their backs, while those pulling tram cars could pull up to forty-five stems, depending on the animal and the terrain involved.[54]

As the commodity chain to various divisions grew in scale and speed, railroads served the company's needs and drove its expansion. Although they were expensive to build, operate, and maintain, the investment paid off with the far greater quantities of fruit that could be moved over greater distances.[55] Linking railways to steamships in company ports smoothed what had been, for Boston Fruit, one of the most problematic points in the commodity chain. Joining forces with the Keith interests in 1899 united the BFC's nascent rail-building efforts with more established railroad expertise. Once built, the main lines of banana railroads could last for decades. This investment paid off as subsequent generations of locomotives with greater horsepower output and better fuel economies pulled much bigger loads over the same road beds. The UFCO dramatically expanded its rolling stock between 1900 and the early 1930s. The figures of this expansion indicate that the acquisition of freight cars and tonnage carried on them outstripped the growth of the company's locomotive pool. Echoing the effect of maritime technologies during the same time, fewer locomotives were pulling many more freight cars by 1930 than they had at the beginning of the century.

The company's heavy investments in transportation required an extensive communications network. Boston Fruit relied on transoceanic telegraphs to communicate between Boston and Jamaica, but written correspondence formed an important coordinating function through the 1890s. From its earliest years, United Fruit linked plantations to ports with telephones. In 1904 the company initiated its first wireless connection between tropical divisions, with stations in Bocas del Toro, Panama, and Puerto Limón, Costa Rica.[56] By the early 1910s, company ships housed wireless sets that enabled continual communication from ship to shore.[57] In the mid-1920s, radio transmitters around the Caribbean connected to the domestic United States through

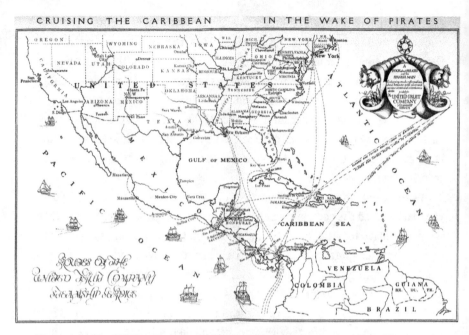

Figure 1.3. The UFCO's empire in 1915 reflected through a tourist idiom. "Routes of the United Fruit Company Steamship Service." UFCSS, *Cruising the Caribbean in the Wake of Pirates*, 16–17.

company-owned receiver stations in Hialeah, Florida, and New Orleans.[58] The company consolidated its control of this communications network through a subsidiary, the Tropical Radio Telegraph Company.

The decision of Boston Fruit and United Fruit leadership to integrate backward into fruit production coincided with a strategy of forward integration into marketing fruit in the United States. Recent scholarship has examined the connections between United Fruit's expansion in the early twentieth century and its efforts to promote banana consumption in the United States. Marcelo Bucheli has documented the transformation of the banana from a luxury commodity to a foodstuff available to working-class budgets. John Soluri establishes links between practices of tropical agriculture and the rise of the banana both in the US marketplace and in US popular culture.[59] United Fruit's forward integration helped create the national consumer market for bananas, altering the nature of that sector from what it had been through the end of the nineteenth century. United Fruit formed the subsidiary Fruit

Dispatch Company as a mass marketer, shipper, and wholesaler of the company's fruit within the United States. United Fruit, like other agribusinesses of the time, developed a business strategy based on high volume and low profit margins.[60] This swift, regular flow of fruit through a tightly controlled commodity chain reflected the broader "revolution in distribution and production" associated with the rapidly growing distributive capacities of transportation technologies.[61]

Conclusions

In the two decades before 1899, United Fruit's main parent companies bridged the gulf between a relatively unorganized trade and one based on tight coordination between production and consumption across vast distances. Despite their successes, they faced a series of challenges and constraints that eventually led them to form the UFCO. Looking to the Boston Fruit Company, dependence on other growers and shippers left the company vulnerable to elements outside its control. Technological limitations, competition with rival fruit brokers for access to independently owned fruit and shipping, and the vagaries of the Caribbean climate added to Boston Fruit's risks. Minimizing those risks pushed the company toward capturing as many segments of the commodity chain as possible. Although Keith expanded his banana properties into Colombia during these decades, Preston and Baker remained confined to limited direct investments in Jamaica.

Only the incorporation of the UFCO in 1899 fulfilled the founders' dream of organizing a steady, year-round supply of consistently high-quality fruit from a variety of sources. Vertical integration and horizontal expansion, strategies born of these experiences, became the bedrock of the UFCO's power for thirty years. United Fruit was able to bring much more capital to bear than its chief predecessor on the tropical fruit and sugar trade. The merger at once united the efforts of competitors and largely eliminated the risky competitive environment of the 1890s. More investment capital enabled United Fruit to engineer a technological revolution in the banana trade. Although Boston Fruit's leadership invested in technological solutions as much as they could, United Fruit represented a new form of US enterprise in Latin America. New technologies and forms of corporate organization brought a much more intensive form of extractive enterprise. In United Fruit's case,

heavy investments in steam-driven transportation collapsed physical distance between cultivation and consumer and dramatically expanded the territory its productive activities could encompass. Numbers tell the tale of this
triumph: between 1900 and 1930, the company's cultivated acreage increased
more than fivefold to just over one half million acres spread over seven
nations. At the base of this system, of course, was labor—tens of thousands
of hands, by the 1920s. And at its apex, pushing the corporate frontier ever
further, strode the icons of the "Conquest of the Tropics": white, Anglo-Saxon
banana cowboys. Their needs and demands would decisively shape the journey from sleepy Coralio to bustling Macondo.

CHAPTER TWO

Tropical Vexations

In August 1919, Bostonian Everett Brown disembarked from a United Fruit Company ship in Antilla, Cuba, ready to begin a tropical career in the transnational's rapidly expanding sugar division of Preston. Brown went from working as timekeeper and draughtsman on railroad construction in Cuba to being promoted to engineer and transferred to Panama, where a few months later he headed a survey crew carving the forested Talamanca Valley into banana plantations. Like many of what management called "the right sort of men," Brown ascended to a supervisory role in the company's racialized labor hierarchy and relished the personal and professional opportunity it represented. Writing home to his wife, he made frequent and eloquent reference to his pride at working on what he called the "raw edge of things," as part of the advance guard of industrial civilization in the untamed tropics. Beneath this sense of mission—a well-recognized element of Western imperialist experiences in general—Brown's world seethed with discontent. The North American engineers and lower-level foremen around him complained incessantly and bitterly about living conditions and their treatment at the company's hands, and as he settled into his position those complaints became his own: poor pay, the high cost of living, a capricious vacation policy that exacerbated homesickness, and rigid, autocratic bosses. What was more, during his Talamanca work, Brown contracted malaria, a debilitating condition that troubled him through the end of his time with the company. In the end, Brown, always aware of better employment opportunities away from the UFCO, took a position with the Santa Ana Sugar Company in Hatillo, Cuba.

That this successful but peripatetic career with the UFCO transpired over the course of only one year stands as testimony to the stubborn reality of life and work in the company's early twentieth-century tropical enclaves: as vitally necessary as management considered them to operations, Anglo-Saxon colonies were often deeply contentious places where extremely high turnover was the rule. By triangulating Brown's testimony with that of other UFCO men and the internal records of the Costa Rica division, a portrait emerges of the broader dynamics and internal tensions that characterized these colonies in the early twentieth century. The raison d'être of these colonies was a racialized labor hierarchy, in which white, Anglo-Saxon first-class employees enjoyed a series of professional and social privileges over the black West Indians and Hispanics who made up the bulk of the company's ranks. Not just an abstract set of traditions imported from abroad, racial difference was constructed day to day in the work and social environment of the enclave; those at the top considered their "natural" authority absolutely vital to company operations. Brown's brief career also highlights the often conflictive relations between first-class employees and management, and the strategies discontented white-collar men deployed to better their condition. Like nonwhite workers all around the company's field of operations, white employees alternately griped among themselves, negotiated with management, made demands of it, organized strikes, or, like Brown, simply moved on to better opportunities. And behind these complaints, many suffered from a variety of "tropical" maladies that could seriously affect one's earning capacity. This chapter explores these tense relationships that decisively shaped the UFCO's vast investment in corporate welfare in the tropics, a form of colonialism that stood at the heart of US experiences of empire in early twentieth-century Latin America.

White Supremacy and Labor Management

Ideologies of white supremacy intertwined with other political and economic motives behind US overseas enterprises in this period. The "natural" authority of white, Anglo-Saxon men had deep roots in US culture, and by the early twentieth century a number of cultural sources buttressed its expression.[1] Scientifically and culturally based notions of racial difference, some of them rooted in the ideology of European imperialism and others more autochthonous products of Euro-American expansion and plantation slavery in North America and the Caribbean, played a powerful role in the perceptions and attitudes of many white Americans at the time, both southern and northern. The acquisition of colonies and protectorates in the Caribbean, Central America, and the Pacific in 1898, and the Panama Canal Zone shortly thereafter had more recently brought to the fore conversations about the necessity of white supervision over peoples who, it was held by many, were incapable of self-governance by dint of their racial biology or history as the brutalized subjects of the decrepit Spanish empire. As Colby has recently shown, the management practices of United States–led industrialized agriculture in the tropics preceded and undergirded those of the US government abroad, in particular in the Canal Zone.[2]

By the early twentieth century, US industrialists had long understood the utility of racially segmented work forces headed by whites, who exploited racial and cultural differences to thwart labor activism and keep wages as low as possible. United Fruit's first generation of management, rooted primarily in the northeastern United States, thoroughly embraced this sensibility. Historical and anthropological scholarship on UFCO divisions has done much to establish that this racist ideology was born of the labor management practices in the industrial Northeast, rather than an importation of Southern Jim Crow segregation, no matter the resemblance. Except for positioning white cadres as a variety of colonial elite—an accurate portrayal, to be sure—scholars have passed over any consideration of management's problematic relationship with first-class employees.[3] In United Fruit's tropical divisions, the white/nonwhite color bar formed something of a bedrock underlying the company's shifting patterns of labor recruitment. The company steadily Hispanized its plantation workforce in Central America after a series of labor disturbances involving West Indian blacks in 1909–1910, and leveraged racial difference to undermine labor organizing. The advance into technical and supervisory ranks by either blacks or Hispanics, who often replaced whites, only developed in the 1920s.

The racial division of labor occasionally blurred when circumstances required. Necessity occasionally forced managers to promote blacks to supervisory positions, though the color bar hung perilously over such promotions. Writing to a railroad colleague in the United States in 1908, Northern Railway Superintendent E. Mullins explained one such case of a vacancy at the head of the rail car repair shop: "At the present time there is a very competent nigger over the men," he wrote, "and I do not want to make any more experiments." Ending the "experiment" was paramount, lest it set an uncomfortable precedent, and so Mullins asked for help: "If you come across an energetic fellow, whom you feel satisfied would fill such a position suitably, would appreciate if you would let me know."[4] Such exceptions were a rarity and the white preference in company divisions prevailed. Company policy was repeatedly expressed in letters of hire to recruits in the United States, which usually included frank statements to the effect that "the overseers, superintendents, etc., are all white Anglo-Saxons," and managers were careful to discern whether potential employees were black or white before hiring them.[5]

Identifying the "right sort" of white man hinged as much on his technical competence and experience as on his ability to effectively manage "colored" or "foreign" labor. When manager John Keith (Minor Cooper Keith's nephew) hired one Joe Smith as assistant wharfmaster in Puerto Limón to oversee West Indian stevedores in 1904, he informed company President Andrew Preston that Smith was a "heavier weight" than his predecessor and "is equal, if not superior, to him in his command of profane language." With Smith on the wharf, Keith noted with satisfaction, "I think our negroes will lead a strenuous life."[6] When Superintendent Mullins sought the "proper sort" of car foreman from Vermont a few years later, he wrote to his colleague James Coleman that "it is, as you are aware, a case of handling negroes." So important was the this ability that Mullins preferred to wait rather than risk filling the position with an unsuitable man—the line between "proper" and "not suitable" resting on the question of controlling nonwhite subordinates.[7] Coleman came through for Mullins, for six months later the latter reported that a J. Binder had just arrived to fill the post. He sent the new man out to his first day on the job only after thoroughly briefing him on "the class of labor to handle."[8]

The proper procedures for managing nonwhite labor found codification in company policy. Drawing from years of tropical experience, the head of the company's engineering department based in Panama, Harry Bestor, created and circulated a set of "Instructions for Field Engineers and Draftsmen" in 1920. Addressed "to the young engineer unfamiliar with the Tropics," Bestor laid out a series of technical practices to its white employees heading surveying crews on the expanding edges of the company's properties. "It is the custom to allow the negroes and natives to do most of the manual labor," the author of the fruit company's manual noted, the supervisory and technical tasks only being suitable for whites. The new recruit would encounter both types of laborer, and each posed its own challenges to foremen: "The natives are usually very quick and are exceptionally good for woodland work," but "are not very rugged or strong." Typically, they required several days' rest a month. "The negroes," on the other hand, "are more regular and steady, but not so quick to learn. They seemingly get along best when employed in the same kind of work, and cannot readily be changed from one duty to another." The author cautioned his readership to avoid the temptation of depending on blacks or natives to clean and maintain the surveyor's instruments, tools he considered far beyond their limited comprehension.[9] A procedural document such as this one encapsulated the shared understandings of the company's tropical management and socialized new expatriate employees to the workings of the racially stratified labor force and the racist ideology behind it. This ideology would have been familiar to anyone involved in plantation labor in colonial contexts for centuries, where the owners of capital and their managers constructed and naturalized the purported inferiority of nonwhite laborers in a variety of ways. Bestor's manual renewed these notions for the particular world of the expanding fruit plantation frontier.

Being entrusted with such a position over nonwhite laborers signified an important rite of passage for some company men. In the fruit company's world at this time, a willingness to handle nonwhite subordinates aggressively served as a key criterion for recruiting and advancing men to positions of responsibility—a performance of white superiority that was as important on the ground as it was in company lore. There was always the Horatio Alger narrative of Victor Cutter, who rose from timekeeper to company president between 1904 and 1924.[10] A central part of Cutter's identity was his much-trumpeted ability to best blacks in a variety of ways, including with his fists.[11] Even more telling is how an individual could experience his initiation into the racial landscape of the company's sphere. Everett Brown, who worked directly under Harry Bestor in Panama and Costa Rica, stepped into this new role when he was transferred from Cuba to lead a crew into the Talamanca Valley in 1920. Surely, he benefitted from his boss's ideas about labor management; the "Instructions" were written for men like Brown, whom the company was then hiring to undertake this wave of expansion. Donning a new Stetson and revolver, he set about plotting a line through the forest at the head of fifteen "native" laborers. When the laborers on his crew went on strike for $1.50 gold a day—a situation Brown described as "quite a circus"—he summarily dismissed the lot of them, even those who did not participate in the stoppage. Bestor welcomed Brown's decision upon his return to headquarters at Guabito, and immediately set about forming a new, more pliant crew for Brown.[12] "Of course it is all new and strange," he wrote his wife after the incident, "and I own to rather enjoying this being a little tin god." Brown's experience with white authority in the workplace, and the day-to-day forms of deference he enjoyed out in the field (such as being addressed by subordinates with hats in hand), played an essential role in ensuring that the lowest level of labor remain subservient.[13]

White supremacy permeated the lives of UFCO employees, both on the ground and as a part of company culture. The company's employee magazine, *Unifruitco*, propagated such notions in the 1920s and early 1930s. Anglo-Saxon men, wrote one UFCO employee from his post in Honduras, possessed character traits necessary to subdue the tropics. He was "cool-headed, per-severing, enterprising, practical," wrote Prospero Alger, and "responsible in large part for the advances made by the modern world in the fields of busi-ness, commerce, and material progress." He was expert at adapting himself to new circumstances, and was imbued with "a singular reverence for law and order." These virtues, concluded Alger, meant that "other races have a great deal to learn from the Anglo-Saxons."[14] On the other hand, recurring portrayals of nonwhite workers in *Unifruitco* spoke to their defects. Cartoons lampooned blacks and Central American *mozos* (field hands), and timekeep-ers and overseers from the company's farms offered their own anecdotes. One such portrayal described Jones, a Jamaican working in Honduras. "Like most Jamaicans," wrote overseer John Erskine, "Jones wanted money and was will-ing to do almost anything but good work for it." The feckless man cut corners in banana planting that led to crop losses and took time away from his paid work in various petty money-making schemes. Erskine conveyed the lessons he learned from Jones: "You must judge everything these men do on its own merits and then forget it—as they will."[15] In this telling, a Jamaican could be made to do good work only with unrelenting supervision, a role that could only be filled by the "right sort of man."

The Problem of Climate

The first set of obstacles to finding and keeping the "right sort" were medical, and would lead the company to create its own medical department in 1912. The impetus for investing in a vast medical infrastructure rested on keeping a nonwhite workforce healthy enough to be productive and male Caucasian bodies healthy enough to manage them. As the United States embarked on large-scale occupations of overseas colonies, protectorates, and properties, the question of white adaptability to tropical environments assumed primary importance in the burgeoning fields of tropical medicine and public health. At the outset of United Fruit's expansion, medical knowledge was in the process of turning from miasmatic and humoral explanations of human disease toward the causative framework of germ theory and parasitology. At the heart of the gradual turn away from miasmatic explanations lay the old question of whether Caucasian bodies could withstand extended life in tropical environments. Following Darwin's ideas of species adaptability to specific environments, many North American doctors still would have heartily agreed with the editorial voice of the American Medical Association, which declared in 1905 that "individuals thrive best and attain their highest perfection when most nearly adapted to their environment."[16] From this perspective, races were likened to distinct species in their apparently different capacity to survive in tropical milieus. Behind this evolutionary paradigm stood centuries of popular and official vexation over "white man's graveyards," hot places where European colonial projects withered as quickly as freshly arrived populations could die of mysterious and often horrifyingly lethal fevers.

Managers in Costa Rica keenly felt the impact of disease on their employees. Writing to his uncle, Minor Cooper Keith, in 1901, John Keith noted that a hospital in the Zent district (near Puerto Limón) was "most urgently needed" because of a "very sickly" season. "Beginning of this week," he complained, "there was not a single white foreman at work on the Limon end of the Northern Railway." Office men, banana receivers, and commissary workers were all laid low, apparently because they could not stand the heat in the company's buildings, and several were sent to the cooler climate of San José to recuperate. Keith noted that the Limón hospital was overflowing, and that medical infrastructure was desperately needed.[17] A few years later, the younger Keith recommended to his uncle that a reliable employee repeatedly struck with malaria be relocated from Limón to the recently opened Guatemala division, "where the climate is better than it is here."[18] Such relocations or repatriations of sick Anglos could prove very costly, for the company bore their cost. Several years later, superintendent W. E. Mullins wrote to the company's new medical superintendent that medical facilities for whites, separate from sick camps for laborers, were under construction in the same area.[19] By that time, United Fruit had heeded years of complaints from its managers on the ground and moved to create its own medical department. Whites' elevated susceptibility to disease in the tropics exercised a powerful influence on the shape of the company's colonial enterprise.[20]

On the other hand, great strides in public health—in particular the near eradication of yellow fever and radical diminution of malaria in United States–occupied Cuba and Puerto Rico—were leading others to exonerate the tropics of their deleterious effects on whites in particular. In William Gorgas's powerful words as president of the American Medical Association in 1909, "the white man can live in the tropics and enjoy as good health as he would have if living in the temperate zone."[21] This well-known declaration by the medical savior of the Panama Canal project served as a foundational belief for United Fruit Medical Superintendent Dr. William Deeks and his subordinates, for it meshed with the racial division of labor then considered vital to the success of plantation agriculture. United Fruit's tropical colonies provided a rich testing ground for the belief that disease resided within the human body and that the tropics could be made salubrious in and around white colonies.[22] Indeed, Deeks had worked under Gorgas in Panama as head of Ancón Hospital, and United Fruit provided him the means to continue his work on tropical health for years to come.

Although a few doubts and debates remained about the salubrity of the tropical climate for whites, the larger turn toward absolving these areas of inherently unhealthy effects was well underway. Occasional mention of the "enervating" effects of tropical heat or the debilitating effects of sunlight coexisted with a broader push to demonstrate the healthy potential of the company's tropics. The dissonance could be jarring, if one tried to make sense of such declarations and the oft-echoed statement that "the heat is much less oppressive in the American Tropics than in most localities in the United States."[23] The medical department's vital statistics demonstrated this potential time and again by favorably comparing morbidity and mortality of various conditions in the company's sphere to that of other colonial contexts and various temperate localities.[24] Doctors even reassured actual and potential employees that their masculinity would thrive in the tropics. In one such study, they proudly reported the nearly 40 percent of married white men working for the company had fathered 383 (white) children while in the tropics, of which 357 survived, a comparable death rate to temperate latitudes at the time.[25] This triumph of white male virility in the tropics—itself long an object of deep anxiety in Western colonial experiences—was meant to stand as potent testimony of the company's ability to neutralize the dangers of tropical environments to temperate physiology.

Absolving tropical milieus of their miasmatic or climatic insalubrity only displaced long-held notions of tropical danger to human bodies—in particular, those of "tropical" races. Situating disease within human bodies powerfully linked transmission to behaviors, and the path to avoiding illness became "moral hygiene," a framework that racialized unhealthy habits as tropical or native and prescribed the means by which whites could avoid them. Moral hygiene, then, added medical imprimatur to the practice of racial segregation in company enclaves. But a key part of rendering the tropics safe rested on subjecting white expatriates—much more than nonwhite laborers—to the disciplinary function of tropical medicine. Privileging individual behavior and morality as a factor in health served both medical and managerial logic, and infused the language of both. Employees who cared for themselves and guarded themselves in certain ways would be healthier and, the assumption went, more compliant to the company's requirements. Writing to one prospective employee in Vermont in 1907, W. E. Mullins, the general manager of the Costa Rica division, levied a typical statement meant to answer questions about climate and health. "One's health," he noted from his experience, "is largely dependent upon his habits."[26] The medical department labored to document the salubrity of the tropics, but, as noted above, of the tropics rendered sanitary by the company's public health regime, where behavior nonetheless remained vital to health. Behavior could buttress the argument that measurable progress had been made in this area. William Deeks offered an assessment of autopsies of "white employees from temperate zones" in 1923, a small group that included North Americans, Britons, Frenchmen, and Spaniards. Deeks noted that these ten men were the only deaths of about two thousand temperate-zone employees, a rate he compared favorably to that prevalent among populations in the north. He discounted two as accidental and another two as "directly attributable to personal habits." Only four had died of "tropical" conditions, and two of these Deeks wrote off as laborers on railroad construction gangs (probably Spaniards), "who undoubtedly paid little attention to hygiene and preventive measures." The remaining two deaths to tropical disease occurred in new divisions, "where a great deal of frontier work is being done, which necessitates living under more or less primitive conditions"—acceptable casualties to be expected in the company's expansion.[27]

The rise of moral hygiene made the policing of white employees a primary mission of the medical department after its formal constitution in 1912. The process began with medical examination of every potential employee before he (or, rarely, she) could begin a tropical career, in an attempt to recruit only those physically and morally fit for tropical service. A key part of an application for a salaried position in the tropics was a health certificate, formalized in 1916. The questionnaire, to be completed by a company-approved medical examiner, was designed to screen out those who suffered potentially debilitating conditions, such as tuberculosis, that could wind up costing the company once the applicant was under contract. Tellingly, near the top of the list were questions about alcohol and narcotics use, and venereal disease.[28] Writing a couple of years later, Deeks stated that nearly eight percent of all applicants for such positions were rejected on medical grounds, a cause for relief at the expense and trouble saved by medical examination.[29]

For those temperate-zone employees who made the cut, they would occupy a curious place in the stratified environment of United Fruit enclaves. On one hand, they stood atop a racialized occupational hierarchy, often in supervisory capacities, earning more and enjoying superior housing and amenities than laborers. Just as company doctors indicted "natives" and "colored" laborers for their failure to accept the company's medical paternalism and their resistance in the face of modern medicine, so did they construct "temperates" as quintessentially good patients worthy of doctors' best efforts.[30] But expatriate colonies were the subject of keen medical worry and much intellectual energy during these years, in no small part because retention among salaried employees remained chronically low for this whole period.[31] The "exoneration of the tropics," then, was not an easy road. It involved subjecting first-class employees to many of the same clinical practices that laborers would endure, albeit in deeply unequal fashion. Whites escaped the most debasing and exposing practices of the medical department (such as photography and display), even though they were offered up as anonymous case studies with some frequency. Temperates were also thoroughly incorporated into the "statistical community" of tropical divisions, with all the invasive examination and sample-taking this project implied, all with the underlying goal of demonstrating their ability to acclimate. Medical practice in United Fruit's sphere shows how white superiority—coded as temperateness—could be constituted and naturalized in the clinic, even while enmeshed in the disciplinary functions of the company clinic. Tropical medicine, which so powerfully coded the inferiority and backwardness of "others," also structured medical notions of temperateness and whiteness in the company's tropical divisions.

Alcohol Abuse

The chief culprit among the bad habits associated with white tropical weakness was alcohol abuse, linked more broadly in the United States at this time to serious moral failing. An editorial in the *Journal of the American Medical Association* of 1915 summed up the state of medical knowledge in this area:

> When the foreign [white] resident of the tropics has learned to guard himself against prevalent unhygienic conditions, to adjust his mode of life and his personal hygiene to the obvious requirements of his new environment, and to avoid the misuse of alcohol, which increases enormously the other unfavorable and detrimental influences, he need not suffer seriously by comparison with his relatives in temperate zones.[32]

Inebriation, it was known, caused men to abandon the care of the self, specifically regarding protection from mosquitoes but more generally and ominously blurring the social boundaries between white and nonwhite populations. Anxieties about the connection between white morality and health haunted even the hopeful language meant for public consumption. Summing up the first decade or so of UFCO medical work in Bocas del Toro, one company doctor noted a connection between malaria and moral hygiene among whites:

> The moral tone of employees has improved with health conditions, and the observation has been made in past years that a large percentage of hemorrhagic malaria, or "blackwater fever," was among white men who were reckless and were in many instances alcoholics. Almost always in a case of death among this class of men these attributes could be traced to those infected. The management wisely observed these facts, and since drastic action was taken against such employees, we rarely have a

case of hemorrhagic malaria, and the records submitted herewith show a decrease in the disease along with the improvement of the moral make-up of employees.[33]

Alcohol posed serious difficulties to white acclimatization, offered another observer, because it undermined "industrious habits" and led to discontent and exposure to disease—chiefly for its ability to erode the boundaries between whites and "natives."[34] The persistence of these anxieties over white morality in the company's medical narratives over several years suggests that such boundary crossings were something of a routine occurrence.

Drunk and misbehaving white employees posed chronic problems for managers in Costa Rica. While company doctors and executives spoke of the moral fiber of employees, management on the ground exercised a more pragmatic approach to alcohol abuse. In 1904, one district supervisor in Zent complained to John Keith about a *mandador* (team supervisor), Mr. King, whose drunken behavior had brought friction with his superior. The man's "very reprehensible" conduct led the supervisor to propose a circular for all regarding drunkenness, a measure Keith frowned upon. It "would be very unwise," he cautioned, "as it is not at all unlikely that at an early date you would be forced to either go back on your Circular or lose the services of a useful assistant who might temporarily fall from grace." Before letting King go, Keith continued, the supervisor should consider just who would take the man's place.[35] Another problem employee, a Mr. Prendergast, ran afoul of his superiors a few years later because "he indulged a good deal in liquor." Superintendent W. E. Mullins shrugged off complaints about him because of his reputation as a "good worker. . . . [who] comes from a part of the country where rascality in the Banana Business is the order of the day."[36] As long as a man's drinking did not disrupt operations, managers in this division tended to overlook it or weigh the costs of a problem employee over the possibility of finding and paying for a replacement. Medical narratives aside, the usually tolerant attitude of managers toward such situations points to their understanding that drinking was an especially tempting or even natural vice for whites in the tropics.

"The U.F.Co. is very good in some ways, but I don't like the way it pays"

Aside from anxieties linked to the health of whites in the tropics, recruiting and keeping those men in the tropics persistently vexed management for

basic economic and material reasons, and confronting each set of these difficulties—usually through negotiations with employees—eventually amounted
to a far-reaching investment in corporate welfare. One point of contention
surrounded the marginal living conditions even first-class employees were
subjected to (conditions for laborers were far worse). Employees rightly coupled such complaints to those about low pay, for living in tropical divisions
was no cheap affair. In September 1906, a group of the Northern Railway
Company's first-class men organized a committee of representatives and presented a series of complaints about poor pay, accommodations, and food to
Superintendent Mullins. The men claimed that the high cost of living, along
with low wages, made it impossible for many to stay in Costa Rica. They gave
Mullins a schedule of salary increases for conductors and engineers, which
included allowances for board. Mullins's response, which he detailed in a
letter to Minor Cooper Keith, must have been disappointing to the petitioners.
On the issue of pay, he offered no concession whatever, because "present
earnings would not permit any increase in wages"; and true to the company's
policy of not entering into anything resembling collective bargaining agree-
ments, he brushed off the men's desire to have their petition become a formal
agreement.[37] Writing to one of the petitioners, C. Strasburger, Mullins added
that the company's wages for railway men were "considerably higher" than
those offered elsewhere, a statement that would soon be rendered untrue by
the high wages paid such men on the Panama Canal project.[38]

The petitioners also outlined a series of difficult living and working conditions, and their complaints reveal that management had overlooked a series
of issues that seriously affected employees' daily existence. In the workplace,
shifts were long and off times too short for rest, the men perceived recent
firings as unjust, and new men were put into situations they could not hope
to resolve without the benefit of experience. Room and board were also dis-
mal. One crew of forty-six men who had been detailed to work on a tramway
was put up in "filthy" rail cars packed with mud; what was more, the foreman
of the project exacted seventy-five cents a day for meals, and "such as were
furnished were quite insufficient."[39] Conditions were not much better in
Puerto Limón proper, where the company relied on the Limon Lodge to house
and board many of its men. Not only was the food and coffee provided poor, it
was served so slowly that railroad men were often late for their shifts. Those
who arrived in town late from working out on the line were not served at all,
since the staff insisted on closing too early.[40] While denying any demands for

increased salary, Mullins immediately set about remedying these "many small grievances" with what he admitted could be "a little more intelligent operation."[41] Engineers and conductors were to have more time to rest after long shifts, as long as it didn't negatively affect the functioning of the railroad, and inexperienced men would be sent out on the line in the company of veterans. In cases of dismissal, the petitioners demanded a man's right to have the case investigated by his supervisors, "except in cases of intoxication." Mullins also moved to make concrete improvements to living conditions. The following year, the company completed a thirty-room building in Puerto Limón, which he felt "would be much appreciated by our employes [sic] and aid in the securing and retention of a better class of engineers and conductors."[42] He also improved the quality of bedding in company accommodations and the food offered to its men.[43] The superintendent's response to this employee petition reveals that he fundamentally agreed with the substance of the men's grievances—he declared as much to his UFCO counterpart in Costa Rica (who was in charge of farm operations and commissaries).[44] Diffusing employee discontent by addressing every complaint except salary reveals management's strategy for dealing with first-class labor: Mullins prevented pay increases from appearing to result from employee demands; assented to reasonable adjustments to work conditions that did not affect operations; allowed the men a limited sense of having redress with management; and, finally, invested in living conditions in lieu of raising pay. What would become a significant investment in corporate colonialism stemmed from a desire to control labor costs and stifle employee organization along the way. It is reasonable to imagine that similar negotiations took place throughout the company's sphere of operations.

The outcome of this episode for the petitioning employees is unclear, but if events in the next few years are any indication, many of them left the company—most likely to work on the Panama Canal. "The rates in the Canal Zone are constantly being increased," Mullins wrote a year later, "and, in consequence, furnish a strong incentive for our men to go there."[45] Indeed, railroad men in Panama were quickly becoming the "labor aristocrats" of the zone, especially as excavation picked up in earnest in 1907.[46] Surely many of the UFCO's railroad men parlayed their tropical experience, however limited, and their proximity to the canal project into such choice jobs. The expansion of canal construction put pressure on the UFCO, and the better pay and living conditions offered by the government made an already difficult labor recruit-ment situation even worse—just when banana production in Costa Rica was entering its peak. Facing a serious labor shortage a few months after the petition, Mullins appealed to John Keefe, the trainmaster of the Central Ver-mont Railway, for all manner of railroad men. Conductors and engineers were at a premium, Mullins acknowledged, and he wrote directly to one prospect offering $135 monthly in gold soon after. He also wanted "some nice clean brakemen and firemen." In contrast to those higher up on the scale, men at these less skilled positions "are better suited with conditions, and the rate of pay means more to them."[47] Keefe came through for the NRC, for a few months later Mullins reported that "all the Vermonters are keeping well and appear to enjoy their new location."[48] So grateful was he to Keefe for these "clean young men and good workers" that he sought out for him Indian curios—bows, arrows, and machetes—and had them shipped to Vermont.[49]

Those "clean" workers from Vermont and elsewhere in the US Northeast, however, brought their own set of expectations with them along with their work ethic. A few years later, their discontent boiled over during a wave of labor violence and strikes that rocked the UFCO's Central American divisions in 1909 and 1910. These strikes originated in the discontent of the company's West Indian work force; in Costa Rica and Guatemala, the divisions most affected, racial tensions mirrored labor tensions and had turned deadly.[50] In early 1910, some eight thousand of the division's Jamaican laborers around Limón organized the Artisans and Laborers Union, apparently with the help of a "rather smart Spanish Lawyer."[51] The union's leadership reached out to their Hispanic coworkers and claimed that both groups were mistreated by the company. This move toward working-class unity seriously concerned UFCO officials. Work stoppages in the banana fields began in late July, at peaked on August 1, Emancipation Day in Jamaica. The UFCO broke the strike with the cooperation of the national government, and by replacing West Indian workers with Hispanics from the central highlands.[52]

Although the UFCO's white overseers were not involved in the strike, the white employees of the Northern Railway were. An overlooked dimension in historical writing about these episodes is the involvement of white first-class railroad employees in the strikes, at least in Costa Rica. Low pay and poor living conditions had continued to plague even the company's "labor aristoc-racy," and there is little reason to imagine circumstances being much different elsewhere. When the Jamaican union struck, the white conductors and engineers presented management with a petition demanding higher pay and shorter hours, a set of complaints not unlike those presented a few years before.[53] Whether or not the Americans coordinated their efforts with the Jamaicans is unclear, although UFCO manager E. Hitchcock claimed that the lead employee representative, NRC engineer and "agitator" M. L. Mathis, acted "in connection" with the Artisans and Laborers Union. NRC superintendent Mullins immediately boarded a train in San José for Puerto Limón, where he met with the men and summarily dismissed Mathis and another engineer for their effort "to create dissatisfaction and uprising among our Conductors and Locomotive Drivers."[54] Eighteen other American engineers and conductors refused to return to work unless their representatives were reinstated, a condition absolutely unacceptable to company management. Mullins exploited the company's close relationship to the Costa Rican government to have Mathis expelled as "a pernicious foreigner and disturber of the peace."[55] The expulsion order was promptly enacted, much to Mullins's satisfaction.[56] Breaking the railroad strike with outside labor proved unnecessary, for most of the remaining strikers "were promptly paid off" and returned to work.[57] Two Vermont men apparently refused, and the company arranged to have a Costa Rican police escort attached to them day and night until they left the country soon after.[58] With an eye to weeding out potentially troublesome remnants in the railroad's ranks, Mullins soon had ten new American railroad men en route on company steamships from New Orleans and Boston.[59] Mullins considered weeding out "tropical travelers"—American labor agitators abroad—a major accomplishment, one that would "forever put a stop to attempted organization amongst white employees in Costa Rica."[60] To his managerial peers facing labor activism in the United States and Canada at the same time, he chided that the means he could use to break strikes were "a little more effective than obtainable in Canada."[61] "We are more expeditious than the cold northerners [sic]," he concluded with satisfaction.[62]

The effects of these strikes were far reaching. In order to break the strikes in the fields and on the docks, the UFCO began hiring sizeable contingents of "native" labor—in the case of Costa Rica, Hispanics from the Central Highlands. What resulted was a major change in the demography of the company's divisions throughout its Central American divisions. After these years, management moved toward creating a racially segmented labor force, in which divisions between mostly mestizo Spanish-speakers and English-speaking black West Indians helped squelch the unity of labor. As to white employees, Mullins was right: no other efforts to unionize appear in the documentary record, although individual and collective petitions would occasionally find their way to management into the 1930s, and a climate of discontent continued to simmer. Managers essentially exchanged the unpredictability of unionization for the more predictable set of difficulties surrounding low retention. Destroying white organizing power meant that control over labor costs for first-class employees would remain in the hands of local management, which would tend to view top-down investments in corporate colonialism as the cheapest and most effective means to that end. That colonial project extended into the everyday lives of its employees. But choosing this path and crushing white organization did not dissolve discontent nor resolve the basic problems of economic difficulty for first-class employees.

Out on the farms, where white overseers and timekeepers earned much less than the railway men (in the 1910s a mandador earned between $100 and $125 monthly after an initial probationary period at much less; a railroad engineer could expect to start at $200). In some part, the company justified a few months at low salary in order to recuperate the costs of transporting the new man to the tropics. Turnover was high on the farms, but first-class men showed no signs of organizing.[63] Perhaps the relative quiescence of these employees, especially during strikes, stemmed from their workplaces and social milieus, where racial and occupational hierarchies mirrored each other. Like other subordinate whites in plantation contexts, those at the bottom of the superior stratum tended to be some of the most strenuous guardians of white authority. White overseers were indeed on the front line of conflict with Jamaican laborers, and it was tensions at this level that had spurred the strikes in the first place.[64] UFCO manager Hitchcock's handling of these men on the farms might have had something to do with their loyalty as well. Even as the strike brewed in the summer of 1910, Hitchcock fought hard with corporate headquarters to secure higher wages for overseers, timekeepers, and banana receivers. Over the course of 1909 and into the summer of 1910 he engaged in a series of sharp exchanges with Charles Hubbard, the UFCO treasurer in New York. Hubbard objected that the UFCO superintendent had raised salaries of several men to what he called the point of "extravagance"—around $125; he also questioned the irregular timing of the raises and the fact that they were not standardized for this rank of employee.[65] Hitchcock, a pragmatic and paternalistic manager, insisted again and again that his ability to grant raises on an ad hoc basis was essential to incentivizing his men. He explained that he often got at least several months' labor out of new recruits as a sort of probationary period, after which he granted them the customary wage of $100 to $125 monthly in gold, depending on the size of the farm to be supervised. Overseers and inspectors were often "a rough element," Hitchcock argued, prone to transient careers. What wages they were offered were the bare minimum that would keep them for even a short time. Without the expectation of raises dangled in front of them, "help would fight shy of the company."[66] Hitchcock's argument fairly boomed with frustration at the distant official. His pleas must have gone unanswered, for nearly a year later, on the eve of the strikes of 1910, he was still making them, hammering away at the UFCO's failure to pay market salaries. Exasperated, he declared that "we cannot expect them to work for us and put their hearts into their labor."[67] Tellingly, over on the company's railroad, William Mullins offered no such pleas to Boston and New York.

Hitchcock's complaints to headquarters also reveal something of the stark economic picture and the poor conditions facing first-class employees in the UFCO's tropical divisions at this time. Typically, a subordinate white based in Limón had to pay so much for room, board, and other expenses that only $17 was left "with which he must clothe himself, buy toilet articles and pay for such amusement as may be indulged in."[68] One married employee, a banana receiver, had worked his way up for three years from a very low starting salary of $50 a month to $110, earned "barely enough to pay their living expenses and live decently."[69] What was more, poor health conditions in the Limón division and inadequate medical facilities drove men away.[70] The lack of suitable housing and the high cost of living continued to trouble American employees for more than a decade. In 1919, management again faced a petition from railway employees demanding $50 monthly raises across the board, free living quarters, and preferential prices in company commissaries. A local manager with an appreciation of the labor market understood that the UFCO's monthly salary for a railroad engineer ($200) was far below those offered for the same work in the Canal Zone ($350) and in the United States ($280). "We cannot expect to secure or hold good men at these salaries," reported the NRC general manager that year, "without providing good comfortable living quarters."[71] As to the much smaller number of married employees, the dearth of company housing was even more problematic, for couples could only seek lodging in private dwellings around the town, characterized by "limited supply," "exorbitant prices," and "general unfitness."[72]

Management's response to these complaints and the history of discontent behind them soon led to a greater investment in infrastructure, all at a time when the company was engaged in a massive expansion into Costa Rica's Talamanca Valley. The NRC manager sought to diffuse this round of employee complaints by granting an immediate $20 raise, acquiring land around the UFCO's hospital complex, located on the shore north of the port, and building bungalows for married men and shared accommodations for single men.[73] Providing such facilities for most first-class employees enabled management to reduce NRC salaries by between $20 and $25 monthly, roughly the cost of "decent" lodging in Puerto Limón.[74] Two years later, the UFCO completed its Community House on Hospital Point, a social center and mess hall, amid the first-class housing complex and the recently expanded company hospital and medical laboratory. The new facility obviated the need for the much-reviled Limon Lodge, source of much employee protest over poor service and dismal food. As the company assumed total control of employee room and board and absorbed the cost of staff, equipment, and furnishings, the cost of board for each man went down from $30 to $25, according to the railway's manager. The total savings that came with the Community House, he estimated, stood at around $5000 a year.[75] As would be the case with most of the company's welfare efforts, men were expected to contribute a share, in this case the revolving stewardship of the facility and the expense of acquiring provisions. This significant investment in corporate colonialism and the greater involvement of employees in the operation of their mess hall apparently dulled organized protest among the division's first-class employees. Until the retrenchments and labor-force restructuring of the 1930s, employee petitions disappeared from the company's records.

Glimpses into the company's other divisions around the same time confirm the difficulty lower-level American employees faced just to get by. In Cuba, Everett Brown might have reveled in his place in the company's racial hierarchy, but his starting salary as a timekeeper and assistant to the engineering department—around $100 a month—made tight personal budgeting vital. With a wife and daughter to support in Massachusetts, he usually sent home at least $45 monthly, leaving little after room, board, and other expenses took the lion's share.[76] After two months in Cuba, he wrote that "It is a pretty tight rub to get along on what I have, [and I] have not been able to do it yet." His only recourse was to borrow from colleagues, a debt that had started to accumulate upon landing "broke" in Cuba in 1919.[77] Not long after landing, he began to note dissonance between the assurances that accompanied his hiring and conditions on the ground. As the expenses of daily life accumulated—laundry, clothing purchases, social life—Brown's complaints gained focus. "They tell good stories at Boston," he explained, "but here they are different." With his responsibilities, there was no way to get ahead, although the Preston division was "a good place for a single man to lay up money."[78] A radical organizer could not have put it more sharply: "this is a very expensive place to live," he groused, "and the company are [sic] using the men as a source of greater income than they have a right to expect." Between the high cost of living, low salaries, and the distance from home, Brown and the men he worked with often felt trapped, unable to wring better salaries out of management, saddled with debt after the passage down, and far from major population centers. "They have us both ways and in the middle," he concluded dourly, and his wife Ethel should prepare for shortfalls back in Boston.[79]

Although the company was already covering infrastructural costs and some transportation involved in corporate welfare measures, the fabric of society in this context essentially taxed first-class employees and justified keeping wages low. In Preston, Everett Brown keenly felt the pressure of keeping up with the social expenses of the first-class community. Company dances and other leisure activities were paid for by subscription, and such functions could cost each man between $4 and $7. For one particularly expensive Halloween dance in Guaro, Brown told his wife that he would try to get out of it, but feared creating bad feeling among his peers. He noted with some bitterness that the single young men had money already accumulated and none of his obligations, so they could spend more freely on such functions and on alcohol.[80] "I have to keep up some way," he felt, at least "enough to keep them satisfied."[81] In the end, he attended that particularly expensive function, though paying $4.30 for one night of entertainment stung. "I saw that it would cause hard feeling if I did not," he worried, pointing out that "It is policy to pay it, for they would make it very unpleasant here if they chose."[82] Brown felt such costs necessary to fit into a new community of colleagues, but paying them also carried important implications for his professional possibilities with the company. Soon after this particular dance, he overheard two of his supervisors weighing him for a supervisory position in the agricultural department, which would have brought a significant raise in pay. Overhearing such a conversation made paying his way into the community an acceptable loss. Resigned, he exclaimed, "I think it is policy just now not to start any antagonism, even if it hurts to pay the price."[83] Although the social opportunities afforded by the company's welfarism formed an important part of Brown's experience (especially in Cuba, before assumed a field post in Panama), he quite accurately and incisively calculated his own contribution to them within a larger calculus of his relationship to the company as a laborer.

Brown found much fewer grounds for complaint in the terrain of the material conditions of living. Wherever he lived with the company, even in camps and other temporary dwellings, he felt well cared for. In fact, as we shall see in a later chapter, he relished in living "on the edge of things." The men around him also might have had many grievances with the company—which he elaborated upon often—but apparently, they found their living conditions acceptable. As Brown followed the expansion of the railroad into Preston's hinterland in 1919, the company put him and a crew of other engineers in camp cars, white bunkhouses on rails with screened canopies over "a nice easy bed, with nice snowy bed clothes."[84] In Guabito, Panama, he had his own room in the Railroad House, a twenty-room facility for first-class men. The food might have been alien to him in Cuba—"dosed," as it was, by the "chino" cook—but it was always enough and of some quality.[85] In Panama, the variety was less than he was used to, but apparently it was fresher, and "does not grow in cans as all the food in Cuba did."[86] Brown's sense of where he stood relative to others in the company's world underlay some of his attitude about living conditions. Heading through Guaro, he noted the contrast between the tiny white colony, "an extra fine estate," and the "native" neighborhood, "the worst backyard you can find."[87] The racial hierarchy woven through the company's tropical world made Brown's living conditions better in another way: by providing him with personal servants, "house boys" whose cost was included as a part of lodging, both in Cuba and Panama. Both in the

field and at home, then, Brown thus found confirmed his sense of racial superiority. Critical as he could be of his bosses, and sensitive as he was to injus-
tices in the workplace, Brown's favorable testimony about material life rings
true. The cost might have been exorbitant, the likelihood of saving dim, but
the living conditions for first-class employees were good in Cuba and Panama. The contrast between his experience and that of his colleagues around
Puerto Limón from around the same years reminds us that the UFCO's world
contained significant variations in living conditions, although some common
threads connected them.

Another set of tensions revolved around workplace culture. The haughti-
ness and imperiousness of UFCO overseers and managers over their black
and Hispanic workers percolates through literature about the company; so
great were these conflicts that they could become bloody. Colby has shown
how violence between white overseers and black employees played a key role
in sparking the labor disputes of 1909 and 1910 in Costa Rica and Guatemala, and violence between white supervisors and blacks or Hispanics sim-
mered through Cuba and Panama during Brown's year-long UFCO career. As
fundamental as these divisions were during this period, they have led scholars to ignore in large measure the fault lines between bosses and subordinate
whites in the workplace. Upon examination, the absence of violence in these
relationships did not equate to harmony. As products of the US business
culture of the time, UFCO managers colored their authority in the workplace
with a paternalistic ethos, an attitude that had important implications for the
company's workplace culture in the tropics. The UFCO and its subsidiaries
tended to hire from their own ranks, and managers usually had several years
of tropical experience under their belts. The generational superiority of these
men, magnified by the perception that tropical duty was rougher and more
arduous than domestic experience, led older men to a set of assumptions
about newer American employees in the tropics: new generations were softer,
less loyal, and more prone to complaining than their previous generations;
they were unwilling to undergo the hardships of the tropics; and they often
failed to be properly grateful to the company and were unwilling to pay their
tropical dues before ascending to bigger and better things. These managerial
attitudes would wend their way into the company's effort to conscript the
loyalties of its first-class men at the height of its corporate welfare campaign
in the 1920s, a campaign to be detailed in a later chapter. The relationship of

Everett Brown with the company's management provides a useful window into the UFCO's workplace culture in different places at different times. His correspondence nearly always speaks to the experience of the men around him, adding to its resonance. No such picture can be exhaustive; my objective is to highlight experiences suggestive of deeper dynamics.

When Everett Brown started working in Cuba in 1919, he enjoyed a brief honeymoon period with his supervisors as he settled into an interesting new setting with deeply engaging work. Within a couple of months, however, he began to complain regularly about his treatment at the hands of management; often these complaints have the flavor of gripes honed after work in the company fellow workers. Most of his grievances about the company revolved around basic issues of labor economy—sometimes related to his own personal interest, and other times tied to the overall efficiency of the company's operations. Three months after his hiring, Brown was promoted and sent to Embarcadero, another UFCO outpost in the cane fields around Preston. He loved the work itself and the field engineers he lived and worked with, but the superintendent of engineers, a Mr. Timlin, was a "full-blooded jackass."[88] At Embarcadero, as he worked on designs for rail trestles, Brown and his peers felt like things were "up in the air" because of Timlin's "poor management"— apparently he overworked the engineers and foisted unrealistic expectations on them, and was "bound to run things regardless of the men."[89] During the 1919 holiday season, Timlin and other managers decided not to grant a holiday for New Year's Day, and Brown wrote home that "All the men have a grouch." "They seem to be after every minute they can get," he explained," and "every one is on edge."[90] As the company raced to complete the sugar harvest and continue expanding its properties around Preston the next month, Brown and his peers shook their heads in disgust. Management's commitment to keeping laborers' wages as low as possible had led to a serious shortage at a time of great need, and his sense was that decisions made far away had led the UFCO to such a situation: "This project is so darned big that at present they are slopping over in handling it. Their system is not elastic enough, they are trying to handle it from headquarters in Boston and not from conditions as they appear."[91] The company's overriding imperative to keep labor costs as low as possible was ultimately a centralized set of decisions enforced from distant Boston. Their effect on employee morale could be far-reaching, especially if a manager like Timlin—unlike Hitchcock in Costa Rica, for instance—took up labor economy with too much enthusiasm.

The UFCO's control over his mobility also bothered Brown. Out in the cane fields in Guaro, for instance, Brown groused at not being allowed a horse to travel on without charge during his off time. Apparently, the new manager had nixed the policy in order to save money and now the men had to pay $2 daily for a mount. Not only was the manager making a better showing of the division's expenses to his own higher-ups in Boston, he was keeping first-class men from having contact with other US companies, which offered better bonuses and higher wages than the UFCO.[92] Much more importantly, local UFCO managers exercised an iron control over vacations, which were a major source of contention with first-class employees. Managers and superintendents, who usually had their own families with them in country, routinely failed to empathize with the need of usually single lower-level employees to travel home with any regularity. Individual managers held on to the promise of vacations and dispensed them on a case-by-case basis, by all indications a company-wide practice.[93] This lack of certainty could be especially maddening to a family man like Brown. Almost a year into his tropical career, now an engineer in Panama, Brown called in a long-held promise for a vacation. After weeks of frustrated requests, the superintendent responded that vacations were granted "as a reward of merit for services rendered and not as a regular occurrence."[94] Unsatisfied with this response, Brown reminded his boss that a vacation had been held out to him as an inducement to come to Panama, and that he would resign if it were not granted. "I have been led to believe it is my due," he grumbled to his wife.[95] In the end, the division manager, Mr. Blair, did not follow through on the agreement Brown had made with the central office of the UFCO regarding a vacation. Blair argued that he would only grant a vacation as a reward for a year's service within his division, regardless of whether a man had transferred in from another company division or not.[96] Brown, disgusted with this treatment and sorely missing his family, resigned from the UFCO a month later.

The paternalistic managerial culture of the UFCO, despite its variations, played an important role in the company's decades-long retention woes. Management on the ground in the tropical divisions exercised great authority over the lives and the mobility of first-class labor, and regarded these men as a significant challenge to retain and discipline. From the perspective of what must have been many employees, the conditions of employment and daily life could make a lengthy career with the UFCO quite difficult. Every source base reveals that Brown's case was not exceptional. He spoke of a steady flow of disgruntled American employees from the company, and joined that flow when he was fed up and had an offer from a US sugar company in Cuba. Even upbeat assessments of the first-class labor situation revealed a dark underbelly. In 1923, the UFCO manager in Costa Rica, M. Marsh, reported to corporate headquarters in Boston with happy news about the white work force in his division. After some years of having to tolerate a "restless and unsatisfactory type of employee," in part because of labor shortages during the war, times were changing and turnover was sharply down. "It would seem," he noted with nostalgia, "that the old-time conditions, when a man came down with the idea of remaining and making good, are returning once more."[97] Showing a hearty enthusiasm for the Fordist ethos of corporate welfare, he touted the success of company-sponsored recreation, morale-boosting activities, and improved living conditions in shaping a new workforce. Although buoyed by a temporary improvement in retention, Marsh's recollection of the good old days and his hopes for the future reveal much more about the anxieties and fantasies of fruit company managers than they do about realities on the ground, before or after the early 1920s. Even at the height of the UFCO's Division Betterment Program—an aggressive corporate welfare drive undertaken by company president Victor Cutter in the late 1920s—white Americans continued to leave tropical divisions at an alarming rate. In 1927, 39 percent of these men in the agricultural department, the majority of them with less than five years with the company, quit for a variety of reasons, most of them medical and disciplinary.[98]

Conclusions

In order to maintain a racial division of labor based on white supremacy, the United Fruit Company and its subsidiaries labored mightily against a series of vexing problems: climatological and cultural concerns about whiteness in the tropics, misbehavior of various stripes, labor costs (including the costs of corporate welfare), labor activism, and growing competitive pressure from the local labor market. In some ways, they fought a dogged battle with subordinates that characterized economic struggles within the US labor force at large; other difficulties were tinged with the particularly tropical nature of the UFCO's enterprise. The issues that arose with those white populations in tropical divisions occupied a great deal of managerial attention in the early twentieth century and steadily pushed managers to adopt a range of corporate welfare measures that, in the context of tropical divisions, amounted to a vast experiment in corporate colonialism. Corporate welfarism in the tropics grew piecemeal out of local labor struggles, and was forged in the tense relationship between management and restive first-class employees. By the 1920s, as former tropical managers such as Victor Cutter rose to the upper ranks of the corporation, these efforts became centralized in the form of a "Division Betterment Program" designed to attract, discipline, and retain the white men considered so vital to the company's operations. The institutional infrastructure of welfarism—hospitals, living quarters, community centers, and athletic facilities—was well in place by that decade. What makes the UFCO's presence particularly "colonial," however, would be the ideological practices that infused those spaces with meaning, a campaign to culturally conscript this troublesome class of employee into the company's mission. The company's relations with its subordinate whites provide a window into the complications and vexations at the heart of the US corporate presence in early twentieth-century Latin America, and show that the problems of colonial governance in the tropics were central to the US economic relationship with the region.

CHAPTER THREE

Corporate Welfarism Meets the Tropics

In 1929 business writer Samuel Crowther noted that United Fruit's success in Latin America rested on the "twin fundamentals" of "health and recreation."[1] After a visit to a banana district of Santa Marta, Colombia, he argued that physical vitality set apart United Fruit's American employees from their failed competitors, in this case the agents of a departed French banana company. Close to where the French "overlords" had lounged amid imported luxuries and foolishly extracted the wealth of the land, dedicated Americans administered a flourishing modern enterprise. The French may have whiled away their many off-hours in an old "chateau" with ostentatious banquets, but their American successors rose early, worked hard, and filled the newly constructed tennis courts in the afternoons.[2] Europeans, concerned only with extracting profits and enjoying the privileges of authority, had declined as colonizers and as men. Effete and vice-ridden, they had surrendered their masculine vitality to the pressures of climate and the comforts of colonial status. Their failed enterprises (this banana company, and, by extension, the first Panama Canal effort) dotted the American tropics. The United Fruit men, on the other hand, remade the landscape they found, eschewing the status of the abandoned chateau for "a dozen or more neat and comfortable bungalows facing well kept streets with paved sidewalks."[3] The construction of this built environment and its triumph over the local ecology was echoed in the vitality of the men who inhabited it. For Crowther, the company's built environment and the community practices that filled it distinguished US business, "which creates as it goes along," from the decadent, "feudatory" French company.[4] What Crowther observed was a mature corporate welfare program that had grown out of years of tension and negotiation between first-class employees and the company.

Now I turn to United Fruit's effort to build and foster such viable North American colonies around the Caribbean Basin. The first section focuses on the construction of built environments that housed thousands of Latin American or West Indian workers and North American employees and inscribed on the landscape the superiority of the latter. United Fruit built a sizeable infrastructure for the welfare of its employees: hospitals, commissaries, social clubs, hotels, parks, and a variety of athletic facilities. These facilities were primarily, but not always exclusively, meant for white managers, technicians, and clerical staff, but performed a vital function as demonstrations of a racialized sense of US technological prowess. The enclave communities that developed in these spaces were also the product of corporate colonialism, for United Fruit labored mightily to shape them and the norms of sociability in specific ways. On a frontier of empire in the early twentieth century, the company's corporate welfarism assumed vast dimensions as an experiment in overseas colonialism.

United Fruit Company Towns in Context

As United Fruit built its tropical divisions over the course of the early twentieth century, its executives could draw from an abundance of examples of company town–building throughout the United States and in parts of Latin America. Company towns had a long history, with precedents in colonial-era trading-company outposts and New England mill towns that had to build communities close to sources of hydraulic power in the nineteenth-century United States.[5] By the early twentieth century, the company town was well-established in industrial societies and on resource frontiers tied to metropolitan economies. In many ways, United Fruit's towns around the Caribbean shared characteristics of design and function with counterparts around the United States, Latin America, and the European colonies of the day. United Fruit's tropical divisions typically contained a company-built town or section of an existing town, with subordinate bases spread over the company's cultivations, which it denominated "farms." A network of trunk and feeder railways fanned out from company ports into agricultural hinterlands. Through mechanized ports, this rail network linked with the company's sea lanes and US or European ports.

At the time United Fruit was building its own towns, its leadership embraced the movement in US business toward corporate welfarism—policies designed to foster harmonious relations between management and labor.[6] A key part of United Fruit's welfarism was its embrace of the "new" or "model" company town. According to John Garner, model company towns shared these features: "(1) a central authority directing planning and construction, (2) a standard house type, and (3) community programs and facilities to edify newcomers while providing social diversion"—all characteristics of United Fruit's towns.[7] In the early twentieth century, company leaders could look to a number of well-publicized model company towns, including Pullman and LeClaire, Illinois, and Milton Hershey's towns in Pennsylvania and Cuba, among many others.[8] Charismatic utopian industrialists usually drove such developments. As part of a broad pattern of corporate community-building, United Fruit's American zones reflected the shift, beginning in about 1900, toward what Margaret Crawford terms "new" company towns—a term describing the widespread embrace of model town design by US corporations. From then until the 1930s, many US businesses adopted design preferences influenced by model towns in the United States and the Garden City movement, whose British proponents sought to ameliorate labor relations through harmonious planned communities. Such plans "explicitly effaced the visual connection between the living environment and its industrial origins" by employing landscape architecture and building styles that softened the edges of the stark, factory-oriented company housing patterns of the nineteenth century.[9] Significant investments in landscaping, recreational spaces, comfortable housing, and a variety of community-building activities showcased the commitment of United Fruit's leadership to supplying its American workforce with the benefits of "new" company towns. This corporate welfare campaign, in motion from the company's earliest years, found its completest expression in the 1920s. Throughout this period, company executives embraced the capacity of built environment to retain and mold a stable, content cadre of American employees abroad.[10]

Besides their practical function as transportation nodes and residences, United Fruit's built environments functioned as what historian Ricardo Salvatore has termed "spectacles of corporate modernity." "Modern company towns . . . in the middle of jungles, mountains, or deserts," he argues, "showed the power of US capital to defeat nature's most awesome obstacles."[11] United Fruit publicists and its US employees often made sense of their activities as spectacles. In particular, they found expressions of what David Nye terms the "technological sublime" in the company's engineered landscapes and built environment. In the industrial-era United States, Nye argues that Americans created an aesthetic concept of the sublime meant "to reinvest the landscape and the works of men with transcendent significance."[12] By the early twentieth century, Americans were seeking the sublime in both natural land-scapes and in the shaping of those spaces with industrial technologies.[13]

A crucial element of Nye's discussion of the technological sublime is that it represented a particularly American way of experiencing and representing the physical world. Part of what made the perspective American was its fundamentally participatory nature. This conclusion bears out in the United Fruit case; spectacles of harmonious unions of technology and landscape in the company's tropics were, to borrow Nye's phrasing, "an experience orga-nized for crowds of tourists."[14] Through their day-to-day interactions with company spaces, both American employees and tourists were participants in and consumers of a spectacle of nature made benevolent and productive by American energies. The participatory nature of such spectacles, however, had boundaries that are perhaps less clear within the United States. Non-white populations of workers inhabited the company's built environment dif-ferently than their white American supervisors. As an expression of technological sublimity, company enclaves were meant to infuse Americans with pride in their company, their nation, and in the Anglo-Saxon race. Tech-nological triumphs were meant to instill Latin American workers with a sense of awe and gratitude while reminding them of their place in the com-pany's racialized division of labor.

Sanitation and Built Environment

In the 1890s and early 1900s, when United Fruit set about to build its tropi-cal divisions, the long-term tropical residence of white Europeans and Amer-icans posed serious problems for governments and companies operating in those environments. The company's first years of expansion coincided with decades when tropical medical professionals had discerned the causes of some tropical diseases but older preventative regimes retained their appeal. Like other European or North American enterprises in tropical climates, several notions of tropical health probably influenced the design of United Fruit towns and housing. The company's "sanitary cottages" or bungalows, built for American employees in tropical divisions, incorporated design fea-tures and nomenclature from the British experience in South Asia.[15] These dwellings were built off the ground and featured several large windows and spacious, airy verandahs. These elements distanced living areas from the soil, maximized air flow, and allowed residents to control, to some extent, ventilation. Residents could maintain steady body temperature and avoid stagnant air, long objects of European tropical anxieties.[16] Copper mesh mosquito netting, a recent American innovation, sealed dwellings while retaining these older functions.

The landscaping of the company's American zones underlined their status as cordons sanitaires carved out of potentially deadly environments. United Fruit drew from the European colonial experience in the tropics, where curtailing the vegetation surrounding dwellings was one preventative measure developed before there was a clear understanding of the relationship between flora and human disease. By beating back vegetation and maintaining closely cropped lawns and hedges, nineteenth-century European colonials observed reduced rates of tropical fevers, maladies later understood to be mosquito-borne.[17] As the role of mosquitoes in spreading disease gained scientific currency, replacing humid, leafy breeding grounds with short lawns and hedges gained further justification as a part of town design.[18] The company also removed potential mosquito breeding grounds through drainage, trash removal, and the application of petroleum to wetlands.[19] Company doctors and executives understood that healthy living conditions in the Caribbean were central to attracting and retaining the cadres of Americans necessary to run plantations. In this argument, only with a healthy population of white managers could the Caribbean lowlands be rendered productive sources of food for North American consumers.[20]

United Fruit's medical infrastructure and its investment in creating sanitary conditions performed several functions. They improved the health of all employees, to be sure, but also extended the company's authority into employee living spaces and projected a set of meanings about the company's role in the tropics. Orderly townscapes, built according to the imperatives of medical science, represented nature tamed by a combination of science, corporate benevolence, and the company's authority over its field of operations. Addressing colleagues in 1924 at a company-sponsored medical conference in Jamaica, Dr. William Deeks placed the company's work over the past decades in a historical context. Deeks situated the company's "energy and foresight" and "skilled direction" of medical efforts as the successors of the futile campaigns of earlier European colonialists.[21] This corporate-driven health campaign, according to Deeks, transcended even the ambitious efforts of the US military, which had overseen similar efforts in occupied areas of the Caribbean. The difference between United Fruit and the military, in this view, was that the company came to stay—its improvements provided the practical and ideological basis of a potentially permanent company presence.

Social Hierarchy and Town Organization

The social hierarchy of the enclave was inscribed in the design of United Fruit's housing and the layout of its towns. The company's towns housed the white managers and technicians who oversaw the production and movement of commodities. Laborers—either indigenous to host countries or contracted from the West Indies—inhabited segregated areas on the margins of these towns. Scholars, writers, and political activists have emphasized this segregation in United Fruit towns as spatially reinforcing the aloofness of American employees from their surroundings and the company's neglect or abuse of its work force.[22] Similar spatial arrangements that underlined class and racial hierarchies characterized company towns across the United States and Latin America in the early and mid-twentieth century.[23] Such segregation projected workplace hierarchies into the realm of off hours and daily life.[24]

The company's nonwhite workers inhabited relatively spare living spaces, often set off from white neighborhoods by railroad tracks. In places, the company housed workers in barracks, especially where a transitory labor force best suited the company's cultivations. Everett Brown observed such dwellings in the Cuban sugar divisions of Preston and Banes, which depended on migratory labor from Haiti or Puerto Rico. From Guaro, he described the division between white and black housing in stark terms: "The town is composed of one line of shacks or stores on one side of the railroad and the white settlement on the other. It is like going from the worst backward you can find into an extra fine estate there—in going from the native to the white quarters here."[25]

In his time with United Fruit, Brown sent home few photographs. Those he chose to send complemented his descriptions of company housing. Along with a self-portrait in front of his copper-screened house, he mailed a shot of "a typical nigger house taken 'down the line' as we call it . . . on the outskirts of town."[26] Brown's drawing of Embarcadero shows the spatial hierarchy of the place. The supervisor, Gartner, inhabited the largest quarters, while

Figure 3.1. "Overseer's House, Atalanta Farm, Costa Rica Division." Original caption reads: "Screened throughout. It will be noted that dense foliage of hedge directly in front of house is further away at sides and to the rear, allowing free circulation of air under building." Annual Report of the Medical Department of the United Fruit Company 1917, p. 81.

Brown and two other engineers occupied smaller individual rooms in the same screened building. Laborer barracks lay to the east, separated from management by two utility buildings.[27] Although the company made much of its paternalistic concern for sanitary worker housing, any observer could see the gulf between two classes of employee expressed in the built environment. The company's critics correctly considered this segregated, unequal housing system a symbol of United Fruit's heavy-handed treatment of its workers.[28] Brown, comfortable with harsh handling of manual laborers, drew another conclusion from his experience: one's housing reflected one's social worth. The company's segregated and unequal built environment invested him in the racialized hierarchy of United Fruit's enterprise.

According to one historian, "the more elaborate housing provided for managers gave physical expression to their power over local workers."[29] Although company housing for managers and technicians lacked the variety of

VIEWS OF BANES.

Figure 3.2. Showcasing the company's model towns in the tropics, in this case the sugarcane division of Banes, Cuba. Spacious streets, modern buildings, sports fields, and parks reflected the UFCO's investment in its enclaves. "Views of Banes." Annual Report of the Medical Department of the United Fruit Company 1913, p. 82.

residential architecture in the United States, differences in status, even relatively small ones within the white work force, would have been immediately recognizable to American employees. In the 1920s the company's Division Betterment Program defined several classes of residence for white employees: superintendent residence; small cottage for married employees; larger married employee residence; standard overseer's house with office; and four-room bachelor quarters.[30] Superintendents and their families inhabited large, multiroom homes with spacious, tidy, landscaped back yards. For this highest echelon of employees, the residence could have more than one story and be quite large. The next class of managers, overseers, lived in smaller one-family dwellings, and single white employees lived in bachelor's housing. Unmarried technicians or functionaries like Brown usually lived in dormitories with colleagues of similar status. In Cuba and Panama, he lived in a variety of living quarters, most often shared between him and two to four others. Within the ranks of white employees, family housing served as an incentive for long service. A supervisor's family residence in Preston impressed Brown

as a place worthy of raising a white family, a potential reward he found enticing. In weighing his prospects with the company, he spoke hopefully about
obtaining such quarters and reuniting with his family.

Domesticating Space through the Built Environment

Attracting and retaining white employees in the tropics required a concerted
effort to make enclaves into the kind of "civilized" places Everett Brown
longed for—environments reminiscent of North American townscapes, cor-
doned off from their surroundings. One cornerstone of United Fruit's strategy
was to domesticate its tropical divisions and to make them culturally familiar to potential employees. The result could look like an American iteration
of the European tropical colony. Emerging from the Guatemalan highlands
into the lowland town of Quiriguá in the mid-1920s, travel writer Arthur
Ruhl noted that upon passing into "the banana plantations, screened overseer's headquarters and spotless hospitals of the United Fruit Company, you
are, for all practical purposes, in a detached bit of the United States with a
'colonial' ruling class as remote psychologically from the land it lives in as
are the Canal Zone Americans at Panama."[31] Like British compounds in its
South Asian colonies, United Fruit made its tropical divisions into culture
areas "modified according to the metropolitan society as interpreted by the
colonial community." Such an effort, as noted one historian of empire, "was
instrumental in maintaining a sense of identity" among Europeans living
abroad.[32] However well-appointed and sanitary company enclaves might have
been before the mid-1920s, after Preston's death in 1924, efforts to improve
enclaves intensified. Under Victor Cutter's presidency, the company made
their American-ness more explicit and publicized the efforts of a Divisional
Betterment Program in the new employee newsmagazine *Unifruitco*. Creating
an enclave "culture area" meant more than just transplanting certain forms
of American life in tropical lowlands. These spaces, described by scholars
and company publicists as American islands, functioned as lenses through
which employees might envision their place in the company's mission to modernize the tropics.

More prosaically, these zones created a sense of community among all
levels of the white work force.[33] Relatively compact neighborhoods linked by
sidewalks and ample public spaces undergirded the kind of close-knit

communities the United Fruit sought to foster. Town grids of blocks bounded by spacious streets and sidewalks provided these employees with a familiar matrix of residential life. Almost exclusively pedestrian traffic encouraged routine face-to-face socialization between US employees of all ranks. "With this compact grouping and such close daily contacts," noted Verson Gooch of Almirante, Panama, "it is easy to understand how the Division develops such strong ties of close association and friendship."[34] Such layouts mitigated the sense of being billeted in a foreign land. Moving to a United Fruit town, for an American, meant stepping into a community of people with similar status and expectations—a strong sense of being "Unifruitcoers" that Atalia Shragai has masterfully documented in UFCO communities from the 1920s until the 1950s.[35]

Walking through most United Fruit divisional headquarters towns in the 1920s, a newly arrived US employee or tourist might have been struck first by the well-manicured lawns, parks, and walkways that surrounded company buildings. Sidewalks and paths invited pedestrian traffic and face-to-face socialization, rather than just direct routes to workplaces.[36] Like other model or new company towns of the time, this town design distanced communities from the productive function of enclaves.[37] Parks such as those in Banes and Puerto Limón interrupted the orderly grids of their surrounding towns and nearby ports and provided tranquil spaces in the shadow of ports and office buildings. Hedges and lawns around company buildings softened the impression of industrial landscapes of port facilities, warehouses, railroads, and sugar refineries. While in Guabito, Everett Brown noted approvingly that the company was in the midst of installing some four thousand feet of concrete sidewalks.[38] Having walked miles over railroad sleepers and muddy roads through company sugar plantations in Cuba, sidewalks represented a welcome addition for an employee who filled many off hours taking walks.

Alongside residential areas, United Fruit built recreational spaces for its US employees in the tropics. The centerpieces of this policy were company-sponsored social clubs, which emerged in the company's early years. Almost every tropical division in the 1920s possessed a club building, which incorporated several functions of social clubs that developed in the nineteenth-century United States.[39] The degree of isolation appears to have influenced the level of such developments. In some divisions, employee social life meshed with that existing within the wider US colonies there. Social pages for those divisions—especially Havana and Colón, Panama—reveal none of the company-built recreational facilities that were so central to social life in more isolated enclaves. Other divisions had separate company zones but existed alongside significant noncompany settlements. In Puerto Limón, Costa Rica, the *zona bananera* (banana company zone) lay about half a mile north of the port, and employees formed the heart of a larger expatriate community. The company's "Community House" hosted social events involving the entire white colony of Limón, whether or not they were company employees. In more isolated divisions, such as those around Almirante in Panama or in the Cuban sugar divisions of Preston and Banes, United Fruit dedicated significant resources to its own club buildings. In enclaves removed from surrounding settlements with US or British colonies, these facilities formed the backbone of social life for US workers.

One analysis of clubs in British enclaves in India could well describe United Fruit's club buildings: "The club, with its familiar surroundings and established rituals, provided the setting for the exchange of . . . social knowledge, the place where community beliefs and sentiments were continuously reinforced and modified, the context in which newcomers were socialised into the folkways of the colonial culture."[40] In United Fruit enclaves, these buildings contained dining facilities, bars, billiard halls, dance floors, libraries, and even musical instruments. The Banana Club building at Almirante, Panama, illustrates the multiple functions such facilities could house. The club's first floor held administrative offices related to the shipment of fruit; the second floor was given to bachelor quarters; and the third floor housed a club room that doubled as a dining hall, at least for unmarried employees.[41] In Puerto Castilla, Honduras, the company built a hotel in 1926 that doubled as an employee social club. The Castilla Hotel and Club in Tela replicated similar buildings in the company's Cuban and Colombian divisions. One of the first priorities in building a new division was the construction of an American club.

Everett Brown's observations of the Guabito Banana Club—not a hotel, but a multiuse social facility all the same—provide insight into the day-to-day workings of this kind of infrastructure. This building provided a focal point of socialization for white employees, housing daily necessities such as meals and off-hours recreation. On a typical work day, American employees took their meals there, and after dinner might read periodicals, chat, and

Figure 3.3. Recreation formed a part of daily routine in tropical divisions. Here, UFCO first-class employees enjoy a game of billiards in a company social club. "Men Playing Billiards, ca. 1920s" UF54.004, Box 54, United Fruit Company Photograph Collection, Mss: 1 (1891–1962), U860, Baker Library.

play cards or pool. The availability of foreign and US magazines and newspapers particularly impressed Brown, who wrote approvingly of the company library. At least in Guabito, United Fruit spent about $200 annually on these reading materials.[42] Aside from occasional excursions to Almirante or Bocas del Toro, the club served as the hub of American social life in this small company town. The club space performed a key community-building function in Guabito, as it probably did in most other company divisions. On a daily basis, this company-funded facility fostered a collegial atmosphere among male employees and cemented their ties to the United States through printed media. Brown's cheerful accounts of afternoons and evenings spent in the club among friends illustrate the community-building function of such places.

The position and stylish décor of club buildings reminded middle-class white employees of their superiority over lower-echelon nonwhite labor. Like company towns in the US South, recreational facilities cultivated the solidarity of white employees with management.[43] United Fruit social clubs embodied a similar strategy. Panoramic views and abundant outdoor spaces dedicated to lounging echoed the enclave's social hierarchy in a context of leisure. Upon entering the Castilla Club in the Tela Division, one would find to the right a "bar and to the left a row of French windows leading to the wide and breezy veranda facing the Bay." "This veranda," continued the writer, "is furnished with hickory furniture of rustic design"—aesthetic luxuries that would have been absent from spaces inhabited by the company's laborers.[44] White employees could lounge and socialize while looking out over their surroundings. After living in a sea of sugar cane in Cuba, Everett Brown happily frequented the Guabito Banana Club, describing it as "a nice cheerful room with a veranda overlooking a part of town."[45] In the absence of air conditioning, verandahs and covered porches amended the interiors of club buildings. Dry, well ventilated spaces provided relief from a climate that many North American employees must have found uncomfortably hot. Like their counterparts in other tropical colonies, verandahs performed the cultural function of providing "a spatial device to express the occupants' status in relation to that of indigenous guests."[46] Open exteriors displayed the leisure time of white employees to the mass of unskilled labor who inhabited the lowest echelons of the company's hierarchy, some part of whom circulated or worked near these places.

Besides providing pleasant walkways and social spaces, the landscaping of company-controlled areas contained a self-conscious expression of spatial order and modernization. In Panama, Brown noticed that older company towns like Almirante and even newer outposts like Guabito to the north were "fixed up nice" with "Well trimmed hedges and trees."[47] The orderly appearance of these enclaves appealed to Brown's notions of civilized space and brought an improvement over the "raw" conditions he had left behind in Cuban railroad camps. In the mid-1920s, Victor Cutter's Divisional Betterment Program intensified the transformation of public spaces in tropical divisions. Once-disorderly spaces of scrub brush or tropical bush were converted into well-cropped lawns. In a 1926 visit to Colombia, Verson Gooch noted approvingly the "reclamation" of unruly spaces:

Somebody is doing a good job here with Bermuda grass. All the area around the Merchandise, M. & S., and Machine Shop buildings was last year nothing but Santa Marta sand, deep and glaring, hot and blowing about. Now they have green lawns all over this reserved area, closely clipped and watered. You've got to see it to believe it. . . . Mr. Pollan [the division head] states that he hopes to cover the entire sand area between the Prado [the company's American zone] and town buildings with a green Bermuda grass covering by the next time I come around a year hence. It is hard to visualize and realize what that will mean in comfort of living at the Prado.[48]

Gooch encouraged his readers to visualize this dramatic transformation of townscape as an extension of United Fruit's larger mission. Like the expansion of banana plantations into formerly "useless" tropical lowlands, the expansion of grass and hedges paralleled the company's agricultural enterprise. The transformational capacities of the company found expression in this intensified effort to manage the appearance of residential zones. Living and working in company towns, American employees and their families inhabited a microcosmic version of the company's tropical enterprise— nature made orderly and productive through the company's transformation of the local environment and its ability to control a mass of unskilled labor.

Domesticating fruit towns also involved a concerted effort to portray them as places where an employee's family life could thrive. The family unit deemed most effective for retention abroad was nuclear, usually represented by a couple and one or two children. The condition and activities of American children in tropical divisions served the company's publicity purposes well, and revealed the anxieties about tropical life that dogged United Fruit's personnel. Despite the company's years of investment in medical infrastructure, sanitation, and disease control through landscape alteration, fears about the long-term effects of tropical residence on children persisted into the 1930s. To dispel these concerns, descriptions of children, especially boys, emphasized their physical health and robust size and the vigor of their activities. After a tour of tropical divisions, a Fruit Dispatch Company employee advised his readers to take notice of the potential for raising healthy children there:

The traveler should find time to stroll through the residential section of the Divisional headquarters of the banana port he visits. Thus he will come back with the proper picture of living conditions provided for North

American employees down south. He should see the youngsters of these families and determine in his own mind whether they are less husky than his own at Cedar Falls. He should stand on the wind-swept beach and watch them swim and play and ride their ponies, and he should determine for himself how well his own little Willy would stack up with them.[49]

In a similar vein, Tela's *Unifruitco* reported in 1926 that the division was "mighty proud of her children, and has a right to be. They are a husky bunch,—tanned by the sun and stimulated by the sea. They ride like troopers, are fearless and powerful swimmers, and real honest-to-goodness kids."[50] A photograph of "husky Almirante youngsters" in late 1925—one of many such images regularly appearing in the magazine—illustrates the company's attempt to broadcast evidence of healthy life in the tropics by holding the most vulnerable members of American colonies up as beneficiaries of the climate.

The image of the tanned, physically fit American, both adult and child, appeared in company literature as a physically vital, outdoor-oriented figure who dominated the tropical environment through vigorous outdoor activity. For young boys in enclaves, scouting provided an outlet for and exhibition of this culture of physical vitality. In at least one company division, Tela (Honduras), employees organized a Boy Scout troop in the mid-1920s. Apparently, the Tela Tiger Patrol formed sometime in 1926, and a charter from the Boy Scout organizing body in London was petitioned for the next year. Begun by Baden-Powell in 1907 in Britain, scouting arose from the British colonial experience and the growing cult of outdoor vitality in the United States and Britain in the early twentieth century.[51] In Tela, male employees volunteered as scoutmasters and consumed the organization's literature and guidelines for establishing troops in far-flung places. Echoing the language of the Boy Scouts, the head scoutmaster noted that "the primary aim is to convey to the mind of the growing boy a higher ideal of physical fitness, moral cleanliness and mental alertness."[52] At least in its rhetoric, the normative culture of scouting, which stressed self-control of adolescent bodies, teamwork within pseudomilitary hierarchies, and respect for adult authority, provided a template well-suited to the policing of child health in the tropics.

This scout troop provided its participants a structure that lent meaning to outdoor activities. On one camping trip 1926, eleven scouts and four scout-masters traveled into "the bush," first on a company train and then by hand-cart. The troop planted its flag at a spot along the Mazapa River and christened the spot "Tela B. S. camp." Over the following days, the boys kept camp, swam, and absorbed lessons in "scout lore" imparted by the scoutmas-ters—lessons that at the time included camp crafts like woodcarving and proper tool use, singing, and absorbing tales that reinforced patriotic virtues and the value of outdoor life and appreciation of nature.[53] Moving into the bush, naming a space, and making a camp also replicated, on a small scale, United Fruit's acquisition of territory—small exploratory missions followed by larger survey camps, logging camps, and, finally, the establishment of permanent banana-growing farms. Scouting introduced company boys to the celebration of an ecology that the company and the scoutmasters themselves were in the process of altering.

Schools formed the cornerstone of childrearing in the UFCO's white enclaves. Where significant white colonies existed, the company maintained one-room schoolhouses that usually taught kindergarten through ninth grade. These children were from the families of upper management or employ-ees whose longevity had earned them accommodations for a family—an employee like Everett Brown could only aspire to such a luxury. Student bodies ranged from ten to thirty students. The teachers were some of few women the company hired during these years, and came from the United States fully credentialed for the classroom. During the peak years of the company's Anglo-American colonies, company publicity touted the quality of these institutions. Divisional reports in *Unifruitco* offered brief sketches of some schools, noting an added library here, a new teacher there. Class por-traits projected an image of health and order for tropical-division youngsters.[54]

Connection to the consumer economy of the United States undergirded this assuring picture of family life abroad. Readers found frequent reference, both written and visual, to the company's Merchandise Department, which main-tained company department stores in tropical divisions. Company commissar-ies have provided much fodder for United Fruit's critics, who have criticized their abusive practices toward laboring populations in enclaves.[55] As with other elements of United Fruit's corporate welfare efforts, the experience of American employees with these institutions was distinct from that of nonwhite laborers and has been overlooked. Company commissaries formed a crucial set of connections between American employees and North American consumer markets. One newcomer to the tropics, an employee's wife, noted with satisfaction that living conditions in Santa Marta, Colombia were surprisingly "American." Besides the living conditions provided by the company, she based this impression on her identity as a consumer. What she particularly enjoyed was regular access to many food staples from home, even fresh produce.[56] Foodstuffs from the United States performed the important function for United Fruit's steamship traffic, filling valuable cargo space that otherwise would have been wasted on runs out of US ports. Refrigerated cargo space had the added benefit of bringing American-grown fruits and vegetables across great distances to employees in the tropics, thereby shrinking the cultural distance between company outposts and the United States.[57] Americans could even find familiar fresh foods served on company farms in the interior, at the UFCO's farthest frontier. United Fruit employee Herman J. Wacker, on a vacation tour of tropical divisions in 1927, was surprised to find American food served on the distant Río Frío Farm in the Santa Marta division of Colombia.[58] The company capitalized on its merchandising efforts to communicate the idea that American families in the tropics would retain their ties to the consumer economy of the United States.

The company's ability to compress geographical space with a network of company stores may well have impressed employees. On the ground, middle-echelon Americans probably understood this logistical achievement but, in the end, viewed commissaries from the perspective of consumers, and not always positively. From Everett Brown, an engineer who had to support himself in the field and his family in Boston, the expense of purchasing goods from the company brought frequent complaint. Once in Cuba, having to outfit himself in tropical clothing constituted a significant expense. Preparing for fieldwork in Panama, he morosely related to his wife the high cost of personal gear for the jungle—clothing, puttees, and a pistol—which the company refused to provide. Being stationed away from headquarters towns also influenced his perception of commissaries, especially at Christmas, when he could not get to Preston to find a gift for his daughter in time for the holiday.[59] Displeased with this situation, he wrote home that "this is a very expensive place to live, and the company are [sic] using the men as a source of greater income than they have a right to expect." He suggested these feelings were widespread, concluding that "they have us both ways and the middle."[60] The Merchandise Department's desire to maximize revenue could undermine the role of commissaries as links to a distant consumer culture.

Crucial to the creation of domesticated spaces was the racial privilege of white Americans in company colonies. Americans inhabited this privilege both in the workplace and during off-hours. Embedded within the small-town, middle-class flavor of household life was a social structure that promised access to nonwhite servants, for married couples and single male employees. For most Americans taking a position in the tropical divisions, the expense of household servants probably lay out of reach in the United States. The company often provided American households at least one servant to do kitchen work, laundry, and landscaping. In Guaro, a Japanese cook and four Jamaican "house boys" served Brown and bachelor employees. While Puerto Ricans or Haitians formed the bulk of the labor force in eastern Cuba's sugar cultivations, Jamaicans apparently predominated as house servants because of shared language. Brown bluntly described the relationship to his wife: "They do anything you want done, wait on tables or anything. . . . The blacks are hired here for that purpose—to be used. Everything is kept clean around the white quarters."[61] Brown's racialized sense of order and cleanliness led him to identify whites with hygiene and nonwhites with the dirty work necessary to maintain that state. This distinction grew from that racialized division of labor and white control of nonwhite labor, both in the cultivations and in living areas.

Both in Cuba and Panama, Brown was pleased to find black servants to care for his domestic life. Not only their labor but their deference emerged as a favorite benefit of working for United Fruit so far from home. Contemplating an eventual return to the United States, he exclaimed, "What am I going to do then, without the nigger to clean my boots and look after things, gee! . . . Some class, what!"[62] He went on to mock the speech of the "house boys," as if to provide his wife testimony of his place at the top of this domestic hierarchy. Later he wrote that such privilege "has spoiled me for work in the states. I rather like having niggers to wait on you and do the work. You don't have to lift your finger for anything[.] I guess I am lazy. Well I like it too."[63] These arrangements were not always smooth—on one occasion, the hierarchy broke down and the house boys walked out (for reasons Brown left unsaid), leaving him and his colleagues temporarily deprived.[64] The racialized hierarchy of daily life heightened Brown's sense of the tropics as a unique professional opportunity. Despite frequent grumbling about low pay, expenses, and distance from home, Brown remained with the company as long as he did in part because of his privileged place in this structure.

The publicity campaign of the 1920s sought to capitalize on this privilege as an inducement to tropical employment. Readers of *Unifruitco* would have known that the company arranged for house servants as a perk of domestic life in the tropics. For the benefit of reticent spouses of potential transfers, one employee's wife, a newcomer to the tropics, reminded readers of this division of labor. Household help was readily available, she noted, but could be "irritating," due to "their childlike minds, their ever-ready alibis, and their special aptitude for misinterpreting the 'missus'' instructions."[65] This tongue-in-cheek exasperation, reading like the musings of an aristocratic socialite, admitted all classes of American employee into a racially privileged perspective and invited them to share in distinctly upper-class complaints about servants. In this newcomer account, maintaining domestic order required constant vigilance and an understanding of the mental limitations of nonwhite laborers. By incorporating inept or potentially unruly labor into the home, this recently arrived American housewife schooled her peers on the role of white American women in the disciplinary and tutelary functions of enclave domesticity. As men would meet the challenges of conquering a difficult environment with vigor and determination, so United Fruit promised women their own sphere in which to exercise a sense of mission. The domestic sphere, usually headed by white American women who controlled nonwhite servant labor, played a central role in domesticating the foreign in company enclaves.[66]

Unifruitco reporters reassured potential tropical transfers that family life would remain intact or even flourish abroad. On a tour of Almirante, Panama, in 1926, Verson Gooch attended the "very pretty home wedding" of an American couple. After a honeymoon in neighboring Costa Rica, he wrote that the newlyweds "will begin their housekeeping in one of the bungalows on 'Harmony Row,' in Almirante."[67] The arrival of newly married employees from the United States also elicited excitement in tropical divisions. Peers often greeted couples at the docks with decorated cars, which bore them to welcome-back parties.[68] Such occasions, captured in *Unifruitco*'s social pages, intended to erode the notion that tropical divisions were remote, lonely outposts. Married life could begin or continue there, and couples would find support and social possibilities among a community of peers.

The company's appeals to unmarried males—in the company's view, the most vulnerable to demoralization in the tropics—fed off this wholesome representation of enclave life. Any *Unifruitco* reader, however, would notice readily the language of sexual possibility that ran through representations of employee life in the tropics. Early in Cutter's presidency, one employee suggested that more young women be employed by the company in its tropical divisions—a suggestion that apparently found ready ears in Boston.[69] By the late 1920s, single white women from the United States found employment in United Fruit enclaves, usually as school teachers or nurses.[70]

The arrival of single female employees to a tropical division represented an important item on divisional social pages. Welcoming the "titian-haired Miss Cavanaugh," to Castilla, Honduras, in mid-1925, the local *Unifruitco* reporter joked that the head doctor had "to use a club to keep the customers away from the hospital since the arrival of the new Nurse [*sic*]."[71] In a like manner, a Santa Marta reporter noted that a recently hired "nice young American nurse" made being sick a cause for congratulations rather than commiseration.[72] Women on vacation from domestic divisions, usually traveling in pairs or small groups, found a similar welcome. In Puerto Limón, the arrival of a party of Boston stenographers on the *Toloa* in spring 1926 excited the local correspondent. He jokingly lamented that the sharp uniforms of the ship's crew gave them an edge in competing for the women's attention.[73] The sexual objectification of female employees reflected their subordinate position in the company's male-dominated hierarchy. Their response to this position remains unknown, but what these episodes reveal is that, by the mid-1920s, United Fruit was remaking its personnel policies based on the recommendations of tropical managers. The company sought to profit from unmarried female employees, both abroad and in tropical divisions, by exploiting their morale-building potential as unattached partners. Their presence in enclaves helped the company's publicists sexualize those places—an important part of the campaign to remake the company's tropics as desirable long-term residences for male employees from the United States.

Employee Sociability

United Fruit communities also came together around employee social clubs, both ad hoc and under the company's sponsorship. The welfare campaign of the 1920s saw a proliferation of United Fruit employee organizations—local athletic associations, learned societies, and "Unifruitco" clubs. As part of the Unifruitco campaign in the mid-1920s, such clubs became more prominent in company publicity and in its corporate welfare efforts. The company, more than ever before, insinuated itself on employee organizations. Not only would company dollars pay for club buildings or ferry employees to functions in neighboring enclaves—company policies demanded that such clubs take on more consciously designed morale-building functions. Speaking of Unifruitco clubs forming around the company's domestic and tropical divisions, one writer spelled out this impetus. "The [Unifruitco] Club should be, above everything else," he wrote, "a medium for the cultivation of friendship and esprit de corps in all departments within our Division. High morale and business efficiency go hand in hand."[74] Crawford Ellis, head of the New Orleans division, described Unifruitco clubs in loftier terms. For him, these associations were meant "to remove the idea that our Company is another one of those 'soulless corporations' which, by the way, are still one of the favorite bogeys of the American people."[75] The employee newsletter suggested that Ellis was the New Orleans chapter's "fairy godfather," a thinly disguised patron who enabled the club to operate "with a noble disregard for cost."[76] Ellis's view reveals that, at its highest levels, United Fruit executives embraced corporate welfarism as a key public-relations tool. These tandem messages about social clubs—that they boosted efficiency and showed the company's "human" face to a hostile public—spoke not only to employees, but to stockholders and to those who would criticize the place of corporations in society.

Ellis and his peers must have taken satisfaction from the participation of many rank-and-file employees in a voluntary association with the company's name built into it. In his New Orleans division, Ellis boasted that the Unifruitco club involved around 65 percent of white employees in 1928.[77] Membership figures for other divisions are spotty but, at least in the 1920s, suggest a high level of participation. In Santa Marta, employees formed a Unifruitco Club in 1926 that soon counted 150 members. Both men and women from the American community filled organizational functions in the club.[78] In Guatemala, employees revitalized the Barrios Club that same year, claiming around sixty members.[79]

The principal purpose of these clubs was to organize frequent functions at which American employees from headquarters towns and outlying areas could gather and socialize. Brown described club buildings as the hubs of community activity, both daily and on special occasions. These spaces, I have noted in the previous chapter, were central to cultivating a sense of collegiality within American communities and to staving off boredom in off hours. Music instruments, billiard tables, and libraries, funded either by employee subscription or by the company, provided for routine recreation.[80] These club buildings also hosted dances and socials, which depended largely on the initiative of local employees. Later, *Unifruitco* would serve as the venue for recounting these events. Local *Unifruitco* reporters, writing under the watchful editorial eye of management, published detailed accounts of parties, dances, and outings, as if to outdo their peers in other divisions. Besides advertising an upbeat picture of recreation in American colonies, these accounts fed into the company's effort to create a sense of shared experience across its field of operations.

That sense of regional community rested, in part, on the lampooning of nonwhites. These occasions underlined the culture of white supremacy that permeated the company's division of labor for the first three decades of the century. Clubs often organized ethnically themed parties and dances—"chop suey" parties, minstrel shows, dances that revolved around some exotic local element, or masquerades. The stark division between laborers and management was always present. At a masquerade party in Truxillo, Honduras, in early 1926, one American employee played on that division. Dressed as a farm laborer—a decidedly unexotic choice—he found himself confronted by angry Americans who wanted "that mozo" thrown out of the club. Once the joke was revealed, alarm turned to amazement at the costume's authenticity and the employee carried home first prize.[81]

Some employees in tropical divisions formed learned societies or organized social functions to educate their communities. In Cuba, the Guaro Men's Club put together a series of "smoke talks" in the mid-1920s. With the blessing of the division manager, the smoke talks would bring together the division's employees and experts who passed through the area on company business. Organizers thought "that desirable contacts were being lost between the many interesting people who visit our division . . . and the personnel of the Company carrying on its work in the field."[82] Company executives in the mid-1920s fostered this sort of contact between disparate parts of the company, with the purpose of making white-collar employees feel like part of a productive enterprise, even if they were confined to repetitive office work. This sort of socialization would help individuals see beyond the limited horizons of their own tasks and share in the company's conquest of the tropics.

Sports and Community

Returning to Corocito, Honduras, on a 1926 vacation, company employee William Fagen "was greatly surprised at the changes that had taken place; the hand of civilization and organization everywhere evidenced." The principal manifestations of that civilization were the "beautiful rolling lawns in front of the houses that answer for golf and tennis courses." The presence of sporting facilities for American employees signaled to Fagen the profundity of the company's transformation of tropical landscapes. Their construction also served the goal of retention. "These pastimes," he noted, "are very necessary for keeping up the morale of employees and they attract a fine class of men to carry on the business of the 'Empire of Bananas.'"[83] Like the other elements of the company's enclaves, these facilities operated as spectacles of modernity. Such spaces reminded viewers of the company's ability to render a previously unhealthy environment sanitary. They also provided places appropriate for the rigorous conditioning of (mostly male) bodies and the building of community through sporting spectacles. Most United Fruit divisions boasted a well-developed athletic infrastructure by the mid-1920s— baseball diamonds, hippodromes, polo grounds, tennis courts, golf courses, and swimming pools. A brief discussion of these facilities as part of the company's built environment is in order; a later chapter deals with the practice and culture of sport among employees, in particular the expression of masculine identities through athletics.

Like the landscaping and park spaces of company towns, athletic facilities expressed the domination of nature through the vision of company executives. Viewing the newly constructed polo grounds in the Bobos district of the Guatemala division in 1925, one described the conversion of the "very uneven and swampy pasture into a really first-class polo ground and race track." Apparently, the impetus for the construction originated with the district superintendent, who exhibited his patronage at the inaugural match.[84] Golf

courses, in particular, expressed the disciplining of landscapes through technology, managerial vision, and community boosterism. "Heavy work" was
required to construct a five-hole golf course near Tela, Honduras, around the
same time. Although some sixty Tela employees had banded together to form
the Tela Golf Club, without the company's "assistance and cooperation," the
course never would have been built.[85]

In the context of the company's tropical enterprise, golf courses, simula-
tions of pastoral order grafted onto existing landscapes, took on added significance. Mayo observes that "the golf course was an asymmetrical garden,
a manicured landscape with a clubhouse that substituted for a British manor
house."[86] Access to such facilities invited middle-class Americans in a once
elite activity; in the tropics, golf courses provided spaces where US employees reproduced their privileged place in the company's hierarchy. Although
they immersed players in a manufactured bucolic landscape, the labor and
technology necessary to create and maintain that space remained a constant
referent.

Athletic facilities also projected an image of community vitality. Returning to Cuba's Nipe Bay in the early 1910s after a twenty-year absence, writer
Frederick Upham Adams noted a remarkable transformation of the area's
landscape. Where there had been "hardly a sign of life or industry" and "a
seemingly worthless wilderness" of "swamps and jungles," now stood a vast
expanse of sugar cane and the recently constructed company towns of Preston and Banes.[87] Those towns contained the signature features of United
Fruit's company towns—modern port facilities, railway depots, orderly street
grids, well-kept company buildings, and comfortable, sanitary housing for
employees. Along with this productive infrastructure, Adams noted the
towns' "parks, tennis and baseball grounds, a well-kept polo field, and other
places of recreation." The two towns, separated by Nipe and Banes Bays,
engaged in a "keen athletic rivalry"—which Adams noted as the surest sign
of healthy community spirit.[88] For Adams, the creation of a North American
town and sugar cultivation in the midst of a wasteland went hand-in-hand as
markers of United Fruit's success in rendering the region productive. The
practice of sport demonstrated to Adams the racially derived vitality that
drove United Fruit's enterprise in Latin America. Like social clubs, sporting
facilities provided gathering places for American communities and places
where their workplace hierarchies could soften through face-to-face

socialization and friendly competition. There, the company's dedication to cultivating healthy colonies and healthy employees stood in evidence.

From the early twentieth century, many American employees in enclaves embraced sports—football, soccer, baseball, cricket, polo, golf, tennis, and outdoorsmanship—as routine forms of recreation. By the 1920s, sport had emerged as a centerpiece of United Fruit's corporate welfare policy. Sporting events provided opportunities to build enclave communities and to foster ties between divisions, as well as advertising the company's interest in employee welfare. Employee interest and company sponsorship united in internal publicity to illustrate a common bond of interest between management and the rank-and-file. Sports, accessible to a majority of Americans in tropical divisions, also served as a relatively democratic vehicle for putting into practice an ethos of masculine physical vitality in the tropics. Reflecting the weight United Fruit's leadership placed on sport, employee T. B. Wall reminded his peers in 1929 that "sport in all its branches furnishes in minature [sic] many of the qualities which go far to insure success in business—physical fitness, leadership, intensity of purpose and comradeship."[89] Sporting served a vital function as a mediator between American masculinity and tropical employment.

At least in some divisions, organized sports had origins in the company's first years. The company's first two presidents either participated in or sponsored some kind of sport. Company cofounder Andrew Preston fostered friendly competition between nearby divisions by contributing a "Preston Cup" to be contested on the tennis court between Banes and Preston, Cuba. The annual tournament began in 1911 but fell into disuse after a couple of years for unknown reasons. In the late 1920s, company employees in Cuba revived the competition.[90] Andrew Preston's personal patronage of the Cuban division tennis competition suggests that company administration encouraged, and at least partially sponsored, sporting activity for American employees stationed overseas from United Fruit's earliest years.

Although Preston smiled on employee athletics, especially if they emerged from employee initiative, in the mid-1920s a new generation of top management increased the company's investment in sport and established it as a centerpiece of its tropical personnel policy. During his stint as a farm overseer in Costa Rica, Victor Cutter (UFCO president from 1924 to 1933) played on the Puerto Limón soccer team in 1905. A graduate of Dartmouth College,

Cutter developed his interest in sports in the context of intercollegiate competition. This Limón selection, of which Cutter was "an active and enthusiastic member," played as far away as San José.[91] While manager of the Guatemala division in 1912, Cutter took up tennis and participated in the company baseball league as an umpire.[92] These glimpses of athletics in United Fruit's early years suggest a wide presence of organized sport in company enclaves before the 1920s.

The much clearer documentary picture starting in the mid-1920s reveals a well-established sporting culture in tropical divisions. Over the course of Victor Cutter's presidency, United Fruit placed even greater emphasis on sport as a key part of employee social life. Perhaps Cutter's perspective as a former tropical employee who participated in team sports influenced the company's embrace of the positive impact of recreation on individual productivity and retention. In any case, in the 1920s United Fruit's management illustrated its attentiveness to wider trends in the US corporate world, in particular corporate welfarism—of which athletics formed an important component.[93] The mid-1920s saw a flurry of infrastructure construction in tropical divisions, an effort linked to Cutter's Divisional Betterment Program. Such infrastructure served as prominent visual reminders of the company's interest in employee welfare, as well as an expression of the company's ability to transform tropical landscapes. The decade also saw the formation of employee athletic associations in several divisions to organize local sporting events.

In the 1920s, company officials carried the message of sport policy to United Fruit's tropical divisions. In one of his tours of Caribbean divisions, observer-at-large Verson Gooch communicated the home office's approval to a meeting of the Preston Athletic Association. Besides offering his personal encouragement "to keep sports in general on a high plane," Gooch "left the impression that the officials of the Company are very much in sympathy with the idea of keeping up a healthy interest in all such activities, and that all practical encouragement possible will be given to that end."[94] The company's sport policy occasionally bore the president's personal stamp, as it had under Preston. Cutter's approval could reach thousands of miles from Boston headquarters. In 1926, he donated the "Cutter Cup" to the Mona Racing Association in the Jamaica division. His name graced the annual horse race and reminded spectators and participants of the company's sponsorship. The company representative who awarded the cup to its first winners spoke of Cutter's dedication to sports as company policy: "He [the representative] went on to say that Mr. Cutter's purpose in presenting the cup was easy to surmise—that those of his subordinates who had made a study of Mr. Cutter's career know that he has the true sporting spirit, which is not confined to sport in sport, but extents to sport in business." The presenter himself concluded with the statement that "the United Fruit Company, its President and its officers are always alive to the fact that the other man has a viewpoint, which after all is the essence of true sport."[95] The notion of "true sport" expressed in the Cutter Cup ceremony alluded to the primary objective of company-sponsored sports—to foster healthy social bonds within the corporate structure through fair physical competition on any field. The level playing field also served as analogue to the ostensibly open field of corporate advancement and to the fairness of the economic system as a whole.

Accounts of sport in tropical divisions sometimes emphasized that the company culture of physical activity demonstrated a triumph over the tropical climate. Following a description of sport and recreation in Preston, Cuba, in 1926, one columnist claimed that the work there was harder than in a domestic division, "but there is always time to play." Contrary to a prevailing belief that equatorial climates induced sloth, "an ideal climate" in Cuba spurred Americans to exercise outdoors as a matter of routine. "Insofar as the 'languorous tropical life' is concerned," the writer continued, that is surely a 'pipe-dream.'"[96] A couple of years later, an account of a baseball game in Limón served to dispel "the theory that living in the Tropics tends to sap the 'wim, wigor, and witality [sic].'" The game, held between recently arrived single men and married tropical veterans, came out in the latter's favor. Ribbing their unmarried colleagues for the loss, one noted that the average time in the tropics for the winning players was over six years, while "some . . . opponents have not been in the Tropics long enough to see a rainfall, and everyone knows it rains frequently."[97] In demonstrating their physical prowess over unmarried men, the married men implicitly proved that their virility had not been sapped by tropical life. These comments, despite their tongue-in-cheek tone, conveyed the message that the climate either had no negative effect on physical energies or that regular exertion provided a means to overcome such effects. Implicit in these accounts, and in some of the company's tourist publicity, lie an inversion of long-held beliefs about the deleterious effects of tropical climates on those of European heritage. From the perspective of publicists and some Americans living in tropical divisions, the long winters of New England kept colleagues from enjoying a healthy life of outdoor exercise.

The culture of physical recreation in the tropics was not always so easy-going—some sport boosters in the ranks insisted that their colleagues routinely exercise as a moral duty. "Maintaining our bodies in physical trim," argued Earle Currier of Banes, "should be considered not alone as an obligation to ourselves but also as a duty to the organization that employs us." Currier reminded his peers of the company's leading role among US corporations operating in Latin America in providing "facilities for open air recreation." "There can be no excuse for a man not keeping well in Banes from lack of exercise," he dourly concluded.[98] Currier encouraged those stationed where there was no such infrastructure to keep fit by daily performing "one-half hour of physical jerks in your room."[99]

Considering the popularity of golf courses, tennis courts, baseball diamonds, and other sport venues in the tropical divisions, many of United Fruit's American employees embraced regular physical activity. As a counter to the potential boredom and isolation of enclave life, the company's investment in sports probably paid some dividends, however difficult they would be to calculate. In Cuba, Everett Brown found tennis an agreeable way to spend off-hours. Sundays or holidays in Guaro would find him playing several sets over the course of the day, interspersed with "shower baths."[100] Like other company-sponsored social events, athletics provided a space where peer relationships could be reinforced and workplace hierarchies could be relaxed and lower-level employees could feel part of a larger whole. In Brown's experience, his interest in tennis and his prowess at billiards helped ease his way in a community of younger peers he occasionally found difficult to penetrate.[101]

A United Fruit man's athletic prowess certainly reflected on his masculinity and weighed positively in his peers' eyes. Reminiscing about his former colleagues from the early days of the Guatemala division, established in 1907 under Cutter's leadership, "old timer" A. Garsaud included a brief sketch of each man he had worked with. The vignettes of more than two dozen colleagues mentioned each man's professional aptitudes and his subsequent advance up the corporate ladder. Tellingly, almost every profile mentioned its subject's athletic specialties as well, or his role in boosting athletics in the tropics. If a man was not an avid hunter, fisherman, or player of golf, tennis, or some other sport, he provided moral support as a "believer" in or "backer" of the value of physical activity.[102] This long-time employee defined prowess in or support of sports as a vital adjunct to professional competence and to one's value as a man.

Although a variety of sports drew employees together, baseball—the most popular sport in tropical divisions—illustrates the social and ideological dynamics of sport in the company's tropics.[103] In the context of the United Fruit's commercial empire in the early twentieth century, American employee/athletes, at least, experienced organized sport less as an escape from than an extension of the company's reach. One historian of the game has argued that, from its mid-nineteenth-century origins, baseball "was an integral part of the cultural matrix of modern business society," a position borne out in the context of early twentieth-century corporate welfare campaigns such as that of United Fruit.[104] Company leaders valued baseball for its putative benefits in the workplace, values social commentators and boosters widely publicized at the time: greater efficiency, decisiveness, pride in individual accomplishment within a team structure, and belief in the fundamental fairness of the business world.[105] Many believed that baseball fostered healthy, outdoor-oriented American masculinity.[106] As a spectacle, baseball also played a favorable role in building communities by boosting civic pride.[107] Judging by their generous sponsorship of baseball, especially among white American employees, United Fruit's leadership placed great stock in the potential benefits of organized baseball in the tropics.

Like dances, parties, and employee outings, baseball games fostered ties of community within and between United Fruit's tropical divisions. Athletic spectacles formed an important part of employee socialization, usually filling an afternoon before a dance or party. Although the company provided the infrastructure and its approval, personnel in the enclaves acted on their own initiative to organize baseball games. Employees in many divisions formed ad hoc teams for competition within the same division, with nearby divisions, or with noncompany teams. Company news items ran detailed play-by-play accounts of games, the lineups of the contending teams, and photos of divisional ball teams. Within a division, a typical weekend series might pit the Single Men against the Benedicts—the married men—or the central office team against farm teams.[108] In the Cuban sugar division, employees formed a three-team league from different areas of the division: the Preston Athletic Club, the Plus Ultras, and the Preston Centrals. In the fall and winter of 1926, these teams played each other on a prearranged weekly schedule.[109] Travel between the home areas of these teams—the neighboring company towns of Banes, Macabí, and Preston—would have been by company bus or train. This sort of intradivisional play formed a routine part of social interaction in United Fruit enclaves. A few years earlier, Everett Brown enjoyed games between company ball teams in Cuba and Panama, to which he traveled on company trains or trucks provided for the occasion.[110]

On occasion, division teams played series against other divisions. The company, through traveling writers, encouraged interdivisional rivalries, even between domestic and tropical teams. In Almirante, Verson Gooch noted that United Fruit's New Orleans baseball players "figure to beat anything in the tropics."[111] The rivalry between far-flung divisions remained confined to jibes in *Unifruitco*'s pages, for short-term travel over such distances was impractical. Neighboring divisions along portions of Central America's Atlantic coast, however, maintained a steady baseball competition with each other. Whenever employees from two divisions met, a series between uniformed ball teams was bound to take place. Many of these divisions lay no more than a few hours by steamer or, in some cases, rail. Holidays, especially the Fourth of July, provided many occasions for such tournaments.[112] Employees played interdivisional baseball spontaneously, not as part of a strict, league-like structure. Baseball constituted an integral part of the social interaction between United Fruit's dispersed communities of tropical employees.

The company and its American employees transplanted the American pastime into tropical divisions and made it an integral part of enclave life. The practices surrounding the organization of interdivisional baseball forged ties within and between divisions. Local athletic clubs met regularly, elected officers, and organized competitions. Committees contacted their counterparts in neighboring divisions and set up baseball tournaments. During such visits, the baseball field constituted a vital place for interaction between employees of different divisions. Hardy Beuchot, secretary of Tela's top-notch baseball club in 1929, discussed the role of baseball in tropical divisions. "Interdivisional baseball as we know it promotes good will among employees of the United Fruit Company. Not only among those that participate in baseball competitions does it stimulate that feeling, but among all the employees of the Divisions represented."[113] For this baseball booster, creating a competitive spectacle fostered bonds among local fans and with those visiting from nearby divisions. Company-sponsored, employee-organized baseball clubs provided surrogates for local, collegiate, or professional team loyalties employees may have held in the states.

Company baseball represented an intersection of employee initiative and corporate personnel policy. Employee subscriptions to local athletic clubs probably covered uniforms, equipment, entertainment, and an unknown portion of transportation costs for such tournaments. Verson Gooch happily declared that the Tela baseball team was "self-maintaining" through "bazaars, vaudeville and minstrel shows, dancing, and boxing bouts."[114] In his desire to highlight employee enthusiasm and community spirit, Gooch took for granted that the company provided facilities, allowed time for travel, and permitted the use of company vessels and trains for trips. Apparently, approval of visits to nearby divisions rested with division managers, who viewed them as important to employee morale.[115]

Conclusions

The United Fruit Company designed tropical divisions and fostered certain forms of community life with the objective of retaining American employees and of projecting a favorable, imposing, "spectacle of corporate modernity." Retention efforts rested on creating townscapes that appealed to the sensibilities of North American employees and rooted them in the company's broader mission. Publicizing extensively this welfare campaign involved the company's American employees, wherever they were posted, in the company's benevolent mission in the tropics. Town layouts, public spaces, and landscaping choices in tropical divisions projected American sensibilities onto the physical environment. A suite of social activities meant to knit together individual communities and disparate enclaves filled out this effort to domesticate foreign spaces and reconcile its first-class employees to long-term employment abroad. Transplanting this template of small-town America into an untamed environment provided United Fruit a chance to sell tropical life to its domestic employees and others. The company's landscape and town designs projected an image of nature made orderly, sanitary, productive, and visually appealing by US enterprise.

Allen Wells, encapsulating recent United Fruit scholarship, has written that company towns "insulated company managers from the rank and file by creating what amounted to foreign islands in the tropics."[116] Wells and others are correct to underline this dynamic in United Fruit towns, where many American employees and their families lived aloof from their surroundings, to one degree or another. The fundamental inequality in experience and perception remained intact. But these boundaries were porous in some important ways. Most manual laborers, especially those who built and maintained the grounds of white zones or who worked in the homes of white employees, saw or spent many of their waking hours in these American "islands." Employees like Everett Brown, in their off time, explored and commented on the living spaces of subordinate classes of labor. The built environment laid down a spatial template in which racial and social hierarchies were to be enacted, displayed, and reinforced. Perhaps a more nuanced view of the company's enclaves would view them as points of intense, unequal engagement between white American employees and nonwhite laborers.[117] For American employees, company towns functioned as lenses through which to experience the tropics and the hierarchies deemed necessary to make the region productive. The built environment was designed to situate the company's manual laborers as the lowliest recipients of the company's benevolence. Demarcating the boundaries between nonwhite laborers and white first-class employees also transpired under another key area of UFCO corporate welfare: its Medical Department.

CHAPTER FOUR

Wandering Foci of Infection

In July 1924, the United Fruit Company convoked a conference on tropical medicine at its palatial Myrtle Bank Hotel in Kingston, Jamaica. Attending the conference at the company's expense were luminaries from nearly every state and private institution engaged in the burgeoning field in Europe and the Americas.[1] As the chief host, United Fruit Company Medical Department (UFCOMD) general manager Dr. William Deeks twice addressed his peers, once to welcome them and another time to outline the medical work of the company he had served for a decade. These were indeed heady times for those laboring in tropical medicine. Parasitology had revolutionized medical science within the professional memory of many. Deeks, who had worked under William Gorgas during the construction of the Panama Canal—to which the near eradication of yellow fever was essential—brought his long experience in the tropics to bear on the relationship between medicine and human progress. Looking back on his tenure with the UFCO, Deeks interpreted the company's expansion through a medical lens. "Agricultural development and commercial activity on a large scale," he declared, "are impossible until medical science brings tropical disease under control."[2] Deeks argued that tropical climates fostered a profusion of parasites that eroded human health, leading to a native population that lacked the "physical and mental vigor" to exploit efficiently the region's tremendous fertility. What was more, he lamented, "the lack of education of the laboring classes makes the problem of reducing infectious diseases a difficult one, but gradual progress is evident, despite the migratory habits of the laborers."[3] The key to unlocking the productive potential of the tropics, he forwarded, was a regime of public hygiene "under skilled direction" and "constant supervision" that could effectively render tropical regions as healthy as the northern latitudes.[4]

Deeks's comments and the context in which he made them call our attention to the powerful medical discourse at the heart of this US corporate colonial project. They also remind us of the fugitive phenomena that haunted Deeks's scientific confidence and sense of mission: landscapes and climates that defied sanitation and transformation, plasmodia and other disease-causing organisms whose complexity and persistence flummoxed researchers, and "tropical" laborers who continually escaped, resisted, and disrupted the company's project.[5] Several scholars have established the importance of medical inquiry and public health practice in the projection of European and US power overseas, taking our understanding far beyond narratives of medical progress over particular diseases.[6] This body of literature has offered much insight into medicine as a technology that had the power both to define and bind colonial subjects within broader fields of political or economic subjugation. This chapter extends the interrogation of medical science and practice to the realm of corporate colonialism in the American tropics in the early twentieth century, to the banana company's most expansive decades. The UFCOMD's paternalistic approach to Central American populations has received scholarly attention; my contribution to this work is to bring into tighter focus the power of its medical project as a constitutive social force and an essential management tool within the context of corporate colonialism.[7] Behind Deeks's comments about the nature of laborers and the tropics lay a culture and practice of medical inquiry built on many thousands of what one scholar of colonial medicine has aptly termed "sociomedical micro-powers" over subject populations: examinations, sample collections, inspections, and experiments.[8] Essential to these practices was the wider web of connections in the scientific world that consumed, confirmed, and often undertook such practices in United Fruit's sphere of operations. It will not be a surprising conclusion that company-driven medicine bolstered the preponderant fact of United Fruit's enterprise during its first three decades: a racialized division of labor premised on white supremacy. The story of how it became so will reveal that medicine in the company's sphere actually stood at the heart of that division of labor, defining and constituting the tropical laborer and temperate employee in the most fundamental, tangible ways.

By the mid-1920s, the scale of Deeks's purview was indeed immense. The company had operated hospitals for its white employees since its inception in 1899, but the rapid expansion of its cultivations and labor force spurred company owners to constitute a discrete medical department in 1912 that could extend its attention to laborers as well. Just a decade later, the department was a vital adjunct to the company's operations. Spread over eight countries around the Caribbean basin, United Fruit's cultivations occupied one million acres and employed around 67,000 people. Deeks estimated that approximately 150,000 people depended on the company's medical service for care, including families of employees, laborers, and inhabitants of lands neighboring company holdings. United Fruit's eight hospitals and many field dispensaries handled around 260,000 visits yearly.[9] The year of the conference, the UFCOMD employed 101 doctors and nurses, themselves by and large, though not exclusively, part of the company's larger expatriate Anglo-American colonies.[10] According to Deeks, the UFCOMD incurred expenses of about $1,000,000 annually, with another $500,000 funding sanitation and landscaping he deemed directly linked to public health.[11] Company doctors also staffed most of the steamships in United Fruit's Great White Fleet, and patrolled the US ports where they docked to ensure that no communicable diseases would trigger costly quarantines. Until the economic contraction of the 1930s and the company's subsequent decades-long divestment from direct production, the UFCOMD expanded apace with the company's agricultural operations. Although Deeks's figures must be read cautiously as language meant to showcase the company's goodwill and largesse, they speak more deeply to the growth of an institution with a reach exceeding that of even the most ambitious state-driven public health efforts undertaken by the United States in early twentieth-century Latin America.

Malaria and the New World Plantation Complex

Although company doctors treated a panoply of diseases, the chief objects of the medical department's public health efforts would be malaria, venereal disease (especially syphilis and gonorrhea), and hookworm. By the early 1920s, the department's information-gathering apparatus was developing metrics for understanding the economic impact of diseases on the company's enterprise. Those three consistently topped the list of "economic diseases."[12] By any measure, malaria posed the most serious challenge to United Fruit's medical establishment, and provides an important window into the medical dimension of social control. Malaria also highlights the limits of the company's ability to fulfill its loftier visions of tropical transformation. In the mid-1920s, despite years of antimalaria efforts, Deeks could estimate that malaria caused 40 percent of all morbidity in the company's sphere, making it "the most important single factor in lowering the efficiency of labor."[13] This report gave quantitative shape to decades of frustration and concern. For more than thirty years, medical scientists had understood that mosquitoes were the vector for malaria, based on the initial discovery of Cuban doctor Carlos Findlay in the 1880s and the subsequent work of Ross and Grassi in the 1890s.[14] These researchers determined that the disease was caused by plasmodia parasites inhabiting mosquito intestines, which passed to the human bloodstream through mosquito bites. The reproduction of the parasites in the human body produced fevers and flu-like symptoms that could lay a person low for weeks and then disappear for weeks, months, or even years, only to return. Patients deemed healthy could go about their lives while serving as carriers. Deaths from malarial fevers were relatively rare where sufferers could be nursed through fevers and administered quinine, an extract of the cinchona tree that was an effective brake to the reproduction of plasmodia in the human bloodstream. But eradicating the sickness posed a thorny problem. Anopheles mosquitoes transmitted different varieties of malaria, and this widely distributed species would fly up to a mile in search of human blood meals. As tropical health experts were learning in the early twentieth century, altering the environment to destroy anopheles and administering quinine as a prophylactic to large populations posed staggering costs and practical difficulties.

United Fruit's experience with malaria forms part of a much longer historical trajectory of malaria's symbiotic relationship to human agriculture. The parasites (the two most common and dangerous, *plasmodium falciparum* and *plasmodium vivax*) have probably been a constant companion of humanity since the dawn of sedentary agricultural societies in the Old World. The colonization of the Americas and what Charles Mann has aptly termed "the restitching of Pangea" set the stage for the biological triumph of these malaria-causing organisms. The American plantation complex, based as it was on African slave labor kept in marginal living conditions, formed the cornerstone of plasmodium habitat. Millennia of adaptation to malaria endemicity provided African populations with the ability to withstand higher levels of plasmodia, and, as Mann has shown, this differential immunity led European colonists to rely ever more on enslaved Africans to labor on plantations from the mid-Atlantic to Brazil. Wherever climate and topography favored the lifecycle of the parasites during much of the year, African slavery predominated. Severe social inequalities inherent in this system played a key role in the biological success of malaria parasites and its preferred human habitats over time.[15] Although malaria had been endemic in some nominally temperate regions—as far north as Boston in North America, parts of southern England, and much of the Mediterranean basin—overall socioeconomic improvement in these places and the expansion of the New World plantation complex elsewhere created conditions ripe for malaria's prevalence as a particularly tropical disease by the late nineteenth century.

The postemancipation expansion of US enterprises in the Caribbean basin, in particular tropical plantation agriculture, created ideal conditions for plasmodia to survive. Tropical lowlands, either improved with irrigation systems or adjacent to marshy environments, provided an abundance of warm and wet breeding grounds for anopheles mosquitoes.[16] The composition of the labor force provided the next ingredient, as a steady traffic of West Indian labor flowed between the Antilles and United Fruit enclaves in Cuba and on the mainland. Like the slave-based plantations of centuries before, this new boom in tropical agriculture replayed the history of malaria in new arenas. Relatively malaria-resistant black laborers might earn wages and be free, but they inhabited a world based on highly unequal and racially stratified labor relations. When West Indian labor activism and various nationalist pressures in Central America and Colombia led United Fruit to Hispanize its labor force in the 1920s and 1930s, the malaria situation deteriorated. Mestizo and Hispanic laborers, often migrating to coastal plantation areas from highland regions, proved as susceptible to malaria as Anglo Americans. All of these laborers, no matter their race, lived at the bottom end of a socioeconomic structure common to the New World plantation complex, in which poor conditions increased susceptibility to disease.[17] And the regional mobility of all levels of company employees between different banana enclaves, surrounding areas, and US and Caribbean ports added to the enrichment of the human habitat for the highly mobile plasmodia. The plantation complex, built around burgeoning consumer demand for cheap tropical fruit in the United States, bound together United Fruit's racially segmented workforce in the explosive growth and perpetuation of thousands of generations of these parasites.[18]

The effort to combat malaria during the first decades of the century reveals much about the power of the medical department and its growing capacities as a disciplinary institution bound to shaping the physical environment and insinuating its authority in the lives and bodies of laborers. In the mid-1910s, William Deeks and other company veterans of the Panama Canal campaigns quickly applied the Canal Zone template of antimalaria measures to UFCO divisions. Even before the arrival of the canal veterans, the company had instituted the cutting of vegetation and the drainage of standing water in and around living spaces. Where ground water could not be drained, the company either filled in, pumped sea water in, or dumped oil to coat the surface and asphyxiate mosquito larvae. Rain collection barrels, the primary source of drinking water in many areas, were screened to prevent mosquitoes from laying eggs in them.[19] In 1921, company sanitary officials opted for the arsenic-based insecticide Paris Green, which could be mixed with sawdust and spread over standing water.[20] In some divisions, surface-feeding minnows were introduced to ground water and even rain-collection barrels.[21] Such vector-control methods required constant expense and attention, as well as the collaboration of entomologists, doctors, engineers, and management. But as public health authorities were learning in the early twentieth century, altering the physical environment had the advantage of bypassing the direct participation of host populations in sanitation campaigns.[22] The second pillar of the company's antimalaria efforts focused on identifying methods of destroying or disrupting plasmodia within human hosts. In company hospitals and laboratories, United Fruit doctors and outside experts developed immediately applicable solutions in this direction: the creation of a viable, reliable, and inexpensive blood test for the parasites; a variety of quinine regimes and delivery methods; and, in the 1920s, chemotherapy with synthetic antimalarial drugs like plasmochin and Erion/Atebrin—all experiments involving nonwhite subjects drawn from the company's labor force.[23]

Despite such efforts, malaria rates remained stubbornly high, and the UFCOMD initiated an "intensive drive" against the disease in all divisions in 1926.[24] That this campaign coincided with a broader investment in corporate welfare programs and bettering working conditions was not accidental. By the 1920s, progressive-era tropical medicine experts, Deeks among them, regularly construed the disease as a social problem. In 1925, he wrote to his superiors to recommend a greater investment in corporate welfare beyond medical measures. "An endeavor should be made to stabilize the population," he wrote, adding that "we must not only build and maintain attractive and comfortable camps, but we must also provide measures for taking care of families of married men, by furnishing them with garden facilities, schools and some forms of entertainment. In other words, we must take an interest in our people if we may hope to retain their services indefinitely."[25] Settling the entire workforce, Deeks believed, would enable the company's sanitary tutelage to sink in. Until the economic realities of the Depression came to constrain such expenditures a few years later, the company poured resources into doing precisely what Deeks recommended, although the stark differences between accommodations and amenities for white employees and laborers of color laid bare the limitations of corporate welfare during this period. High labor turnover for all classes continued to plague United Fruit throughout the 1920s.

More significantly, the antimalaria campaign revolved around expanding the reach and power of the medical department and making a spottily applied sanitary regime a nearly daily imposition. Overstretched medical personnel had failed to arrest climbing malaria rates, it was judged, so the energies of "every intelligent organizational unit," including the agricultural department, were added to them. Overseers, timekeepers, and lower-level foremen were invested with sanitary and medical powers, thereby enhancing their ability to surveil and control workers in their charge. These newly constituted socio-medical authorities worked in concert with "field malaria inspectors," who routinely visited every worker's dwelling in order to monitor sanitary conditions to catalogue the health condition of entire families—a significant expansion of the company's power to intrude upon the private spaces of its laborers. Well beyond the direct supervision of doctors, any febrile cases were administered quinine on the spot and ordered to bed rest.[26] The results of these inspections were recorded on standardized documents and folded into the company's trove of data about laborers' lives. Medical officials' reports after 1926 affirmed again and again the necessity of ever-greater authority to be exercised over laborers and surrounding populations. Laborers refusing to submit to quinine treatments could have their pay withheld, or, where the cooperation of the local government could be secured, fines could be levied.[27]

Despite millions of dollars invested in research, sanitation, treatment, and social control within its colonies throughout the 1920s, the company's advances against plasmodia in its divisions were modest.[28] A summation of the intensive antimalarial campaign of the late 1920s printed in the last

annual report of the medical department in 1931 indicates that malaria morbidity seemed to improve measurably, but its incidence was still significant.
Behind these mixed results, division superintendents continued to echo long-
standing complaints about the impossibility of reducing malaria to insignifi-
cant levels. Heavy rainfall, standing water created by agricultural operations,
intransigent laborers, unwilling local patients, heavy labor turnover—all of
these factors militated against a fundamental change of the pathogenic landscape in tropical divisions, and doctors knew it.[29] In sum, the most important
realities of banana and sugar production—a reliance on a cheap, tightly controlled nonwhite labor force and the intensive transformation of the landscape—helped offset whatever pharmaceutical or public health measures the
company could throw at plasmodia. Reporting in 1924, H. C. Clark, the medical superintendent at Tela, flatly acknowledged that "the natural conditions
determining the location of a large banana plantation and its proper cultivation, are the very conditions that favor a high incidence of malarial fevers."[30]
Seen another way, however, the parasite can be considered an ally of the
company. It was this organism, after all, that spurred the medical department to expand its reach over laborers and the surrounding population and
carry the authority of public health to the farthest reaches of these US corporate colonies.

The United Fruit Company Medical Department

To understand the deepest impact of the UFCOMD, we must continue to turn
our attention away from efforts to combat certain diseases and focus on its
function as an institution, a vital ally of company managers in their effort to
discipline laborers. The UFCOMD's institutional expansion can be mapped as
a steadily intensifying construction of medical authority, an accumulation of
"socio-medical micro-powers," which enhanced the ability of company doctors
to catalog and define subjects and to fix them within a far-reaching community of medical inquiry. In short, doctors rendered patient populations "legible" to several audiences within the company and beyond.[31] These powers
also carried a disciplinary impulse that made the company's authority a matter of daily routine, reaching into the most intimate spaces of patient bodies
and lives through a variety of practices. The spaces where these practices
took shape found their most robust form as the 1920s dawned. At the tip of

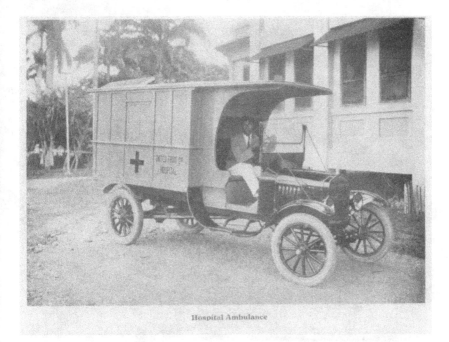

Hospital Ambulance

Figure 4.1. Automobiles and rail-mounted field dispensaries amplified the company's ability to treat, measure, and control its laborers. "UFCO hospital ambulance." Annual Report of the Medical Department of the United Fruit Company 1922, p. 145.

the medical department's tendrils, reaching all the way to what were commonly referred to as frontier zones, was a far-flung network of what had, in earlier years, been known as sick camps. In 1920, the medical department suppressed that insalubrious term and adopted the functional institutional vocabulary of "hospital dispensaries," usually supervised by a physician, and "field dispensaries," operated by "runners," "*practicantes*" (physician's assistants) or "dispensers," drawn from the better-educated members of the company's labor force.[32] These field dispensaries, often mounted on rail cars, extended the reach of the medical department far from hospitals going back to at least 1915.[33]

The organizational heart of this network had become the new space of the base hospital by the early 1920s. By then United Fruit's medical department had developed something of a template for its medical infrastructure in the tropical divisions. A wave of construction brought a reinforced concrete main

Figure 4.2. "Sick Camp, Talamanca, Bocas Division: Showing methods of caring for labor on new development works." Annual Report of the Medical Department of the United Fruit Company 1917, p. 79.

hospital to every division except Jamaica, where private physicians and the colonial government could be counted on to treat serious cases and maintain public sanitation. Typical of these buildings was the new 160-bed facility at Puerto Castilla, Honduras, nearing completion in 1922. In designing such a hospital, doctors and architects worked together to account for "special problems not met with in Northern latitudes." Its design and placement near the seashore mitigated tropical heat and maximized ventilation, making it "ideally suited to a warm climate." But the racialized organization of space within the building revealed its most distinctly tropical feature; the possibility of interracial contact the "special problem." "Ample provision must be made," wrote the medical superintendent, "for the segregation of all classes of employees, who differ radically in race, color and social status." He added that "more attention must be given to the segregation of different classes of patients in our hospitals in the tropics than is necessary in Northern latitudes."[34] The medical logic of segregation in clinical spaces echoed that of living areas, where racial separation was deemed a matter of necessity. Tropical populations, it was widely held by medical experts, were considered a "vast reservoir of infection" in the words of one medical superintendent, and had to be kept at a significant distance from white habitations.[35] Hospital design, then, cemented the racialized division of labor in the company's sphere at large.

An essential part of new company hospitals was the laboratory; in Tela, Honduras, and Puerto Limón, Costa Rica, for instance, these state-of-the-art facilities were even equipped to undertake work in serology, bacteriology, and pathology.[36] Tropical laboratories formed the nexus where the treatment of disease joined the deeper imperative to gather data, study, and construe laborers and employees as part of an "ordered statistical community."[37] Every node in the system, from the most distant field dispensary to the main hospitals in port towns, functioned as a data-collection point; in some way, nearly every patient entering company medical facilities instantly became an object of study. Annual reports tell the story of how company medicos steadily established their authority—indeed, the medical necessity—to penetrate ever more deeply into the most intimate spaces of laborer and employee bodies. By 1924, the year Dr. Deeks addressed his peers in Jamaica, the medical department's annual reports noted that "it is impossible to emphasize too strongly the importance of careful and complete laboratory examinations of all patients treated in tropical localities." To wit, the report charted the growing numbers of blood, stool, and urine samples collected from one year to the next by division, divided between those collected at hospitals and in dispensaries. The 39,508 blood samples, 33,524 urine samples, and 28,753 stool samples collected from 29,766 hospital patients that year, for instance, offer stark testimony of the company's power to impose its will on its ailing workers, not to mention of the impressive apparatus for managing the sheer flow of human bodily products through its facilities.[38] The purpose of displaying such surveys was to establish a statistical narrative of the parasitological terrain of the human population under the company's purview. The ability to undertake such ordering was as essential to United Fruit's colonial project as it was in the US government's administration of the Philippines or the Panama Canal Zone.[39]

New Hospital of the United Fruit Company at Limon, Costa Rica

Figure 4.3. The linchpin of the company's medical network: the divisional hospital, complete with state-of-the-art treatment facilities and laboratories. "New Hospital of the United Fruit Company at Limon, Costa Rica." Annual Report of the Medical Department of the United Fruit Company 1921, p. 19.

The organizational capacity to collect data and fashion reports from them rested on a series of practices that in themselves constructed the company's power over its subject populations. In other colonial contexts, historians writing in a Foucauldian vein have described such practices as "disciplinary." Mandatory examinations and taking of samples, observations, submission to medical photography, including new x-rays, undergoing experimental treatments for all manner of ailments—all required a fundamental surrender to an authority constructed by medical science and assumed as a matter of absolute mortal necessity. The company's power over workers—if we understand it as a "gaze" capable of not just surveilling but shaping behavior—thus found its way into workers' bodies nearly at will. The medical department's power also becomes clear when we consider the question of whose voice shaped the reporting based on these disciplinary practices. Utterly absent from the scientific reports drawing from such data was any mention of exactly how they were collected or what their subjects may have thought about them;

whatever happened on the ground, or in the clinic, doctors wrote as if they were inquiring into the workings of a silent mass devoid of anything but a collective, zoologically construed capacity for motivation.[40]

Robust technologies of representation and distribution ensured that the data gathered in this manner circulated widely and garnered the imprimatur of participation in a wider scientific conversation about questions of tropical health. The Annual Reports of the UFCOMD, published between 1912 and 1931 (when they were discontinued as part of the general contraction of the company during that decade), formed the centerpiece of this effort. From modest beginnings providing narrative overviews of medical work for the benefit of stockholders, by the mid-1920s the reports had become impressive repositories of data and vehicles for scientific publication, distributed to specialists, institutions, and libraries in annual print runs of five thousand manufactured in Boston.[41] By then, the reports had become venues for publishing the findings of company doctors and other experts conducting empirical work in UFCOMD hospitals, as well as reprints of especially relevant pieces published elsewhere. The statistical component of the reports had also multiplied over the years, providing a division-by-division accounting of vital statistics, hospitalization, morbidity, and mortality rates of various illnesses, and data related to sanitary work (e.g. "number of rats killed," "steamships fumigated"). Taken as a whole, the annual reports registered the scale and scope of the company's investment in public health and built an armature of scientific authority and necessity around the medical department as an institution. Beyond creating and distributing the annual reports, Dr. Deeks made sure that the flow of printed medical knowledge went both ways. Reference libraries in all company hospitals kept current subscriptions to relevant journals in the field, some of them publishing venues for the research generated in the tropical divisions themselves.[42]

The active connection of the UFCOMD to the wider scientific community went far beyond the transmission of printed knowledge; the company's medical enterprise operated in a state of continual crossfertilization with the public health and tropical medicine communities in the United States, and to a lesser extent, those in Europe and Latin America. The fluid traffic of experts to and from other state-driven colonial projects in the tropics fundamentally shaped the medical department's personnel roster. Experts schooled in new field of tropical medicine in the United States (at Harvard, Johns

Hopkins, and Tulane) with experience in the medical work of the US military overseas (notably in Cuba, the Panama Canal Zone, and the Philippines) brought those experiences to United Fruit's colonies, and infused the corporation's medical work with a well-developed set of procedures and a deep sense of authority and mission.[43] Most prominent among several tropical veterans was William Deeks himself, once head of the Isthmian Canal Commission's Ancón Hospital under the administration of sanitation chief William Gorgas. Deeks was a key figure in hospital administration and malaria control for the Isthmian Canal Commission prior to moving to United Fruit in 1916, where he was hired as general manager of the medical department. His Panama experience prepared him well. In 1908, he supervised the construction of a new medical clinic at the old French hospital complex at Ancón, and soon after coauthored a published study of malarial fevers in the Canal Zone.[44] Having worked at the highest levels of the sanitary effort during the terminal phase of canal construction, Deeks played a key role in creating a public health infrastructure capable of treating tens of thousands of patients spread over a vast area.[45] The institutional organization he brought to United Fruit during his first years there mirrored that of the ICC, even in its terminology: two main hospitals stood at the head of several medical districts, each overseen by a "district medical officer" (a physician), and provided several field dispensaries, complete with railcar clinics. The whole institution was vested with far-reaching authority in order to combat outbreaks that would slow progress on the canal, much like its corporate successor under Deeks's hand.[46] It is no surprise that Deeks's eventual successor upon his death in 1931, Dr. R. C. Connor, had succeeded him as head of Ancón Hospital prior to being hired by United Fruit in the mid-1920s.[47]

The UFCOMD's connection to the wider tropical medicine community even permitted it to have on its payroll men with feet in two institutional worlds. Dr. Richard P. Strong, a veteran of sanitary campaigns during the US occupation of the Philippines, and founder of Harvard University's School of Tropical Medicine in 1913–1914, was one such figure. A foundational act of the formation of this prestigious school was a thorough collaboration with the banana company. In 1914, Strong was appointed Director of the Laboratories of the Hospitals and of Research Work of the United Fruit Company, a position he held jointly with his tenure at Harvard. This position permitted him and the program's students access to company facilities around the

Caribbean Basin, which had the added advantage of being based in widely varying tropical subclimates. Upon his appointment, Strong undertook a tour of all eight company divisions and cemented the collaboration in person. "One cannot fail to be struck," he wrote to his Harvard colleagues in 1914, "by the abundant opportunities for study and research which exist in many of these localities."[48] (A few years later, he might have made the same sort of declaration privately about the hunting and fishing possibilities in UFCO outposts.) Strong brought his long experience to bear on the improvement of United Fruit's labs in terms of equipment, staffing, and methods, all while serving as a conduit for channeling a steady flow of medical students and visiting researchers through the doors of these facilities. The use of colonial populations as objects of study and trial was nothing new to Strong, and his sensibility in this regard undoubtedly shaped the culture of inquiry in United Fruit's sphere.[49] Medical Department personnel rosters from the 1920s indicate that the company maintained four or five prominent tropical-medicine experts in consulting positions, though they were based in North American medical schools or the Panama Canal Zone.[50] Such institutional cross-fertilization made the UFCOMD an important node within the wider, informally constituted world of North American tropical medicine during the first decades of the century. These crosscolonial connections also shaped the nature and culture of scientific inquiry within the company's sphere at a crucial moment.

Moral Hygiene and the Construction of Racial Difference

Incorporated in 1899, the United Fruit Company undertook its greatest decades of expansion at a turning point in the field of tropical medicine. Newly generated knowledge about disease transmission—specifically germ theory in the mid- and late nineteenth century and the discovery of the mosquito vectors of malaria and yellow fever in the 1890s—was then in the process of displacing older climatological or environmental frameworks. New generations of medical scientists, armed with germ theory, the microscope, and the administrative powers of modern colonial enterprises, would steadily establish the locus of disease within human bodies rather than in the climate itself. The new line of inquiry, according to medical historian Warwick Anderson, eventually brought about "the exoneration of the tropical milieu," although debates over the salubrity of tropical climates would persist well into the twentieth century.[51] Indeed, in United Fruit's sphere, the exoneration was a qualified one. In the mid-1920s, William Deeks touted tropical fertility and productive potential, but added that "in these areas the perennially warm, humid climate also favors the development of the transmitting agents of tropical diseases—undiscovered and unknown enemies, against which no man up to a recent period could fight."[52] In another venue, he noted that "the enervating effects of a constantly warm and practically unchanging tempera-ture tend to reduce the energy and the vitality of the inhabitants."[53] Otto Brosius, company doctor at Almirante, Panama, echoed his colleague's lin-gering climatological anxieties in his personal observations of the ill effects of tropical sunlight, which included unexplainable weakness, anxiety, insom-nia, and digestive distress.[54] Such perspectives are striking in their blending of the latest pathological understanding of disease transmission and exam-ination of the different wavelengths of sunlight with mysterious effects more akin to an era when tropical miasma (bad air emanating from the soil) murk-ily explained just about any condition contracted in those latitudes. For Deeks and Brosius, the remaining anxieties about the tropical climate com-ingled with the firm belief that such ill effects could be remedied with the right know-how and the will to implement a far-reaching transformation of living conditions in the tropics.

Absolving the tropical milieu of its insalubrity would take far more than a shift in understanding the etiology of certain diseases. In US overseas colonies, an emerging notion of tropicality would be mediated through tech-nology; tropical environments could only be absolved to the extent that they could be transformed and rendered healthy. Sanitation and public health formed a central part of US colonial projects in the early twentieth century, for pressing reasons of interest: safeguarding the health of white officials and soldiers, maintaining economic activity, and ensuring quarantine-free ship-ping lanes. Widely touted investments in sanitation infrastructure and public health also showcased the benevolent paternalism of US occupiers and made plain the inferiority and backwardness of their colonial charges.[55] Juxta-posed photographs of public spaces having undergone sanitary transforma-tion were common enough to be considered tropes of US accounts of projects in the Pacific and Latin America, and they made several appearances in United Fruit reports and propaganda. One particularly elaborate photo essay published by the medical department in 1925 showed a progression of sixteen images of dwellings and their surroundings, meant to contrast "Primitive Life Versus Organized Society." Native laundry practices, food stores, and dwellings were ordered from most primitive to the latest in the company's design of sanitary town spaces. Probably authored by Deeks, the essay issued a powerful visual and textual indictment of "natives," whose ignorance, unhygienic habits, and lack of "energy and vitality" had rendered them a vast reservoir of infection.[56] Every avenue of improvement was premised on dramatic technology-driven transformation of building technology and landscapes. Such representations highlight the importance of sanitary transformation to the potent narratives of technological dominance that undergirded US expansion in the early twentieth century.[57] A strident sense of confidence in the capacity of technology to render tropical milieus healthy lay at the heart of US notions of tropicality then operating in the fruit company's colonies.

Making the tropics healthy through sanitation, however, was only part of the battle. Situating disease within human bodies meant that its transmission would be linked more powerfully than ever to behaviors and habits. "Moral hygiene" became the idiom for indicting unhygienic "natives" and "coloreds" and for exhorting individual whites living in the tropics to correct modes of behavior. The link between wellness and morality had its roots in the early nineteenth century, but germ theory and parasitology added an important dimension to the dangers of errant behavior.[58] Health, in this view, rested on fundamental questions of character and morality—and native populations living in poor conditions could be found woefully lacking in both. Tracing the application of these ideas to the US occupation of the Philippines earlier in the century, Anderson has established that germ theory and parasitology effectively racialized pathogen distribution and drew sharper lines between colonizers and local populations. Similar conclusions have been reached based on research into the US occupation of the Panama Canal Zone.[59] To American residents of the Philippines in the early twentieth century, tropical medicine "reinforced fears of racial contact" and made "'native' bodies and spaces objects of surveillance and reform."[60] In United Fruit's sphere, the preoccupation with moral hygiene encompassed all levels of its work force, from nonwhite laborers to subordinate whites, and company officials and doctors leaned heavily toward equating health to easily racialized criteria of character, morality, and conditioning. These broader shifts in the medical definition of tropicality and tropical illness were hammered out, among other places, in company hospitals and laboratories.[61] It was in the medical narratives that emerged from these spaces, and in the thousands of seemingly innocuous clinical acts upon which they were built—and ultimately in the bodies of medical subjects themselves—that the company constituted its racialized division of labor.

A preoccupation with the racial composition of the labor force infused nearly all medical discourse produced in United Fruit's sphere during these years. The medical idiom of expressing and constituting racial difference, however, was in flux. The transition was apparent in the shifting statistical language of the medical department. Prior to 1924, all UFCMD statistics were ordered by race along a white/colored binary. Local officers might occasionally parse these categories in detailed studies, such as one superintendent in Guatemala, who broke down "colored" laborers into three categories in 1912: West Indian negroes, Caribs, and Central American natives.[62] But on the whole, statisticians flattened the racial and ethnic diversity of the company's ranks (even in its white ranks) into more "legible" binaries, an administrative language that simplified complex social realities in order to better control them.[63] The move away from racial biology toward a more adaptive framework became apparent by the mid-1920s; race came to share equal space with notions such as "time in tropics" or "tropical residence," as in one malaria survey in 1924, although in this instance the whiteness of the survey's subjects was implicit.[64] The department changed the statistical binary itself in 1924, adopting a temperate/other dyad. Race was never really jettisoned as a part of these definitions. "Temperate" encompassed "white persons born in temperate zones"; "others" included "all individuals, irrespective of color or race, except white people with nativity in temperate zones." "This method will make possible, for those interested," the report explained, "a determination of the effects of climatic conditions on people born in temperate zones and residing in a tropical climate."[65] The new distinction better served the overarching direction of medical inquiry in the company's sphere discussed above, tilting as it was to the exoneration of the tropical climate and the rise of moral hygiene. The concern with white adaptability, however, was never free from a need to fix and to define "otherness" (which could be equated to "tropicalness") in concrete racial language.

Company doctors, like their colleagues in the Philippines, drew steadily away from racial physiology and developed more and more elaborate expressions of "essentialized race culture," although conversations about racial biology rattled around medical reports well into the 1920s.[66] Laborers' purportedly nomadic habits constituted one dangerous, essentialized tropical characteristic and generated great frustration for company doctors.[67] "The natives are restless and nomadic by nature," wrote Deeks in 1925, "they do not remain settled in one vicinity for any length of time." Deeks's statement made sense: in one division, he noted, the entire nonmanagerial labor force had turned over in the space of two months, and the situation was not much better elsewhere.[68] What Deeks neglected to note, however, was that this problem stemmed from the economic realities of company's enterprise. Continual pressure from Boston to keep wages low, poor and difficult work conditions, and the company's antiunion policies all contributed to high turnover at the bottom end of the labor hierarchy. Laborers of all races and in all divisions negotiated the plantation economy and simply survived by moving frequently, a dynamic common to postemancipation plantation economies in the region.[69] Doctors, however, pathologized these economic decisions through the lens of moral hygiene: as a moral failing inherent to those born in tropical environments and too ignorant to adopt the discipline and stability necessary to live healthily in them.

The company's move toward localizing and racially segmenting its labor force, initiated in the 1910s, could hardly have pleased company doctors with any tropical experience. At this time, United Fruit responded to a series of nationalist pressures around the Caribbean basin and to management's fears of labor militancy of black West Indians, and started hiring more nationals to work in its various tropical divisions. The shift nonetheless raised the alarm of medical officials, who tended to view West Indian blacks as more robust and healthy than mestizos or Hispanics.[70] Plantation zones had always seen a constant influx and egress of workers, but as the years went on more and more in the mainland divisions came from neighboring highlands to lowland fruit-growing regions. Dozens of statements from doctors working all over the company's divisions complained bitterly about the migratory nature of these laborers, who acted as "wandering foci of infection," in the words of the medical superintendent of Costa Rica in 1920.[71] One superintendent in Tela, Honduras, explained an uptick in malaria in 1922 as "probably due to large numbers of laborers brought from the Interior." "These men," he lamented, "usually arrive in poor condition and coming from high, dry climate to low coast lands, they have no idea of how to take care of themselves, and contract malaria when acclimated laborers enjoy good health."[72] Even when treatment might lower the levels of plasmodia in a patient's blood, once out of the hospital, he would most likely leave the company's employ only to have his place taken by a previously infected new arrival.[73] Nationalist pressures to Hispanize the workforce and the drive to keep labor as cheap as possible consistently flummoxed the best efforts of the company's own medical corps.

Some United Fruit doctors also noted that their subject populations possessed a primordial propensity for violence. The trope of the senselessly, inherently violent non-European other in colonial contexts and in Latin America in particular has a long history.[74] What set this view apart in the banana company's world during the 1920s was that laborers, especially "Central American natives" or "native mozos"—read: Hispanic mestizos—were biologically predisposed to violence. Alfred Gage, of the Quirigua Hospital in Guatemala, presented this premise in 1925, based on years of observation. Not surprisingly, Gage confirmed his initial impressions of this population and based his conclusions on fundamental contrasts between them and Anglo-Saxons. Firmly in the tradition of racial pathology, Gage asserted that whites possessed significantly greater immunity to pneumonia, measles, dysentery, and influenza than Guatemalan laborers. Conversely, whites were much more susceptible to all manner of wounds, where mozos possessed "remarkable resistance to [. . .] terrific wounds from firearms, cutting and piercing instruments, etc."[75] His awe was palpable; this power of resistance was, to him, "abnormal" and "little short of miraculous." There was no clear explanation for these differences, so Gage filled the gap by positing that "the nervous systems and receptive centers of these people are not stimulated by wounds of the same extent as the Anglo-Saxon." What was more, many wounded mozos entered the hospital in a state of what the doctor termed "alcoholic anaesthesia," a stupor so deep and acute that they would not even recall having received several severe wounds.[76] The following years, Gage's colleagues confirmed his hypothesis of the "remarkable" and "surprising" resistance of native laborers to machete wounds, and the anesthetic role of alcohol in such cases.[77] This anecdotal clinical pathology of wounds easily translated into a broader social definition of "the mozo laborer." The machete itself, in Gage's account, appeared as nearly a natural appendage of all laborers, an item "without which no mozo feels completely dressed." Political upheavals also brought a flow of quickly cured gunshot wounds under the gaze of company doctors, a detail Gage offered up as supporting evidence and accepted wisdom in company hospitals.[78] And one colleague in Honduras, writing a few years later, lamented the glee with which he had heard hospitalized laborers describe violent deaths in labor camps, a behavior he attributed in the most virulent of terms to indigenous blood—constituted, in his report's title, as "the lower class of tropical American patients."[79] Medical discourse in the company's tropical divisions constituted violence as both a biological and cultural trait of its laboring populations, a persistence of racial biology owing perhaps to an endemic lacking an explanation in germ theory.

At the deepest level, pathologizing racial difference in the era of moral hygiene often revolved around the body's most intimate functions: eating, defecation, and sexuality.[80] William Deeks attributed an outbreak of bacillary dysentery in Truxillo, Honduras in the early 1920s, to the dietary practices of local Miskito Indians, "who are very fond of eating various classes of food, such as crabs, etc., which are prone to carry infection."[81] The cleanliness and personal hygiene of laborers also came under sharp scrutiny, especially those working in close proximity to "high-grade" employees as servants. Following years of high incidence of amoebiasis in Santa Marta, the company invited experts from the University of California–Berkeley to conduct a study with the collaboration of the company's personnel. The team focused on 347 individuals drawn from all classes of employees, and collected and examined stool samples from all of them in the hospital laboratory. The experts knew that infected stools were the only vector of transmission of amoebiasis, and acknowledged that a range of factors could facilitate its spread, among them poor sewage infrastructure and social conditions. What is striking, however, is how this study and the medical department more broadly focused exclusively on the personal hygiene of "the *distributor of cysts*"—identified explicitly as "club servants" and "food handlers." The relatively high incidence of positives among servants and cooks compared to that among white employees led the investigators to pinpoint poor handwashing among kitchen staff as the cause, a conclusion that carried with it their characterization as "ever-present sources of contagion."[82] Other potential avenues of transmission were the truck gardens kept on company property, where ignorant gardeners apparently fertilized with night soil, and flies, which proliferated in fecal matter and mixed freely with populations unconcerned with proper house screening.[83] Even the drinking water in Santa Marta was suspect, but only because "the native population bathe and wash their clothes in these streams and ditches, and it is conceivable that the water supply may thus become contaminated."[84] The study concluded that a more aggressive public health regime encompassing enforcement of hygienic norms in all realms of life "may do much to counteract the baleful influence of the cyst-distributor."[85] The data compiled from laborer and servant bodies fed the racialized characterization of the disease carrier, reducing the cause to one immediately identifiable factor within a much more complex social environment shaped by the company's enterprise.

The study of venereal disease, especially syphilis, provides another window into the racial pathologization of intimate spaces in the company's sphere. A new testing method allowed the medical department to implement a series of syphilis surveys around the company's divisions in the 1920s, and the results established the disease as second only to malaria in causing "lowered vitality and resistance" in tropical divisions, although it was not generally considered a "tropical" illness.[86] Even though white employees were usually found to have syphilis rates higher than those determined in the United States, the font of infection in these reports was the laboring population and "natives" living near company plantations. "Their moral attitude and indifference" were to blame, wrote one doctor in 1922. William Deeks's indictment of laborers' behavior was even more blistering. "The question of dealing with [venereal disease] is especially puzzling among an illiterate and nomadic people," he reported in 1925, "in view of the laxity of marital relations, the high rate of illiteracy, a low standard of morality, and the absence of any responsibility to society."[87] While company doctors construed laborers as essentially immoral, white employees—undoubtedly important members of the syphilitic community—escaped such opprobrium. The shame of white employees, it appears, could even intervene between their bodies and the company's clinical gaze, thereby enabling the virus to propagate in more bodies. Company regulations had long allowed doctors treating whites to consider venereal infections "a private matter between themselves and the patient"; in many cases, no records were even made of many such diagnoses, although first-class (white) employees were required to pay for any consultation and treatment out-of-pocket.[88] When it came to protecting the sexual activity of white male employees, the powerful discourse of moral hygiene fixated on the more dangerous promiscuity of "tropical" races.

Most vexing for the banana company's doctors were the various ways laborers ignored or actively subverted their medical authority and tutelage. The fear of mobile laborers as malaria vectors revolved as much around their "low mentality"—their intransigence and ignorance in the face of modern medical knowledge—as it did around their infected bodies.[89] Since most came from regions without modern sanitary regimes, upon entering the company's cordon sanitaire, these populations failed to understand the necessity of preventive antimosquito measures, such as maintaining house screens and keeping living areas free of water-collecting trash. In the early 1920s, Deeks's frustration with such ignorance led him to advocate investing in window screens only for the "better class of native labor," in other words, "those sufficiently intelligent to appreciate the value of screening and to keep the screens in order."[90] Workers also tended to resist the company's efforts to police their bodies through mandatory tests for plasmodia and through cinchonization, the prophylactic administration of quinine. Doctors on the ground experimented with various delivery methods, including mixing bitter-tasting quinine with rum, disguising it with sugar, and administering it in intramuscular injections. According to company officials, laborers almost never voluntarily completed the typical two-week course of quinine treatment necessary to reduce plasmodia to nonsexual levels in human blood—probably because of the drug's extremely bitter taste and unpleasant side effects, but also because once the fevers died down, they did not see the sense in continuing with regular doses.[91] They explained workers' choices through the discourse of moral hygiene as a symptom of a deeper backwardness, a "natural antipathy [. . .] in regard to taking quinine."[92]

Company doctors also construed as dangerous the workers and the "native" populations near company divisions because their adherence to "tradition" so readily undermined modern medical practice and public health. Doctors wrote often of trying to overcome the stubborn customs of the "ignorant" societies of the tropics, from their fears of air circulating at night to their purported resistance to drinking well water.[93] Concerned about typhoid in the Cuban divisions, the company's medical superintendent lamented in 1928 that "an old custom, bred deeply into the people's nature," was helping spread the sickness. Locals, it seemed, tended to "meddle with sick people," visiting their sick neighbors daily and coming into contact with the pathogen.[94] Local healers could pose an even greater challenge with their alternative explanatory frameworks and treatments. One district medical officer, himself a Cuban doctor, attributed the persistence of malaria in the company's sugar plantations in part to the proximity of Cueto, a town where various local physicians apparently made a bustling business in "patent medicines" and "proprietary preparations" to laborers suffering from fevers.[95] Around the same time, "medical sabotage" militated against the company's opening of the Chiriquí Division on the West Coast of Panama in the late 1920s. "A practitioner, speaking the idiom of the people," complained a company official, "came in and began telling them [laborers] of the 'heating nature' of quinine." As an alternative, the man offered workers large injections of some unnamed concoction. Not surprisingly, the company soon was able to enlist "a splendid system of discipline and control by native police," in effect leveraging its own discourse of public health with local authorities against the likes of the practitioner. The effects of this conflict on malaria prevention are unclear, but the idiom in which the officer described it is telling: "we had to struggle to maintain prestige until this undesirable influence was counteracted," he noted with some satisfaction.[96]

Reading behind the frustrations of United Fruit's doctors provides a window onto the world of laborers' motivations and their resistance to the company's medical authority. It would be inaccurate to claim that laborers universally rejected the company's paternalism. Laborers could demand a deeper presence of the Medical Department, as was the case in the famed Colombian strike of 1928, when poor camp sanitation and health care made the list of the strikers' complaints.[97] Less than an embrace of the company's medical authority, however, these demands should be viewed as part of a broader strategy of the Colombian strikers to demonstrate the company's neglect of worker welfare in several areas. The prevalence of complaints about custom, ignorance, intransigence, folk medicine, migratory tendencies, and the maddening tendency of workers to move about unprotected at night reveal that laborers negotiated the company's control in a variety of ways.[98] Some of these strategies can be viewed as "everyday forms of resistance," ever simmering around the company's efforts to prescribe and control behavior. Chomsky's work on the rich Afro-Jamaican world of the company's Costa Rica division is deeply suggestive in this regard. There, early twentieth-century labor struggles hinged on the resistance of workers and the surrounding West Indian community more broadly to the company's medical authority. Some of the principal leaders in that community described their opposition to the company through the idiom of Obeah, a West Indian practice combining spiritual and physical remedies.[99] The prominence of Obeah in the labor disturbances of 1910 were doubtless long in the memories of company managers and doctors. Taken together, an abundance of company narratives about the baleful influence of traditional medicine in several divisions show that United Fruit's laborers often sought alternative explanations and treatments for what ailed them. The company's medical campaigns thus operated in a perpetually contested terrain, where its subjects often evaded the grasp of Western corporate medicine.

The medical department's ability to constitute laborers and surrounding populations as morally suspect disease vectors intertwined with its growing capacity to measure, define, and lay bare laborers' bodies to a clinical gaze. Starting in the 1920s, the department's annual reports became a venue for case studies and autopsy reports, meant to offer up for observation the disease landscape of the laboring population to the tropical medicine community at large, covering everything from snake bites to yaws. Discussion of cases involving white subjects occasionally appeared, but by and large, the subjects to be disassembled in the laboratory and reconstituted on the page in clinical detail were "others," as the company defined them. It was for this group that the most invasive practices of display were reserved, those involving medical photography. Nameless workers and dependents, male and female, alive and dead, were disrobed in some measure (or all), posed in ways that better displayed their particular condition on the surface of the body (often "curious" cases), or even its internal workings laid bare at the microscopic level or via X-rays.[100] Medical photography could also illustrate more broadly "the physical condition of the average laborer in some of the tropical countries," subject as they were to "lowered resistance due to improper diet, unsanitary environments, and infection by one or more debilitating diseases."[101] Laboratory photographs combined with case studies or autopsy reports served as a potent representational technology for bracketing the "typical" physical

TYPICAL LABORERS' WARD, IN HOSPITAL, SANTA MARTA, COLOMBIA.

Figure 4.4. Segregation of white and nonwhite patients assumed heightened importance in the tropics, where whites were vulnerable to contact with "wandering foci of infection." "Typical Laborers' Ward, in Hospital, Santa Marta, Colombia." Annual Report of the Medical Department of the United Fruit Company 1917, p. 84.

conditions or diseases of tropical milieus and the frontiers of medical oddity, which constructed in a new pathological idiom a much older sense of difference between "normal" temperate environments and excessive, rife tropical ones.[102]

By the 1920s, then, United Fruit's doctors had developed something of a social diagnosis of tropical populations in the company's sphere of operations. Deeks and his colleagues combined culturally defined moral shortcomings, generally poor social conditions, a lack of modern sanitation, and the diverse pathogenic landscape of tropical America into one overarching explanatory framework for the region's backwardness. A series of surveys in the 1920s established that an underlying endemicity of hookworm and venereal disease, coupled with generally poor nutrition, made workers especially susceptible to even more debilitating conditions like pneumonia or malaria. A viable, modern sanitary regime such as the company's offered some hope, but "low mentality" led most in these populations to evade or resist such paternalistic efforts. This medical narrative of backwardness and the necessity of a United States–driven public health regime grew directly out of the clinical culture of company hospitals and laboratories, out of thousands of examinations, sample collections, photo sessions, and sanitary inspections. A subject population so constituted also justified and rendered natural the stark contrast between these "others" and the "temperate" cadre so keenly required to manage their labor.

Conclusions

The racialized division of labor at the heart of United Fruit's Anglo-Saxon empire from 1899 until the early 1930s was intimately intertwined with medical practice and inquiry. The company's vast network of base hospitals, field dispensaries, and mobile clinics served a certain economic logic: it was far cheaper to invest in medical infrastructure than to engineer deeper social improvements that could have diminished the incidence of disease more broadly, a dynamic common on colonial resource frontiers at the time.[103] What is more, that medical enterprise had the benefit of being a highly visible, tangible manifestation of the company's largesse and benevolent mission. Although Deeks and his medical department firmly believed in their ability to transform the tropics into a salubrious breadbasket, a wider lens of history reveals that malaria and other illnesses that so absorbed their attention actually operated in symbiosis with this corporate colonial project. Medical inquiry itself functioned in concert with corporate power, benefitting from its service to the company's economic prerogatives and laboring mightily to cultivate the its continued patronage. As studies of state-driven American colonial enterprises have shown, the burgeoning field of tropical medicine, spurred to new heights by the turn to germ theory, operated as a vital component of US power abroad, and the banana corporation's sphere formed a key node in this wider suite of overseas engagements.[104] Inherent in the battle against disease in the company's tropical divisions lay a series of routine medical practices that disciplined nonwhite laborers by insinuating the company's authority over their bodies and their lives in myriad ways. The narratives generated from these practices shaped everything from the segregated design of company towns, living spaces, and hospitals to the ideological justification of the racially stratified labor force. Corporate tropical medicine, however, operated on a contested terrain where the agencies of humans and pathogens shaped the company's enterprise in concert with the most strident of doctors "engaged in the peaceful strife of science."[105] As for the white Anglo-Saxon men at the head of the labor regime, their reconciliation with the tropical milieu went well beyond the purview of the Medical Department.

CHAPTER FIVE

Becoming Banana Cowboys

I n August 1919, Boston draughtsman Everett Brown landed in Preston, Cuba, anxious to take up his new position on the United Fruit Company's rapidly expanding sugar plantations. A week after arriving, Brown wrote to his wife, Ethel, from Guaro, a "typical frontier town" only few miles to the southeast of the orderly Preston. Most traffic moved on the hoof, and, being Sunday, Cuban cattle punchers and Haitian and Jamaican laborers crowded the sugar outpost's saloons, stores, and streets. Contemplating this "regular wild west" scene, he declared, "This is not a place for a white woman it is raw country in every way." Brown's described Guaro as a particular kind of masculine space, which rough living conditions and "niggers and Cubans galore" made unfit for white women and the trappings of American domesticity. For a white male engineer, however, this extractive frontier promised to provide "a fine experience professionally." He stood to gain both practical field experience and the manly cachet that the company's culture attached to triumphing over the dangers and discomforts of its frontiers. Within a week of arriving in a United Fruit enclave, white, suburban, middle-class professional Brown made sense of his new tropical career as a masculine frontier vocation. The experience would prove transformational.[1] Among employees like Brown, a masculine ethos of tropical work often found expression through a North American frontier metaphor, with its readily recognizable tropes of white supremacy and dominion over unruly, hostile, unproductive populations and environments. This chapter explains why such constructions of white masculinity became so important to the corporation's effort to build a profitable tropical enterprise. A discussion of Brown's career follows as a window into the vital role this gender ideology, as cultural imperative, came to play in the company's internal culture by the late 1920s.

Historical scholarship on US expansion has embraced the notion that ideas of masculinity have played a central role in it. Much of this work offers important insight into the sphere of the state and government. So it is that we better understand, for instance, how appeals to "McKinley's backbone" and anxieties about white manhood helped propel the country toward war in the 1890s; how lowly privates deployed in Haiti were "culturally conscripted" into Washington's agenda for that nation; and how fears about white male debilitation in the tropics shaped US colonial medicine in the Philippines. Such studies elucidate how notions of masculinity shaped US expansion and motivated those in positions of power, from presidents to the rank-and-file men deployed overseas. Constructions of American masculinity emerge as the underpinnings of the violence at the heart of state-sponsored overseas interventions. The literature's focus on the state, though valuable, reflects the broader state-centric tendency in scholarship on US expansion and US–Latin American relations more specifically. Bringing a focus on masculinity to bear on the expansion of private enterprise, in particular a long-standing concern such as United Fruit, can push inquiry in new directions. For instance: more than military occupations and even the Panama Canal Authority, United Fruit faced the long-term problem of hosting sizeable white expatriate colonies. Our understanding of violence and its relationship to imperial masculinities can also be complicated by the story of United Fruit's men. Physical violence played a role in their experiences with racial others, to be sure, but it was much more significant as a creature of imagination and fantasy, as a set of dangers that situated the tropical hand apart from and above laborers and one's office-bound peers back in the states. On the other hand, the importance of violence in company culture suggests that economic expansion cannot be understood separately from the ideological forms that infused military intervention. In either case, the experience of company men and how the company managed and motivated them (they were not conscripts, after all) can tell us a great deal about the vital role notions of masculinity played in making overseas enterprise profitable.[2]

The entire UFCO enterprise, as we have seen, depended on a large, racially segmented labor force. True to the racialized thinking of the day, the company recruited a nucleus of white Anglo-Saxon men to supervise and organize the work of a much larger workforce made up of nonwhite laborers. As several scholars have noted, United Fruit's demand for labor reshaped the human geography of the Caribbean basin in the early twentieth century. Jason Colby's recent study of United Fruit's labor practices provides a useful periodization of these developments across the company's early twentieth-century field of operations. Initially favoring black laborers over Hispanic or mestizo locals, company recruiters shipped thousands of West Indians to the

Caribbean littoral and Francophone blacks to Cuba. Following labor unrest in 1909, company officials turned to recruiting more Spanish-speaking locals where they could; their objective was to disrupt labor activism through segmentation of the labor force. Exploiting tensions between Hispanic and West Indian laborers, however, fell victim to the rise in Hispanic nationalism around the region in the 1920s. By the end of that decade, company officials from Guatemala to Colombia were heeding calls to exclude West Indian labor and were well on the way to recruiting a solidly Hispanic workforce.[3] Through all of these shifts, company management treated its "second-class" laborers imperiously and often brutally, the best known such case being the company's collusion in the 1928 massacre of striking workers in Santa Marta, Colombia, at the hands of the army—a prominent episode in Gabriel García Márquez's *One Hundred Years of Solitude*.

Although several scholars have produced valuable studies of the company's treatment of laborers, scholarly work on the company, with few exceptions, has largely overlooked the experience of American men, like Everett Brown, who spent part of their lives in the United Fruit's tropical divisions as foremen, timekeepers, doctors, engineers, and scientists. By the mid-1910s and 1920s, white American men working abroad for United Fruit numbered between one and two thousand, probably falling somewhere between until the general contraction of the company's ranks during the Depression and World War II and its gradual postwar divestment from direct production of bananas. (In the same period, nonwhite laborers on the payroll grew from more than twenty thousand to more than fifty thousand.) A sampling of one thousand salaried white employees in 1924 indicated that almost three-quarters were Americans, with Britons, Canadians, and other Western Europeans making up the balance. Although privileged compared to nonwhite laborers, these employees faced an upper management that could be intransigent, tight-fisted, and unpredictable. As the third segment in United Fruit's tropical labor force, skilled expatriate employees posed a series of problems specific to their status as white American men. That attrition among these men lingered around 60 percent annually in the mid-1920s spoke to the seriousness of such problems.[4]

Facing persistently poor retention of tropical division employees led company president (1924–1933) and longtime tropical veteran Victor Cutter to question the manliness of new recruits who failed to overcome the difficulties of tropical employment. No doubt recalling his own experience in the company's first years, he chided the new generation of men for becoming too accustomed to the company's generous corporate welfare regime. "Luxury," he told an audience at the company retreat in 1927, "easily gets in the blood." Providing American employees comfortable, sanitary housing and community facilities had its disadvantages—it could make white men soft and alienate them from the masculine vitality of earlier generations.[5] Cutter's view of American men in the tropics spoke to what some historians have termed a crisis of early twentieth-century Anglo-Saxon masculinity. That crisis, the argument goes, resulted from the apparently debilitating effects of white-collar work, an "overcivilized" urban existence, and a reaction to the growing vocality and political influence of immigrants, peoples of color, and women in American life. The masculine qualities valued in the company's internal culture and later taken up by company propaganda spoke specifically to these anxieties.[6]

By the mid-1920s, United Fruit's leadership confronted cultural and social isolation, the "softness" of young men, and the medical and moral dangers of life in the tropics as problems of social engineering. Acting as an interventionist, progressive-era colonial government in its tropical divisions, the company was well positioned to reconcile white, middle-class masculinity to white-collar tropical work. Better men could be made by investing not only in infrastructure but by fostering a masculine corporate culture that spoke to the vulnerabilities, ambitions, and fantasies of its employees. Crafting this culture on a frontier of corporate empire meant formulating notions of what it meant to be an American man in the tropics. The pervasive metaphor of the "banana frontier" functioned as the principal ideological mechanism of this effort to engineer a better class of white tropical employee. Born not of Boston boardrooms, this tropical iteration of the frontier idea had its roots in the day-to-day experiences of men like Brown, and provided an important cultural imperative articulating their power over their surroundings.

The company's critics have often argued that its management of tropical enclaves reflected a set of practices drawn from the plantation and apartheid cultures of the US South. The racialized division of labor and Jim Crow social regime many observed in United Fruit towns led to such conclusions. Recent scholarship on United Fruit sheds much-needed light on these critiques and this aspect of the company's labor practices. Company plantations, although

structured in part around racial thinking akin to that of southeastern slave-
holders, were not transplants. The racialized division of labor in company
enclaves owed more to the labor-segmentation strategies of northeastern
factory owners and the need to manage the criticism of Hispanic nationalists
than it does to a reliance on the practices of the Jim Crow South. A consideration of the frontier myth in company culture and its relationship to masculine identity deepens this argument.

As a touchstone of corporate identity and employee culture, the western
frontier offered an accessible narrative untroubled by the north-south divide
and the history of slavery. Narratives about westward expansion abounded
in the American culture of the late nineteenth and early twentieth centuries,
infusing political discourse, popular culture, and a whole array of public displays of Americanness at home and abroad. A popular literature subgenre of
the period even centered on the adventures of heroic frontier engineers. A
Rooseveltian understanding of the frontier's importance to national identity,
in particular American masculinity, held wide cultural currency. As Richard
Slotkin describes in his analysis of Theodore Roosevelt, one's masculinity
could be reconstituted by "regeneration through regression"—a notion of the
frontier premised on "the passage of a highly civilized man through a revivi-
fying return to the life of an earlier historical 'stage.'"[7] The Rooseveltian
concept of the frontier tinctured white-collar work and tropical life—sites of
anxiety as they related to white masculinity—with the "barbarian virtues"
then the object of much discussion in the United States. This transformative
aspect of the US frontier metaphor made the voyage overseas quite intact,
and inflected how American men would make sense of their work in tropical
enclaves much more than the narrower referent of the southern plantation.[8]
The company's tropical frontiers might resemble the racial hierarchy of the
US South, but the otherness of black and Hispanic laborers would be cast in
the framework of an expanding frontier of civilization.

Everett Brown's Tropical Career

True to the tendency toward high turnover, Everett Brown's career with
United Fruit lasted almost exactly a year, from August 1919 until September
1920. He started as a draughtsman in Cuba, and six months later gained
promotion and transfer to the Panama Division. In each division, his work on

railroads and plantation surveying kept him on the fringes of the company's operations, well outside the better-developed headquarters towns. Although he privately expressed anxiety about his position with the company and his relationships with supervisors, Brown apparently had enough success and political acumen to find his way into positions of greater responsibility. By the time he left the company, Brown stood at the head of a survey crew expanding the company's domains in the Talamanca Valley between Costa Rica and Panama. A case of recurrent malaria, the company's unwillingness to grant him a vacation, and a more attractive offer of employment spurred him to end his stint with United Fruit. Although frequently critical of his supervisors and office politics, he clearly loved the kind of work the company gave him and relished in the transformation it offered him professionally and personally.

The satisfaction Brown found in the tropics emerged in large part from his gendered understanding of the company's sphere as a series of frontiers expanding into wasted or wild spaces. Although distance from his wife and young daughter pained him, it was the absence of white women that, in part, defined the opportunities of company's frontiers for Brown. What made such spaces unfit for the likes of his family was the preponderance of black and Hispanic laborers and the danger they represented. "Raw" was the term he used to describe such places, whether the Cuban railroad camps where he and a handful of white engineers lived in simple bunkhouses surrounded by hundreds of Haitian laborers or around Guabito, Panama, where a segmented labor force lived and worked in an often-tense environment. For Brown, demography even more than the lack of modern amenities defined a frontier as "raw," where civilization's hold remained tenuous. "I would not know what to do with you here now," he wrote to his wife, Ethel, from Cuba, "for there is . . . no place where a woman would be put up here it is a man's camp pure and simple." Negotiating such deprivations and potentially dangerous races remained, for Brown, the exclusive province of white American males. The burden of confronting that raw space formed a centerpiece in Brown's understanding of his own place in the tropics.[9]

Reminiscent of North American frontiers, Brown portrayed United Fruit's raw edges as violent places—and, true to the frontier metaphor, disorder emanated primarily from people of color. Their inherently violent nature, he believed, had to be restrained with an abundance of armed company guards, who maintained racial order with a rough kind of frontier justice. Most men, himself occasionally, "packed a gat" (carried a sidearm), even around camp. After "someone started to shoot up the town one night," he related from Guaro, he saw the company guards drag the perpetrator by his office. Later, he wrote to his wife, "they laugh and say it was taken care of." A few months later, in Guabito, Panama, he described a rash of incidents around the time of his arrival. In one case, the company's railroad superintendent had been beaten by a West Indian worker. "The nigger ought to have been shot on the spot," he noted bitterly. He continued, "So you see we have some excitement here. There have been 5 shootings here since I came. 2 have been fatal, all niggers. They have machete fights every day almost. Someone gets cut up. This is life on the edge of things."[10]

Brown's sense of racial order proved to be more than bluster. At the head of a ten-man survey crew in Costa Rica's Talamanca Valley (at the time, the northernmost reach of the Panama division), he readily assumed a sense of racial entitlement inherent to the frontier metaphor. In this view, any threat to the company's authority from disorderly elements invited an aggressive retrenchment of the racialized labor regime. When some of the laborers on his crew suddenly struck for higher wages, he fired the lot of them—for good measure, even those who hadn't taken part in the strike. After this episode, with a new crew on hand, the work of extending the grid of railways and future banana plantations continued. Later on this foray "up the line," Brown encountered a group of Talamanca Indians, who lived on lands leased to the company. His survey line cut straight through their village, an intrusion that soon led them to "move their villages and ranches to the hills as we advance." Brown viewed this dispossession as the necessary price of progress. "They are a rather degenerate race and fast dying out," he explained, pronouncing them "too lazy to brush the flies off." Unproductive landscapes had to be tamed for the good of civilization and the backward races that inhabited those places had to be swept aside in the process.[11]

Assuming such a sense of racial authority went hand-in-hand with assuming a masculine professional identity wrapped in the language of frontier adventure. On the company's raw edges Brown found a space where he could take on the trappings of the frontier engineer, a heroic male stock character in late nineteenth- and early twentieth-century US fiction. Whether this literature informed Brown's perspective remains unknown, but his engineering colleagues provided a ready-made narrative of masculine engineering adventures into which he could step. "No need for story books here," he wrote Ethel, "we have men, plenty, that can tell true stories of their work, that beat any book ever written." These men had worked all over the world as itinerant field engineers, work that took them all over Latin America, Asia, and Africa. He felt thrilled by access to "the real inside stories of things that never get printed." His brushes with danger and primitive conditions in United Fruit's employ allowed Brown his own role in the larger story of intrepid engineers working on the world's colonial railroad frontiers. Upon being promoted and transferred, his membership in this community of itinerant tropical professionals appeared complete: as he departed Cuba for Bocas del Toro, Panama, "the real honest to God tropics," he cheerily signed off as "your tramp, Everett."12

Brown experienced his new professional self as an invigorating personal transformation. Once in Panama, his work of surveying new banana plantations took him out of company offices and into the field north of Guabito into Costa Rica. The jungle conditions required that he buy gear that was unnecessary in his office work. "From now on," he wrote his wife, "you can imagine me in kayki [sic] pants (riding) leather puttees and one of my old shirts with a wide rimmed stetson hat and sleeves rolled up and shirt open at neck. I look some like a native the sun gives me quite a color. Shall probably wear a six shooter on the survey. Have a 'snake kit' in my pocket."

He took up the vocation of the frontier engineer with gusto, his white-collar trade now dressed in manlier attire, ready for the rugged outdoors, and seasoned with a hint of danger. Brown found this new assignment physically invigorating. After describing a day in the field covering many miles on foot, he happily wrote home, "You can see by that, that I am in fine condition better than I have been for years."13

The engineering frontier of United Fruit's tropics, then, represented a distinct kind of professional space than urban offices back in the United States.14 Not only did it hold the potential for personal transformation, but the possibilities for recognition and advancement were also much more open than anywhere in his stateside experience. "It is different down here—one feels as though the bars were down and you could go as far as you like or as you have brains for," Brown concluded after two months in Cuba. "I like the feeling of making your way among men who know things, and have done something," he wrote a couple of months later, and speculated, "I am in a position here where I guess they are trying me out for something better." Being part of a team of engineers who included him in their discussions of the Cuban division's overall structure elevated Brown's own sense of professional self-esteem, and probably laid the groundwork for his promotion and transfer to Panama. After the transfer, his work as survey crew chief brought even greater autonomy and recognition from superiors. He related his meetings with them to his wife, and felt that they took his ideas seriously—apparently the first time in his professional life he felt like an integral part of an engineering team. This work on the company's frontiers offered Brown a sense of belonging to a masculine cohort of professionals engaged in a grand enterprise. From Panama, he proudly noted his ascent to this community. "Down here," he wrote, "you are not lost in a crowd as in the states. Here everyone is known all through the tropics."[15]

Even before working on surveys of Costa Rica's Talamanca Valley, which he did toward the end of his United Fruit career, Brown found engineering work in the tropics quite different from what he had done in the United States. Not only did he find like-minded peers; being on the "edge of things" made his work for the company seem more real and tangible. Having arrived recently in Cuba, he wrote home about the quality and importance of "work here [that] is very accurate and is to be for record at Boston." After a few months, the impression of being a part of work he deemed significant had grown. "This is the raw side of engineering where things go," he cheerfully exclaimed, concluding that "I would not miss it for a good deal." Those raw conditions that separated him from his family, often painfully, provided incentives beyond just earning a living. Making surveys—for railways and plantation layouts, mostly—and being involved in supervising their construction invested Brown's work with a vitality and importance that he had found lacking in stateside work.[16]

The frontier metaphor provided Brown with a vocabulary that expressed the transcendental importance of his work with United Fruit. Not surprisingly, a series of apologists and publicists repeatedly conveyed this message to the US public, Latin American audiences, and the company's own employees. The conquest of the tropics, went the argument, rendered unproductive places a new breadbasket for North American markets and provided opportunity for local populations. As he ascended to positions of responsibility,

Brown invested his work with such a sense of mission. Repeatedly he described the transformation of "virgin forest," "real wilds," and "wild sections" into cultivation, and relished being on the cutting edge of the process. For Brown, the advance of the company's frontier went something like this, at least in the far reaches of the Panama Division:

> Monday I shall start a crew packing concrete monuments into camp to be used in marking the different farm divisions. The timber cutters are following the survey closely in two weeks more the [Talamanca] valley will be cleared. The cutters have reached the camp, underbrushing to be followed by the men who fall the big trees. The railroad is being pushed into the valley very fast in three or four weeks we shall be in rail communication with the outside world, also in three weeks time I shall be in camp 12 miles further in the mountain, if things go as they are planned.

Playing a personal role in this process, Brown found a sense of commitment that transcended his usual day-to-day concerns about distance from family, money, and personal advancement. "We break into the wilderness and make things ready for civilization," he wrote proudly to his wife. "That is the reason it is attractive to me. It is what I have had a longing for all my life."[17]

Back in Boston, Brown's wife, Ethel, and young daughter, Susie, endearingly registered his transformation into a frontier engineer from afar. His letters provided a steady flow of images and stories of company towns, Indian villages, banana plantations, and the "virgin forest," imagery that nested in the imagination of the family. To his wife, writing in the summer of 1920, their nearly year-long separation "has been in a good cause—if you feel it has made you a 'real engineer' as you tell about, given you travel and the breadth that comes from seeing other lands and other people, and above all improved your health." Besides these benefits, Ethel noted the loftier dimension of his work. It "must be interesting to see civilization such as railroads, camps, etc. approach as you beckon thro' the wilderness," a grand project she ventured would make her husband "feel like a pioneer." Having listened to her mother read aloud her father's letters, Susie also imagined her father's adventures on the banana frontier from afar. One day, Ethel found the girl sitting in their living room with her eyes closed, intensely focused. She described the scene to her husband: "'Oh mamma,' she says, 'If I shut my eyes I can see pictures.

I'm seeing a picture of my papa now. . . . dressed just the way he wrote us, in the camp her wrote us about—and now I can see him riding a mule.'" The special properties of the banana frontier—its professional opportunities and regenerative possibilities—helped assuage the pain of separation for Brown's family.[18]

Little more than three months after taking charge of the Talamanca Valley survey, Everett Brown left United Fruit. Becoming immersed in the company's masculine culture had helped him adapt to work in the tropics and to appreciate the region's fresh opportunities as his own. He had transformed himself into a rugged frontier engineer, and through his work had gained a sense of his own role in overcoming human and environmental obstacles and, in his view, spreading the reach of civilization. A recurring malarial infection, contracted in the survey camps of the Talamanca Valley in Costa Rica during the summer of 1920, took the shine off his surveying work and probably hastened the end of his tenure with United Fruit. After struggling for weeks with fevers, the unpleasant effects of quinine doses, and the boredom of being confined to office work, Brown felt "run down" and "badly in need of a change of climate," an opinion seconded by his superintendent and a company doctor. In their view, such casualties were to be expected wherever the company undertook pioneering work. He sailed to Boston and quit United Fruit, probably already having lined up work as head engineer with the Santa Ana Sugar Company, a US concern that had recently bought plantations in eastern Cuba. Santa Ana's higher pay and the real possibility of housing for his family cemented the decision. After six weeks back home, Brown returned to Cuba cured of malaria and confident in his ability to continue work on another corporate frontier. His correspondence closes amid preparations to move his wife and daughter to Cuba. Gone were his worries about the place's "rawness" and unsuitability for white women—views perhaps tempered by time but surely shaped by becoming a new man on United Fruit's banana frontier.[19]

Frontier Masculinities and Company Culture

Victor Cutter's ascent to the company's presidency in 1924 brought the culture of the banana frontier to the center of the company's operations in Boston. Massachusetts-born and educated at Dartmouth College, Cutter began his rise through the company's tropical ranks in 1904 as a lowly timekeeper. The man himself was an icon of the company's ideal masculine culture—bold, large in stature, athletic, not hesitant to use violence against laborers—physical qualities melded with his college education and upward mobility. Cutter undoubtedly considered his career a model for new company men, for upon taking up the presidency he promptly publicized his biography, among other venues in *Unifruitco*, a monthly magazine directed at the company's American employees at home and abroad.

Unifruitco's first period of publication, 1925–1931, nearly coincided with Cutter's tenure; it later resurfaced in the 1950s. The employee magazine went hand-in-hand with the company's increased investments in corporate welfare, a broad-based effort to cultivate employee loyalty and invest the company with "corporate soul." Although an organ of corporate propaganda, *Unifruitco* provides a valuable picture of enclave life told in the voices of those who lived there. Their narratives always served the company's interest and reflected the kind of masculine company culture leaders like Cutter wanted to propagate. The idiom of the North American frontier dominated how Cutter and others framed the company's tropics during the last years of the company's great expansion.[20]

That frontier narrative structured accounts of the company's growth since the late nineteenth century. Romanticized accounts of the company's "pioneer days" claimed that the company succeeded during those early years through "old virtues," a stew of steady nerves and steely determination in the face of an untamed environment. Describing Honduras before the development of company ports, one recalled that loading banana boats by lighter "called for iron nerve and courage. . . . When a norther started to blow, it took quick action and a clear head not alone to save the gas boat and lighters . . . but also to guard against the loss of life." The rigors of harsh weather and the lack of port infrastructure made the movement of fruit a life-threatening enterprise that molded a generation of company men suited to tough conditions. This periodization of the company's history emphasized the dramatic transformation of tropical divisions in the intervening years. President Cutter himself looked back on his own early career with the company in Costa Rica as "pioneer days," even in his sober assessments of United Fruit's development written for stockholders and executives.[21]

Well after the pioneer days of the banana trade, the frontier metaphor held its resonance in depictions of United Fruit's advancing edges and the possibilities it held for new employees. In an imagined conversation between a tropical veteran and a naïve and skeptical newcomer—a fixture in early issues of *Unifruitco*—an old hand struggled to convince his junior colleague of the company's higher purpose, a mission wrapped in the language of the frontier. At last, the greenhorn shakily grasped the point. "Work like this is really pioneer—just as much as the early frontiersmen," he conceded, "the same old stuff, in the twentieth century, as the early Conquistadores had—the chaps who were the first to explore these countries and who bucked hardships that make conditions today look like pink tea." Such pieces circulated the idea that working for United Fruit in the 1920s provided a kind of experience lost to modern society, a test of masculinity in a place outside of modernity and its comforts. "Whatever it is, it's real," concluded the newcomer, satisfied with his place in the company's "big scheme of colonization, sanitation, and commercial development." The frontier metaphor, grounded in the masculine pioneer figures of other eras, lent an aura of transcendence to the company's activities, a cultural imperative to possess and transform places for the good of humanity. The naïve greenhorn represented the newly arrived American who had yet to grasp the transformative possibilities of the tropical frontier. Acclimatization, some bout of tropical illness, and passage through rough conditions formed one part of his trial; by proving himself physically capable of tropical life, he could then assume his role in the company's larger mission. In narratives designed to assuage the anxieties of potential tropical men, older generations of tropical men tutored new arrivals through difficulties and guided them through a metamorphosis into proven tropical hands.[22]

That process of becoming a tropical man promised to provide professional opportunities unique to tropical divisions. In these white-collar frontiers, one's manliness could translate into upward mobility. Helping the newcomer snap out of his "grouch," the veteran noted that "we don't expect to be out here forever, you know." The potential benefits of roughing it could come later. As an example in the flesh, he pointed to the division superintendent:

Take the Chief; he's got a mighty comfortable house in town; rides around and, while I don't doubt that he works his think tank harder than we do, nevertheless he has a lot of comforts that we don't. *But* he didn't land that job fresh from the States. Oh no! He's gone through the mill, just as we are doing; he's bucked mosquitoes, sandflies and the other pests we're putting up with. I'll say so. Bucked 'em under harder conditions than we have. Been in the bush for months at a time; not even an occasional night in town for weeks at a stretch.

The superintendent was no effete pen-pusher sent down from Boston or New York; he had passed through the crucible of the company's frontier and emerged a better man, one possessing the confidence and managerial vision necessary to oversee a whole division. Confident that the company's leadership would reward such a transformation, the veteran concluded that "if a chap sticks to it . . . he comes out ahead" and assured his new colleague that proving himself in the tropics would give him "the jump on the stay-at-homes."[23]

Once having embraced the rigors of the banana frontier, the greenhorn could become a "banana cowboy" or "banana herder." This character in company publicity included any American on the lower rungs of tropical management, usually overseers or farm bosses—any supervisor directly involved in organizing banana cultivation or harvest. As an element in company lore, the association of overseers with the cowboys of the western frontier predated the *Unifruitco* employee-relations campaign begun in the 1920s. In Honduras in 1913, employees wrote and distributed *The Banana Herders Gazook*, a newsletter that showcased this association. In this publication, the banana herders raced across a banana plantation on horseback, endured "hot weather . . . to one who is not accustomed to the Tropics," and poked fun at a fellow herder promoted into the "Pen Pushers Union of the General Office." The departure of this colleague—written as a tongue-in-cheek obituary—highlighted the separation of field men from office workers. The *Gazook*, generated outside the purview of the company's public-relations apparatus, illustrated that American employees needed no direction from above to craft frontier-inflected work identities.[24]

Editors of *Unifruitco* tapped into and amplified these organic frontier identities. Tropical division employees produced their own renderings of this particular character, usually lighthearted drawings that poked fun at colleagues. Often, cowboys puzzled over stubborn mules or fumbled through encounters with women. Seasoned cowboys also wowed new arrivals to the tropics with tall tales. "With a power born of knowledge," rhymed one veteran, the cowboy will "pick out some nice new tenderfoot and start a cowboy college. / 'Say, son, watch those tarantulas, they're big as a frying pan; / Did you ever hear of a crocodile that used his tail as a fan?'" Despite their levity, such representations helped circulate to the company at large the visual language of the banana frontier, its unrestrained male sociability, its transformative possibilities, and the racialized labor discipline that kept the business running. Typically, the banana cowboy surveyed the landscape around him from a horse or mule, wearing a wide-brimmed Stetson, high leather boots or puttees, and a cartridge belt and revolver. These accoutrements and the use of a mount set white overseers above and apart from the workers they controlled, themselves always faceless and distant in these representations. The ubiquitous sidearm reminded readers of the potential for danger in this occupation, either from wildlife or unruly laborers. The cowboy vocation, with its cultural referent in the North American frontier tradition, undergirded the outdoor ethos and personal liberation company publicists attached to tropical employment. "The best part of this tropical life is the freedom," claimed one, who continued, "You are in the open much more than is possible in the States."[25]

Figure 5.1. The iconography of the western frontier meets the tropics: An American banana cowboy oversees a UFCO sugar plantation in Cuba. Submitted to *Unifruitco* by employee Hamorsky. Caption: "The Start of the 1927 Crop." *Unifruitco*, April 1927, 511.

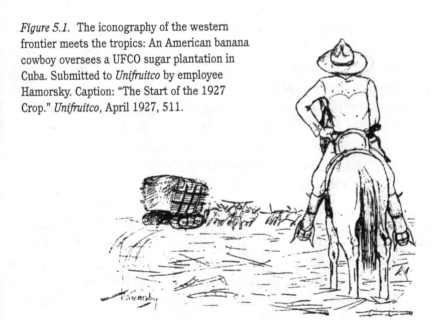

The outdoor ethos and equestrian skills of banana cowboys found an outlet in company-sponsored rodeos and horse or mule races. Typical of such an
outing, one field day in 1926 at Puerto Castilla, Honduras, featured banana
cowboys who "strutted their stuff" for colleagues. Such occasions made light
of stubborn or lazy mules and featured more serious displays of cowboy prowess, such as horse races, "buckjumping" contests, and other feats of horse-
manship. Verson Gooch's account of the Guabito, Panama, races reveals
management's view of horse and mule racing. "Besides providing good clean
sporting events," President Cutter's traveling assistant wrote, "it is found
that racing, with the necessary care of animals, develops efficient stockmen
all over the division, and the proper care of livestock the year around."
Rodeos in the United States at the same time organized displays of masculine
physical prowess in a context in which technology and corporate organization had rendered such skills increasingly irrelevant to the livestock industry. A similar nostalgia characterized banana rodeos, but the culture of
masculine vitality projected in such displays served the internal public relations efforts of a modern corporation. Through the figure of the banana cowboy, company publicists invested the company's frontiers with a democratic
and adventurous spirit. There, the shared rigors and dangers of the frontier
space promised camaraderie between American colleagues and upward
mobility for men willing to embrace its challenges.[26]

In the early twentieth century, hunting and fishing formed another part of
the masculine sporting culture in United Fruit's tropical divisions. There, the
sport of taking and displaying game grew in popularity as it did in North
America at the time, from what Tina Loo describes as "the conjunction of the
expansion of the middle class, anti-modernist ideology, and the apparatus of
mass marketing."[27] This confluence made possible the expansion of game
hunting among the professional classes of North American whites and provided one avenue for the formation of what she terms "bourgeois masculinity."[28] Similarly, sport hunting and fishing provided the company's supervisors
and office men a way to define themselves as men. United Fruit's publicity
apparatus exploited the practice to add another dimension of male-centered
excitement and vitality to its tropical divisions. In the areas around company
properties, many American employees dedicated their off-hours to bird, tapir,
and alligator hunting or tarpon and yellowfin fishing. Such trips provided
occasions for male sociability outside the workplace. The return of successful

fishermen and hunters to company towns with trophies, events frequently pictured in *Unifruitco*, showcased their triumph over the tropical landscape. Like adventure travel and work on the banana frontier, well-publicized hunting excursions promised potential tropical employees a brush with danger and a chance to test one's fortitude away from the comforts of modern life.

The taking of fish and game was also central to the maintenance of professional networks beyond the bounds of the UFCO. The introductory photograph to this book reveals that such connections were essential to the relationship between Harvard University's School of Tropical Medicine and the UFCO, specifically in the camaraderie between UFCO medical superintendent of Honduras, Dr. R. B. Nutter, and Harvard's Dr. Richard P. Strong. Nestled amid the men's correspondence about specific medical and institutional questions, one finds endearing personal letters hinting at fond outdoor memories. These medical professionals poured much time into exploring the hinterlands of Tela, both in the hills and on the water. Nutter reminded Strong of these adventures in his personal notes, and enticed his colleague to return for "more time with the king fish," in one instance.[29] Shared adventures in the outdoors formed a touchstone of such relationships.

The coastal waters and estuaries of tropical divisions provided rich opportunities for company fishermen, and a chance to test their mettle in the face of danger. That test often assumed a tongue-in-cheek quality, embracing hyperbole but never masking the accomplishments of sportsmen. In a tribute to tuna fishermen of Preston, Cuba, one of them penned, "A fig for the seas and the howling gale, / As we fish from our storm-tossed bark, / Whenever we fish, we fish for whale / And our bait is a ten-foot shark." Printed beside the poem stood two company men, "who manage to hook the big ones every time," displaying their catch of three-foot-plus tuna.[30] Near Almirante and Bocas del Toro, Panama, the Chiriquí Lagoon and the Manatí River, both protected from the open sea, served as especially fruitful waters for company men on outings. According to one Almirante columnist for *Unifruitco*, the area offered fishing for both active men and "easy chair type[s]."[31] Visiting company dignitaries and residents of the company towns frequented the lagoon on bird hunts and fishing trips. These outings could put the fisherman into potentially perilous situations. "To add excitement to the game," noted the Almirante man, "the sawfish of evil temper is a major inhabitant of these waters and is respected by all who know him," including local Indians. This aggressively territorial riverine species reportedly attacked cayucos (dugout canoes) that entered its space, infusing fishing with a danger usually reserved for the hunting of large predators.[32]

Hunting outings in the tropics also assumed a flavor of danger. Alanson Morehouse, a consulting engineer in Puerto Castilla, Honduras, recounted one such trip in 1927 with former Tela Railroad Company employee George Boyd. Since leaving the company's employ, Boyd had put to use hunting skills and knowledge of the Black River environs he gained while working for the United Fruit subsidiary. By the late 1920s, Boyd apparently made a living killing egrets, an aquatic bird much prized by US milliners for three of their long tail feathers. Morehouse joined Boyd on an expedition through the mangrove swamps along the Black River, an area "infested with alligators and snakes." Morehouse, despite being the lesser outdoorsman, cheerfully rose to the challenge of negotiating the mangroves. "The spirit of adventure or desire for gain," he claimed, "will cause one to undergo many hardships and dangers." The perils of the journey, according to him, were not hypothetical—just a few weeks earlier an alligator had attacked an American there.

The hero of the narrative, Boyd, cut a Rooseveltian figure—a robust, mustachioed outdoorsman pictured boldly striding through shin-deep water with a shouldered shotgun. The author, in awe of his companion, drew a direct connection to the Rooseveltian ethos of frontier hunting. "The intrepid hunter," read the caption, "might be taken for the redoubtable . . . T. R."[33] Deep in the swamps of Honduras, Boyd remained committed to what Morehouse saw as the higher virtues of hunting. Boyd "always made a practice of shooting on the wing, not only through sportsmanship but also because in thus shooting the plumes of the egret receive far less injury."[34] Whether or not Boyd practiced such high-minded shot selection, Morehouse's portrayal projected him as a sporting ideal—not primarily concerned with taking animals, but with testing his skills. The birds, of course, were not dangerous, but their environment was, and his insistence on firing only at birds in flight made the docile egrets something better than helpless prey. As with other accounts of company men exploring tropical environments, the modern technologies making the trip possible receded into the shadows of the narrative.

Sport fishing and hunting, at least in the company's internal publicity, was almost never a solitary activity. Men forged bonds outside of work by exploring nearby waters or forests in pairs or small groups. Taking game and displaying it upon return to town reinforced company men's willingness and ability to dominate the local landscape. For office-bound employees, especially, an intense engagement with the tropics as a predator promised the kind of physical regeneration only accessible to American men. Hunting or fishing also shaped masculine relationships within families. Pictured with his son and their catch of tarpon, Limón employee Sam Kress offered the local *Unifruitco* columnist these lines:

> A boy is at his best—
> Out fishing,
> He learns the beauties of the stream
> Gets a chance to really dream
> A boy becomes a Man—
> Out fishing.[35]

"Like father—like son," read the title of Kress's verse. Publicists embraced episodes like this father-and-son fishing trip because they built on the argument that the tropics could be a healthy childrearing environment. Outdoorsmanship, in his view, provided something more than recreation, sociability, or even masculine revitalization; it formed a necessary part of becoming a tropical American man.

Another type of tropical veteran, the "tropical tramp," made occasional appearances in company publicity. This figure emerged from the dramatic growth of US travel in Latin America during the early twentieth century. Tramps were those who gained deep knowledge of Latin America by traveling or living off the beaten track and, in their view, acquiring a more authentic tropical experience away from the well-worn paths of tourists. In United Fruit's tropical culture, the tramp was a veteran employee who had developed an especially intimate tie to the tropics—a relationship built on a feminization of the landscape: "there's never a land that holds a man with a clutch that never yields—[. . .] / With a hold as strong or an arm as long as the slumbrous [sic] land that lies / And dreams her age-long Summer through beneath the tropic skies." The hold on the tramp stemmed from his desire to find adventure and seduction in the tropics. The poetic tribute continued: "'Tropical Tramps,' we pitch our camps and live wherever we can. / Our road we take through the jungle brake o'er the ceiba's twisting roots; / We follow our dreams on a thousand streams." Embracing the Rooseveltian cult of the strenuous life, the tramp sought a revitalization of masculine energies by passing through the hardships of a primeval environment. His disregard for modern comforts underlined his intimacy with a fascinating but potentially dangerous landscape. The tramp's romanticized attachment to this landscape worked in tandem with the company's conquest of the same, as a form of what Rosaldo terms imperialist nostalgia—the longing for that which one is complicit in destroying. The tramp completed his affair with the tropics by returning home having emerged from the transformative space of the tropics regenerated, a better and stronger man for having tried himself abroad.[36]

The banana cowboy and the tropical tramp served as the chief vehicles of an "invented tradition" of tropical service to United Fruit. They provided a lens through which rank-and-file US employees could understand their own place in the corporation. Such traditions "inculcate certain values and norms of behavior by repetition, which automatically implies continuity with the past." These tropical characters existed, in part, to construct an aura of generational succession in tropical-division ranks. New arrivals could expect to be mentored and mildly hazed into tropical life by such old timers, who themselves had undergone the same passage. Nostalgia for tropical life also established emotional ties to an imagined past. In poetic tributes, which centered on intensely personal accounts of the emotional transformations wrought by tropical life, cowboys and tramps usually looked back on their time in the south with longing. Once "back on the beaten track to the paths our childhood trod," the tramp would start to miss the tropical landscape he had left and he would be left with a "ceaseless yearn." The cowboy, often linked to some amorous adventure, might find his version of tropical nostalgia fraught with longing for some "Spanish" girl. "Come you back, Banana Cowboy, come you back to Rincon Bay . . . Where the old bananas play," beckoned one imaginary beauty to a departed cowboy. Back home, all the former cowboy could do was reminisce and go about his modern life. "But all that's left be'ind me long ago an' far away," he sighed, "An' there ar'n't no taxis runnin' from New York to Rincon Bay." The recurrence of these figures in *Unifruitco* and the structure of their tropical memories suggested that American men who would accept tropical service would be stepping into a tradition of masculine regeneration through the rigors and seductions of life abroad.[37]

The masculine figures drawn from the banana frontier succeeded in the tropics through mastery of the self as much as through mastery of surroundings. They embodied the ability to weather the purportedly greater temptations and dangers of tropical environs (especially homesickness, sloth, and alcoholism) without succumbing to them. Surrendering to these urges could harm more than just a man's morale or effectiveness—it could render him vulnerable to specific illnesses and the more diffuse process of moral and physical degeneration associated with tropical residence. Judging from the attention given to failure in *Unifruitco*, in the reports of company doctors, and even in the admonitory essay printed on the back of all employment contracts, many American employees fell short of the company's ideal. The frontier metaphor played a key role in structuring this vocabulary of failure.

In a series of cautionary tales that ran in the early issues of *Unifruitco*, the failure of some American men to adapt to tropical service stemmed from an unmanly surrender to the difficulties of distance. Nostalgia and longing for home, as we have seen, informed how American employees experienced distance from the United States. A tender desire for the comforts of home formed one dimension of the masculine caricatures of the tropical tramp and banana cowboy, but such feelings never entered the newly pathologized territory of "nostalgia." The embrace of the adventure and hardships of tropical life represented the triumph of these characters over their childlike or feminized longing for home. In 1925 one writer, imagining a conversation between a veteran and a newcomer, encouraged tropical initiates to "buck" poor conditions, including longing for home. "If a chap sticks to it, bucks the first few weeks of home-sickness . . . he comes out ahead," promised the columnist. A year later, George Cox cautioned new men to avoid the trap of homesickness. "Do not come to the Tropics if you must carry with you all of your home ties," he warned. Although a phase of homesickness was expected, an inability to "keep your thoughts down in the Tropics" would lead to alienation from peers and professional failure. "Then," he noted ominously, "the best thing you can do is to pack up and get out." For Cox, the homesick man was unmanly for his failure to grasp the freedom and the physically invigorating possibilities of tropical work.[38]

Influenced by experts in tropical medicine, United Fruit's recruiting and retention campaign of the 1920s included gendered warnings about the dangers of alcohol abuse in the tropics. In the tropics, admonished Victor Cutter, alcohol abuse could "down" a man quickly and precipitate the weakening of an American man's physical vitality and character, a view shared by company doctors. To these commentators, alcoholism represented a weakness in one's masculine character and a surrender to the temptations of excess. Thus could internal publicity subtly tempt potential employees with the availability of alcohol outside the United States while the Volstead Act remained on the books. "Lay[ing] off the booze, at least to the point of not requiring it as a regular ration," wrote one tropical man in *Unifruitco*'s inaugural issue, represented a man's best chance to earn promotion. For some commentators, access to liquor reflected the greater personal freedom of the tropics. "There is plenty of liquor in the Tropics," assured George Cox, "but it is not a curse as so many fictionists like to describe it." Like homesickness, however, a man demonstrated domination of self by avoiding drinking to excess. He also set himself apart from and above laborers, who, by dint of their biology, were particularly vulnerable to alcoholism. Guatemalan Indians, blacks, and the Chinese, according to Cox, were "orderly and quiet" unless "white eye (strong native liquor) gets the upper hand." That same year, a company doctor confirmed this popular perception that "the laboring class of native is an acute, and not a chronic, alcoholic."39

The tropical climate also elevated the danger of laziness—a trait popular perception and company doctors attributed to the racial makeup of all populations of color. George Cox warned his readers of this curious effect, one he linked not to climate or heat but to racialized customs. One "ambles" rather than walks, he noted, since "it is not the fashion to hurry in this part of the world." Surrounded by local people "quite content to dream and work as little as possible themselves," the American penchant for hustling through the work day stood out as a curiosity. In a later installment, Cox elaborated on the dangers of such surroundings for the white American male. The "naturally lazy" man should stay home, he argued, "for this is the laziest-feeling place on earth." Retaining one's sense of purpose and hustle formed a part of what he deemed living "sanely." Above all, an American man had to avoid the "siesta habit." The mastery of the Caucasian masculine self would produce a triumph over sloth, and set the employee apart from his racial inferiors.40

Anxieties surrounding nostalgia, alcoholism, and sloth found expression in the visual language of the banana frontier. One illustration, submitted to the employee magazine by a Truxillo Railroad Company (Honduras) employee in 1926, mocked the failed banana cowboy. "An Indoor Overseer who came to

Figure 5.2. A caricature of failed American masculinity in the tropics. Submitted to *Unifruitco* by Truxillo Railroad Company (Honduras) employee V. E. Fewell. Caption: "An Indoor Overseer who Came to the Tropics to Seek an Outdoor Life." *Unifruitco*, August 1929, 45.

the tropics to seek an Outdoor Life," read the caption beside a man goofily lounging in a hammock under a sign that read "Mañana Farm." The overseer puffed at a pipe, exhaling puffs of smoke laced with his fantasies labeled "vacation" and "pipe dreams." Gazing into the distance, he contentedly neglected his duties—a railway alarm sounded off unnoticed and a pistol belt lay abandoned on a stool. Fueling the man's unproductive fantasies were his alcoholic "liquid diet" and an adventure magazine. Distracted from the manly professional identity offered by the banana frontier, he found all the excitement he needed in the pages of the magazine. Rather than conquer the tropical environment through physical vitality, dedication to work, and self-discipline, this failure succumbed to homesickness, alcoholism, and laziness.[41]

In its early twentieth-century "conquest of the tropics," United Fruit and its men brought to bear the cultural capital of another recently concluded conquest, that of western North America. That referent carried with it an implicit teleology: the necessary and nearly inevitable subjugation and transformation of ostensibly empty or unorganized peripheries by the agents of civilization and industry. The "banana frontier," then, seemed an especially apt description of the company's advance into wet tropical lowlands where bananas grew best. Company towns, usually constructed precipitously where little or no population had dwelled previously, brought to mind the railroad and mining towns of the North American frontier. The frontier myth implied a way of relating to landscape quite appropriate to the managerial gaze of an extractive enterprise in the age of vertical integration and overseas expansion: "nature" was to be harnessed by the science of tropical agriculture, rendered more productive, and made to suit the material necessities of modern civilization. The frontier referent also structured the racial ideology underpinning US empire in general and United Fruit's operations more specifically. Who better to undertake this grand enterprise on a new overseas frontier than the energetic race that, within living memory for many, had closed the western frontier? Such men were, by dint of this inheritance, the natural managers of a large nonwhite labor force, a hierarchy that echoed the subjugation of Native Americans or the white control of black, Latino, or Asian labor in the US West.

Brown's experience and the company's campaign to create the right sort of men bring into sharper relief the relational and performative function of gender identities—functions that were pronounced in racially stratified, often contentious enclave environments. Maintaining the racialized boundary between management and labor was a gendered practice of everyday life enacted by men like Brown. Various Others—laborers, women, and failed men—shaped the contours of that frontier-inflected masculine ethos. First were the laborers: in taking on frontier identities, company men projected an image of everything they thought Black or mestizo laborers were not: physically vital, healthy, hard-working, purposeful, capable of at once dominating and being seduced by nature, and capable of comprehending their work experience as regenerative and essential to the progress of humanity. This masculine company culture was also meant to portray an image of virility and strength to women. In Brown's case, his wife (not surprisingly, he never hints at other sexual or romantic interests) received a detailed accounting of his transformation. As episodes of malarial fever laid him low in the summer of 1920, Ethel worried about her husband's health but found consolation in his newfound confidence as a "real engineer." Finally, these masculine identities spoke to other American men, infusing company culture with a series of normative prescriptions for proper white American maleness in the tropics. In the languages of the banana frontier, "stay-at-homes" or failures could see themselves defined as men who lacked the manly fiber to take on the banana cowboy vocation or who, once in the tropics, let down their guard and succumbed to vice and laziness, the principle failings of nonwhite laborers.[42]

The specters of failure and degeneration, then, haunted United Fruit's masculine culture at its most confident and expansive. As a structure of feeling, the banana frontier was infused with early-twentieth-century anxieties about white-collar masculinity, tropical health, and racial boundaries. What is more, that so many of United Fruit's American men failed to stay more than a year with the company hints at the tenuous hold of the company's masculine culture over its core constituency. By this metric, then, the effort to make better men often met frustration, and did indeed generate much concerned discussion among executives about a crisis of masculinity within the company. But, as Bryce Traister has cautioned, this apparent crisis—indicated by such statistics and by stubborn anxieties—ought not distract us from what he has termed "an American masculinity remarkable for its satisfied ego, its imperial drive, its individual power, its sexual aggression, and its assumption of citizenship as a matter of birth and God-given right." From this perspective, the shortcomings of tropical employees fade: during these decades, United Fruit enjoyed its most profitable years, steadily expanding both its Latin American properties and its US market share. Whatever the misgivings of the boardroom, enough tropical managers and technicians reconciled themselves to tropical life to ensure the company's profitability—even if, like Brown, they only stayed with the company a short time. Finally, the culture of the banana frontier reveals a fundamental continuity of empire: the gendered framework of the North American frontier myth underwrote the building of United Fruit's tropical empire. By becoming banana cowboys in distant tropical enclaves, company men immunized themselves from the degenerative effects of the tropics, regenerated flagging metropolitan energies, and found upward mobility—all the while policing the racial boundaries in the "wild west" of a new imperial frontier.[43] Those "raw edges" also excited the curiosity of those seeking to push the frontiers of scientific knowledge.

CHAPTER SIX

Serving Science on the Side

One sweltering April morning between 1910 and 1914—the exact year is unclear—two American travelers stepped off the United Fruit Company train at remote Quiriguá Farm, Guatemala. The men had traveled up the line for dozens of miles from the company's new base at Puerto Barrios, taking in signs of the company's bustling enterprise along the way: past newly opened banana plantations, a recently constructed company hospital at Virginia, and orderly housing for overseers and laborers. Where the railroad ended, they were met by division superintendent Victor Cutter, who was to escort the men on a visit to the Mayan ruins of Quiriguá, a major pre-Columbian settlement that happened to lay on lands the UFCO acquired in 1909.[1] Already that morning, the energetic Cutter had taken another American couple on a tour of the ruins, and despite having been up since 4 a.m. and the oppressive midmorning heat, he cheerfully ushered his next guests to the site. The banana frontier faded behind the party as Cutter drove them on a rail-mounted trolley car along the Motagua River to the branch terminus, then up a narrow path through the forest. Cutter's guest expressed his excitement and astonishment by reenacting a Western ritual of archaeological discovery. "Turning a corner we suddenly found ourselves in a cleared space," he recalled, "face to face with the ruins which the forest for centuries had hidden and successfully baffled the curiosity of most intruders."[2]

Although they couched their visit as an adventure into the mysterious unknown, these visitors encountered a site under intense scrutiny, a place where powerful economic and cultural agencies of empire intersected. Not only was Quiriguá incorporated as part of the banana company's expansion into Guatemala—itself the product of a web of political relationships with the country's elite—it was a major site on the rapidly evolving frontier of North American cultural and academic interest in Latin America. Upon entering the clearing, the party was met by Dr. Edgar L. Hewett, a prominent archaeologist on a field expedition for the Archaeological Institute of America. With funding and help from the UFCO, the AIA had begun excavations at Quiriguá in 1910, and returned yearly throughout that decade and on several other

Figure 6.1. US tourists from the *SS Carrillo* touring the ruins at the company-owned Quiriguá complex. The 75-acre reservation was set aside from banana cultivation and became the object of intense archaeological and touristic interest in the 1910s and 1920s. Frame from an anonymous 16mm film of a United Fruit Company cruise to Guatemala, ca. 1920, in the author's possession.

occasions until 1941.[3] For two sweat-soaked hours, Hewett offered the men his best reading of the site, which his audience compared to what they knew of Egyptian or Greek antiquity. Awestruck by the scale of the structures and stelae slowly emerging from the vegetation and earth, the guests wondered about their connection to the many living indigenous people who served as Hewett's laborers and servants, whom the archaeologist concluded were "quite ignorant of anything concerning their ancestors," a recurrent theme in Western representations of pre-Columbian antiquity. Beaten down by the heat, the party retreated back down the line to Cutter's headquarters at Virginia, where they concluded their Guatemalan travels by touring banana plantations for two days.

The availability of Quiriguá to visitors and academics alike, and its later popularity with UFCO tourists, would have been impossible without a more personal agency of empire: Cutter's own. Cutter's promotion to the helm of the new Guatemala division in 1907 cemented his interest in archaeology and his avid collecting habit, for it was in laying out the company's new plantations that the Quiriguá ruins were uncovered—not discovered, for they had been registered by Western travelers and explorers in the nineteenth century and were surely well known to local inhabitants.[4] Cutter had an intimate relationship with the site, one forged in a career of leisurely exploration that consumed much of his free time. This amateur archaeologist played a central role in exposing Quiriguá's sites and relics to Western eyes. Cutter was not alone in this habit: many of United Fruit's first-class employees assiduously explored their surroundings as amateur scientists, archaeologists, and ethnographers. Cutter's experience and the broader culture of leisure exploration in the company's domains demand that we push well beyond the confines of United Fruit's towns and plantations and the brackets of the work day if we are to understand more fully the culture of corporate colonialism, its crucial contribution to the UFCO's authority, and its relationship to a broader North American enterprise of knowledge.

The colonial project at the heart of the United Fruit Company's tropical world structured enclave life in a series of ways that buttressed its racial division of labor. The built environment, the gendered corporate culture of the tropical workplace, and medical science worked together to bind an enclave's inhabitants in a set of social and labor relationships grounded in an ideology of white, masculine, Anglo-Saxon authority. The company's control over its milieu, although always complicated by "fugitive" populations and organisms, rested on much more than the formal authority of management. Its power was also embedded in a variety of informal conduits weaving through employees' expressions of personal identity, their leisure activities, and in particular their ways of experiencing and knowing their surroundings. This chapter carries this story to the furthest fringes of the banana frontier by examining how employees explored, collected artifacts and specimens, and catalogued places and people, often far afoot of company property. There exists a robust literature on the relationship between amateur and institutional worlds of science, but historians have yet to consider in much depth how these worlds interacted under the aegis of corporate colonialism.[5] What follows is a series of stories that show how personal, amateur pursuits of ethnography, archaeology, and natural science interwove with United Fruit's interests in the region. The generation and circulation of cultural expressions produced by such adventurers and hobbyists—written narratives, photographs, collections of pre-Columbian artifacts and tropical insects—played a vital role in naturalizing the company's expansion and glossed it with a benevolent, disinterested curiosity. The knowledge generated in this context could also result in conclusions not necessarily friendly to corporate interest.

Leisure exploration served the corporation's interest in part by connecting the UFCO to broader academic and scientific communities in the United States.[6] The nineteenth and early twentieth centuries saw a steady intensification of the relationship between science and European and North American colonial projects of various stripes.[7] State-sponsored expeditions made up of military personnel and scientists played a vital role in US expansion into western North America and Latin America going back to the early nineteenth century. By the turn of the twentieth century, a robust museum complex and institutional apparatus in the United States was dedicated to exploration, the collection of specimens and artifacts, and their display—an interlocking series of practices, technologies, and institutions comprising a "representational machine of empire."[8] The US public was drawn ever more into Anglo-American expansion west and south by a dramatic expansion of print media and by an exhibitionary complex that framed tropical organisms and the racial others of these spaces in hierarchical frameworks and naturalized Anglo-American dominion over them.[9] The rise of corporate capitalism and intensive direct US investment abroad, which peaked between 1890 and 1930, deepened these dynamics. An intense nexus of activity involving US business interests, the US government, and a panoply of academics and experts characterized this period and made Latin America the object of intense scrutiny, feverish academic interest, and wide popular appeal.[10] Largely overlooked in historical writing about this period is the role of leisure exploration and amateur science in furthering this enterprise of knowledge and, in important ways, US business interests. Leisure exploration differed from mass tourism in that explorers mostly traveled outside of established tourist itineraries, engaged their surroundings intently and systematically (sometimes for years), and generated collections and narratives meant to address questions about tropical nature and humanity.[11] United Fruit's sphere in this period provides an important window onto such a culture of inquiry and its relationship to the corporation's interest, and US interest in Latin America more broadly.

Stewards of the Past

Victor Cutter's interest in antiquity and his decade-long collaboration with US archaeologists in Guatemala provides early evidence of the powerful role company hobbyists played in shaping scientific inquiry within the company's sphere. Surely Cutter knew of the ruins' existence, for upon taking up his headquarters at Virginia in 1907, he soon set off to locate them. A friendly biographical sketch written upon his ascension to the company's presidency in 1924 recalled the search. After traipsing through thick undergrowth shadowed by towering trees, Cutter eventually "came upon the huge monuments, covered with aged growth, and buried in a tangle of vegetation." Like his visitors to the site a few years later, Cutter's biographer couched the experience in the mystique of Western rediscovery by highlighting the moment of the first glimpse. What was even more significant was that the gaze was cast by Cutter himself, for Quiriguá was "probably unvisited for many years by a white man."[12] In fact, Quiriguá was well known to locals and to Westerners interested in Mesoamerican antiquity, several of whom had visited the ruins in the previous century, albeit without excavating it. The racialized discovery story concluded with the shunting aside of Cutter's "so-called guide," an unnamed local, who receded into obscurity and insignificance.[13]

Progress in clearing the site proceeded as Cutter managed the laying out of plantations and settlements in the newly opened Guatemala division. The dynamic young manager established the seventy-five acre Quiriguá Ruins Reservation and opened it to archaeologists, and himself assisted in their excavations while he oversaw the felling of the rest of the Motagua Valley's forests to make way for fruit plantations. Cutter's presence and his own years-long "close study of the old Mayan civilization" ensured the banana company's collaboration with the Carnegie Institution and the Archaeological Institute of America, the first organizations to focus on Quiriguá.[14] So great was Cutter's role in uncovering Quiriguá that he was made a fellow of the Royal Geographical Society in 1912, surely on the recommendation of the archaeologists he was helping at the time.[15] The digs of the 1910s attracted prominent figures in the field of American antiquity, including Edgar Hewett, Jesse Nusbaum, and Sylvanus Morley, the latter of whom produced a guidebook to the site and made significant advances in understanding Mayan glyphs there.[16] Early expeditions focused on clearing vegetation and mapping the massive temple complexes, necessary steps before below-ground excavation could begin in the mid-1910s. The fruit company helped fund two of these expeditions, and supported others logistically, in no small part by paying laborers to keep the ruins cleared of vegetation and the land around them well drained.[17]

The desire to collect, display, and represent antiquities played a central role in the early development of the Quiriguá reservation, and those practices generated narratives that buttressed the company's interests. The site became a favorite spectacle in the nascent tropical cruise industry, in which the UFCO was a key player. Early on, Cutter must have recognized the site's potential as a tourist attraction, for he dedicated part of his time as manager to guiding visitors there. By the 1920s, company itineraries for Guatemala promised passengers on the Great White Fleet the chance to gaze upon living indigenous primitives while contemplating the mysteries of the long-abandoned city. One tourist party in the mid-1920s even filmed its visit to Quiriguá, its towering restored stelae clearly the highlight of the visit. Sylvanus Morley, who made many expeditions to the site after 1910, noted in the mid-1930s that "no other city of the Maya civilization is as accessible to the visitor as Quirigua."[18] By then, company steamships, railroads, hotels, and guides hosted a steady traffic of tourists and experts. Tourist displays showcased the company's benevolent role in salvaging the ruins from overgrown oblivion, an archaeological echo of the belief that the UFCO-led banana industry rescued and rendered "empty" tropical lands a productive breadbasket. Both projects rested on racialized assumptions about the necessity of Anglo-Saxon stewardship over Central American lands and history.

Using the company's transportation network, archaeologists and private collectors transmitted representations and artifacts of Quiriguá back to the exhibitionary complex within the United States.[19] Edgar Hewett's colleague at the School of American Archaeology in Santa Fe, Jesse Nusbaum, undertook a photographic survey of the ruins in 1913, and these images became the basis for Morley's *Guide Book* more than twenty years later. An expedition in 1914 sought to create glue-molds of Quiriguá's "finer sculptures" for public display at the Panama-California Exposition in San Diego. The gelatin-based molds were used to create concrete-cast replicas, which were later transported to the SAA's museum in Santa Fe, New Mexico.[20] Academic publications by Morley, Hewett, and others pondered the meaning of glyphs at the site, its role in Mayan history, and hypothesized about the reasons for the city's abrupt and decisive decline in the ninth century CE. These experts, and the tourist promoters who echoed their arguments for a larger public, tended to voice great admiration for the architectural and artistic achievements of ancient Mayans, and strove to equate the marvels of American antiquity with those of the ancient Mediterranean. Developing a narrative of the "mystery of the Maya," however, held up their modern-day descendants as markers of the region's backwardness, hopelessly removed from past grandeur by centuries of Spanish oppression or by dint of their racial decadence. The display of Mayan antiquity rescued from the ignorant neglect of locals and the ravages of tropical nature was thus a deeply ideological project that reinforced the corporation's authority over the milieu and provided its intervention there with an armature of benevolence.

The most assiduous collector of artifacts was Victor Cutter himself. During his time as manager of the Guatemala division, Cutter amassed a "varied and elaborate group" of artifacts uncovered at the site in his private collection. Pre-Columbian pieces intermingled with Guatemalan baskets and painted gourds made for tourists, perhaps finding a home in the Cutters' own bric-a-brac exotica displays, by then popular fixtures of middle- and upper-class homes.[21] These items were displayed in Cutter homes over the years, eventually making their way back to Musa, the Cutter estate near Boston, when Victor became UFCO president in 1924.[22] In 1938, he lent the collection to the museum at Dartmouth College, his alma mater. After his death in 1952, his widow donated the collection permanently to the museum (now the Hood Museum of Art), where the artifacts are housed to this day.[23] The travels of these artifacts and the story behind their acquisition speak to the cross-fertilization between corporate colonialism and professional archaeology, with leisure exploration forming the nexus between them. From their origins in the soil of Quiriguá and the nascent tourist markets of Guatemala, through decades of display in affluent Cutter homes in Guatemala, Jamaica, and the United States, and finally to the US museum complex, the collection took on its own meaning beyond being the relics of one man's curiosity. Cutter's dedication to finding and displaying objects made by the hands of living and dead Mayans suggests that he valued their purported authenticity—their hand production outside of modern mass production—as much as their aesthetic value.[24] The acquisition, care, and display of such a collection also conveyed a powerful statement of the doctrine of salvage, the notion that Western intervention was necessary to rescue the patrimony of humanity from the ignorance and neglect of locals.[25]

Other employees shared Cutter's interest in indigenous antiquity and dedicated much of their leisure time to searching out its traces. (Cutter himself collected in the shadow of Minor Cooper Keith, who had amassed a large collection of pre-Columbian antiquities, which he eventually willed to the American Natural History Museum and Brooklyn Museum in New York City.)[26] Like Cutter, these men worked for the company on the steadily advancing frontiers of its enterprise around the region. Their efforts, couched in a language of scientific curiosity and the rescue of antiquity, could not escape the clumsiness and acquisitiveness of much amateur collecting. In 1921, a UFCO railroad construction crew at Río Seco, near Banes, Cuba, stumbled on a large cave made up of six chambers, the largest of which measured one hundred feet in diameter and more than sixty feet in height. The men immediately noticed that skeletons littered the cave floor, along with several heaps of debris. They tried to "salvage" the bones, but conditions in the cave had left them extremely fragile and they crumbled to dust when disturbed. The crew had better luck with potsherds, and extracted several pieces.[27] This find captured the interest of UFCO employee M. Carrington, whose work at the forefront of the company's rapidly expanding sugar plantations afforded him ample opportunity to explore and collect. Within a few years, Carrington knew well the various sites around Banes, and wrote of amassing a large personal collection of bones, stone tools, and broken pottery. In 1924, his efforts culminated in an expedition into the far reaches of the company's massive properties, for which he secured a company pack mule and an assistant. During this trip, Carrington and his unnamed companion explored thirty-five caves in the area and significantly expanded the collection to include some intact human skulls, small figurines, and painted potsherds. The fate of the collection is unknown; we can surmise that it remained in the possession of Carrington himself.

There is no evidence that Carrington collaborated with outside experts in his archaeological hobby, but working in isolation did not prevent him from forming narratives based on his finds and reenacting Western tropes of discovery. One site near Banes, known as La Loma de los Muertos, was regarded with apprehension by locals. "Superstition still clings to these mounds," Carrington wrote, "and on digging into them I was solemnly assured that on certain nights these mounds gave forth a dull, blue light." Undaunted, he excavated and found middens of shells, potsherds, and bones. The dig allowed him to brush aside the locals' ignorance. "Needless to say," he scoffed, "the light did not appear for me."[28] The artifacts Carrington accumulated led him to the conclusion that Cuba's extinct indigenes inhabited the "savage" rung on the ladder of human civilization. Their "crude attempts at decoration" on potsherds and figurines provided the evidence. Either the designs were meaningless symbols, or at best echoes of Old World antiquity: some "bore a surprising resemblance to the Sphinx," while "other symbols could represent snakes and could easily go back to the snake gods of the ancient Egyptians."[29] Carrington's years exploring Banes and gathering remnants of indigenous civilization may not have formed any known connections with a wider scientific community, but his personal immersion in local archaeology glossed with curiosity his own sense of authority over the landscape and its inhabitants. Publishing his account in *Unifruitco* invited his coworkers to share in that sort of project.

Had Carrington been stationed in Tela, Honduras, he surely would have welcomed the arrival of Wilson and Dorothy Popenoe, who became the most prominent advocates of leisure exploration in United Fruit's tropical divisions in the 1920s. A botanist and renowned "agricultural explorer" working for the USDA, United Fruit hired Wilson Popenoe in 1924 to head its main tropical research station at Lancetilla, near Tela on the northern coast. Although a botanist, Popenoe brought with him a hearty interest in the human landscape of tropical America, both past and present. Just before leaving the USDA for the fruit company, Popenoe published "Regional Differences in the Guatemalan Huipil" with the prestigious International Congress of Americanists, a work based on observations he made while gathering plant stock in the late 1910s.[30] He also brought to Honduras his young English-born wife Dorothy, who was even more fascinated with antiquity than her husband. In the course of the Popenoes' long tropical career (although Dorothy would die after eating poisonous fruit in 1932), the couple generated several publications about the region's human past, aimed at the UFCO's first-class employees and, later, at a broader US public.[31]

While in Honduras, the vibrant Dorothy threw herself in archaeological work. She surveyed the pre-Columbian mountain fortress of Tenampua in 1927, and the following two years she excavated the Playa de los Muertos site on the Ulua River—incredibly enough, while bearing and raising five children between 1925 and her death.[32] While in Tela, the couple spent their leisure time exploring and collecting artifacts around the Ulua Valley, eventually producing an illustrated survey of their distribution and their conclusions about the area's ancient inhabitants. As at Quiriguá, the expansion of the UFCO's

infrastructure inadvertently spurred a wave of private archaeological exploration. At one site near Lancetilla, workers clearing a bluff for a meteorological
station uncovered a sizable deposit of stone tools and potsherds on the mound—
thereafter an important site of interest for the Popenoes.[33] Dorothy's work at
these sites was far from amateurish: she maintained a correspondence with
luminaries in the field, including the Peabody Museum's A. M. Tozzer and
George Vaillant, the latter curator of Mexican antiquities at the American
Museum of Natural History after 1930. Tozzer, in particular, was a font of
encouragement and validation, occasionally providing Dorothy with small
grants from the Peabody.[34] Her careful stratigraphic studies of pottery at these
sites played an important role in establishing a chronology of human habitation
in Honduras.[35] Once the Popenoes purchased a colonial-era home in Antigua,
Guatemala, she produced a pamphlet narrating the founding of the once-grand
colonial city, published by Harvard University Press in 1933.[36]

Dorothy Popenoe came into Mesoamerican archaeology during a blossom-
ing of North American interest in the region's antiquity, and her work
reflected the ideological constraints and priorities of that context. On the one
hand, her excavations sought to address fundamental archaeological questions, in particular those related to the chronological sequencing of pottery
techniques. On the other hand, she was a collector and played an important
role in the traffic of antiquities north. Neither priority would have been possible without her close association with the upper echelon of the UFCO in
Central America. Although Honduran legislation had dampened a once-
bustling export traffic in artifacts in the early years of the century, by the
1920s the growing power of the fruit company and its deep influence over the
Honduran government elevated it to supreme importance in the practice of
archaeology. It was through the connections of company officials with local
and national authorities that excavation permits were granted to foreign
archaeologists, and Dorothy Popenoe labored under such auspices.[37] The
UFCO's preponderance even led local authorities to turn a blind eye to a
robust export market in pre-Columbian objects centered around the company's sphere of operation, a market in which the Popenoes—particularly
Wilson—were avid participants for years.[38] That Dorothy worked within
a context of the imperialist context of early twentieth-century North American archaeology becomes clear when we consider her role in trafficking artifacts into the US museum complex, particularly Harvard's Peabody

Museum—activities she and other archaeologists of the time justified through the doctrine of salvage.

The racial politics behind her work become even clearer when we see the intrepid Dorothy at leisure. In one of what must have been innumerable casual explorations of the Ulua region, she was ferried down the river by a local man, Concepción Morales. Dorothy marveled at his quiet confidence and ability as a boatman as he steered the cayuco through the swirling waters. At the same time, she took careful note of the river's banks, which at every high water revealed strata of potsherds and stone artifacts, all of their "mysteries" pulling at her keen curiosity. Morales's stolid indifference and stark distance from the "secrets" of these objects then took the fore; according to Popenoe, it stemmed from his racial inheritance, benighted by the long-distant Spanish conquest and the racial mixture that ensued. "You might have inherited the secret from your mother and your mother's mother," she began, "but perhaps the blood of your fathers, the conquerors, runs too strongly." Contemplating his silent visage—for in her account the man never has a voice—she saw "no expression but that suggestive of hopelessness."[39] Such a paternalistic view was not without notes of respect, but it decisively invested the Western archaeologist with the authority to explore, manage, and acquire the past in lieu of the benighted local population.

The Popenoes spurred a robust culture of amateur inquiry in Tela, one that merged archaeology with agronomy and natural science. In December 1925, along with other interested employees, they started the Ulua Society, a club "along strictly unpretentious lines" dedicated to "the increase and dissemination of knowledge concerning the Ulua Valley, with special reference to its early inhabitants, its physical characteristics, its natural products and development."[40] The founding declaration, probably penned by the Popenoes themselves, echoed with a racialized sense of scientific mission: "The pioneers are not all dead. Those who live and work on the Caribbean Coast are pioneers in a very real sense of the word, for they are struggling with a new environment—new not only to those born and bred in the Temperate Zone, but new also from a standpoint of science, which is nothing more than organized knowledge of one's surroundings."[41] From its inception until the early 1930s, when budget retrenchments decimated the research division and ended publication of *Unifruitco*, the Ulua Society enlisted the participation of first-class employees in a broader scientific enterprise.[42]

Figure 6.2. Dorothy Popenoe's banner for the Ulua Society, reflecting her and husband Wilson's wide-ranging scientific interests. *Unifruitco*, April 1926, 552.

At its core, the society provided a venue where first-class employees collaborated with and were exposed to the work of academic professionals.[43] Indeed, its informal charter published in *Unifruitco* proclaimed that "it will be the aim of the society to assist visiting scientists in carrying out any investigations they may desire to undertake."[44] Agricultural supervisors, "who are constantly making observations on the animal life of the valley, archaeological sites, climatology, useful plants and operations connected with banana culture" represented an important perspective on the landscape, both as contributors to the society and as guides.[45] The society's inaugural publication indicates that this kind of intermingling of company amateurs on the banana frontier and academics based in the United States was already common. These contacts must have been more than just courteous. When two prestigious tropical-health specialists, Harvard University zoologist Dr. Thomas Barbour and canal-zone pathologist and UFCO doctor Herbert Clark, undertook a "snake census" in the Ulua Valley in the mid-1920s, UFCO foremen around the division helped them collect more than 3,400 specimens—several of them deadly and common, among them the feared fer de lance. The snakes were dispatched, packed in jars of formalin, loaded on company ships, and shipped to Harvard College.[46] What is unclear in the record is the role of local laborers in the enterprise. Either they were not engaged as assistants or collectors, or (more probably) their work was subsumed to that of US scientists in their written accounts. In any event, this particular investigation ultimately served the UFCO's interest by helping company doctors develop and stock effective antivenin, thereby reducing costly hospital time and the costs of treating snake bites.

It is little wonder that such an organization flourished under company auspices, given UFCO president Cutter's personal history in Central America and the Popenoes' intense interest in exploration. But the Ulua Society can also be understood as a creature of the prevailing corporate culture of the 1920s. Publicized as a civilized addition to frontier life, clubs like this one ultimately served to discipline first-class employees by occupying their off-time and involving them personally in the loftier fringes of the company's mission, those tied to improving the tropical milieu. A talented artist, Dorothy Popenoe played a key role in advertising this sense of mission to employees. Her three-paneled banner, which headed the society's regular columns in *Unifruitco*, centered the reader's gaze on the company's purview in northern Honduras, flanked by iconography of scientific endeavor. Popenoe's own etchings of Mayan glyphs and sketches of pieces she had excavated decorated the frame and the foreground of the breezy tropical scene—a tidy melding of the visual idioms of science and tourism, aimed squarely at first-class employees in the tropics.

The Popenoes' personal interests undoubtedly influenced those around them with an interest in the human past of Central America. The experience of Marston Bates, an entomologist hired by Wilson Popenoe in 1928, offers one such case. The young Bates, recently graduated from the University of Florida, brought a roving curiosity with him to Honduras, and flourished in the environment of Lancetilla. A Floridian who had grown up outdoors collecting all manner of insects, he found naught to complain about in the tropics and threw himself into exploring his surroundings whenever he could. Although he would distinguish himself as a leisure explorer of insect habitats (more on this later), Bates eventually found himself drawn to the "ancient" past of Antigua, Guatemala. He found himself in the partly ruined former seat of Spanish authority in early 1930, when he was transferred there via promotion to head up the UFCO's Servicio Técnico, an agricultural extension service created to help Guatemalan export-crop growers in technical matters. Where Honduras drew him in for its insect life, his interest in Guatemala would focus on certain elements of the human landscape.

Earning the trust of his superiors allowed Bates to freely indulge this personal curiosity as he fulfilled his functions for the company. In October 1930, he set off on a car tour of Guatemala with an American friend from the UFCO freight department, one Mr. Brunkard. The "Brunkard-Bates Expedition," as he dubbed it, loaded into a Dodge "fully equipped for exploring the wilds of the Guatemalan highlands" and set off into the countryside.[47] Bates's inventory attests to the enthusiasm of the explorers and to their variegated sense of mission:

> We packed our extensive and well-planned equipment into the available space, and then squeezed ourselves into such odd corners as remained. We looked very much like a family starting out for the winter in Florida, or for cross country camping, what with blankets and thermos jars sticking out at all sides. To itemize, we had: complete photographic equipment, including ten film packs; one bag each of personal effects three heavy blankets, in case we had to spend the night out; enough good for at least two good meals; a supply of United Fruit Company circulars and advirtising [sic] material; lots of paper, note books, and pencils; apparatus for the collection of insects, such as nets, vials, cyanide bottles, forceps and scalpels; hospital equipment, including material for anything short of a major operation; and altimeter, and a complete set of Poe's works.[48]

Although he could never leave his insect-collecting hobby aside for long, on this trip Bates—equipped with a company camera—voraciously recorded picturesque land- and townscapes and the indigenous peoples he encountered. No mere tourist, Bates had his sights set on publishing travel writing with substance, even worthy of *National Geographic*.[49] Things did not always go as planned for the explorers: the Dodge had to be extracted from a river ford near Tzanjuyú.

The Brunkard-Bates Expedition made the necessary introductions on behalf of the company to Guatemalan and German coffee growers, while Bates all along focused on gathering ethnographic sketches. Like most US travel writers and tourist promoters of the time, he sought with singular determination signs of the picturesque, either in nature or humanity. The men sought out promontories, crawled through ruined churches with

Figure 6.3. Brunkard and Bates working through an inconvenient moment in their expedition, near Tzanjuyú, Guatemala, October 1930. Photograph #721, Guatemala folder, Box 22, Marston Bates Papers, Bentley Historical Library, University of Michigan, Ann Arbor.

flashlights seeking hidden tombs, poked about small-town markets, and witnessed indigenous festivals up close. Monumental curiosities and majestic landscapes moved Bates to wax eloquent, as when, taking a rest on the shores of Lake Atitlán, the men "watched the changing mists on the volcano[e]s" and "speculated on the steely depths of this mirror-like sea."[50] As the men ambled through the towns bordering the lake, colorful indigenes going about their domestic labors inhabited the magnificent backdrop. Near Santiago Atitlán, Bates wrote, "The lake-side presented a brilliant spectacle as we neared the town. The rocky shore was covered with women, in their bright red dresses, washing: for all the world like a flock of some brilliant kind of bird."[51] In Penajachel, the pair came upon the festival of Saint Francis of Assisi, well underway, and Bates later recorded what he saw and heard in his journal. A local guide—perhaps a hotel attendant from their lodgings, perhaps someone else—helped the visitor make sense of the revelry and capture such details as the different sorts of music played.[52] The resulting entries reveal Bates applying his taxonomic sensibilities to a human landscape without the cultural and racial disdain so prevalent in early twentieth-century writing about the region's indigenous cultures. The next day at the festival, the "very picturesque" celebrants dressed in "brightly embroidered" costume, moved him "to splurge heavily," laying out $30 for an outfit complete with "trousers, jacket, head cloth, and sash."[53] He would follow up this fieldwork by compiling Mayan vocabulary lists and translating into English a Spanish text of Quiché legends he had acquired.[54] Clearly, this was a man deeply committed to understanding his human surroundings without seeking to judge or transform them.

Marston Bates's respectful interest in indigenous cultures remained, however, thoroughly within the primitivist framework then predominant in the wider field of white representations of indigenous peoples. Writing about representations of Indians in the US Southwest in ethnography, tourist spectacle, and art, historian Leah Dilworth has described the workings of this aesthetic in the early twentieth century: "The iconography of these representations (both written and visual) presented images of Indians as ruins, ritualists, and artisans; that is, Native Americans were represented as people doomed to vanish or as living relics of the past, as performers of colorful ceremonies, and as makers of pots, baskets, blankets, and jewelry. These images were more about their makers than about Native Americans and imagined a primitive that was a locus for idealized versions of history, spirituality, and unalienated labor."[55]

Bates offered no explicit proclamations about race, but he greatly preferred to experience aesthetically pleasing people and places—preferably those free from the spoiling influence of modernity. Looking over the plaza at Antigua, for instance, Bates pondered the town's colonial past but found the place "ruined for photography by the multitude of light and telephone wires strung about."[56] Markets were less interesting if Indian handiwork was missing from the scene, and he stopped taking pictures at festivals where there was "nothing very picturesque."[57] But on the whole these small, heavily indigenous towns deeply impressed the amateur ethnographer because they often fulfilled their observers' preconceived notions about primitiveness. For Bates, the right kind of scene to record on the expedition would capture subjects contentedly at home in their primitive context, unpolluted by deculturation or the influence of the outside world. "The freshness and cleanness of the Indians," he observed in Santiago Atitlán, "contrasted greatly with the slovenly type that we know about the cities."[58]

By creating an ethnographically flavored expedition memoir and following it up with many off hours of private research into Guatemala's past, this company employee captured something of the premodern world that he saw surviving outside of modernity. The capitalist transformation of Guatemala, then in full swing primarily at the hands of United Fruit, is conspicuous in its absence from this private expedition account. Nowhere did Bates record his thoughts about racial destinies, but undertaking such a project with the taxonomic and collecting urge so central to his work in entomology reveals his implicit debt to ethnographic and touristic practices of the time (including, it merits mention, the tourist promotion of the UFCO itself). He was, in short, selectively compiling his own personal exhibit of a living past. At least within the culture of United Fruit's tropical divisions, the expeditioners Bates and Brunkard were walking in storied footsteps.

F. H. Baron and the Search for the "White Indians of the Darién"

In Panama's remote Darién, a curious reenactment occurred in 1927, three years before the Brunkard-Bates Expedition. United Fruit Company agent F. H. Baron led thirteen men along the route taken three years earlier by the adventurer Richard Oglesby Marsh, whose expedition to find a lost tribe of white Indians in the Darién region had vaulted him to controversial fame. "We thought we'd sort of casually look around," Baron wrote later, "and maybe astonish ourselves at the sight of one of them."[59] Baron's sanguine attitude toward the Darién—a rough piece of country for outsiders to this day—was directed at Marsh, who had made much of his party's jungle tribulations in the US press. The fruit company man was breezily trying to upstage his adventuring celebrity contemporary. The first leg of the journey went smoothly. After steaming all the way from the company's base at Bocas del Toro on the Caribbean coast, through the Panama Canal, and down the Pacific Coast, Baron stopped at Yaviza to form his party. Soon after heading upriver from Yaviza "and leaving behind us the last traces of civilization," however, the expedition hit a snag at a site they called Camp Blair: several local porters refused to continue up the Sucubti River, a tributary of the Chucunaque, for fear of hostile Indians. The situation in the base camp grew tense and confrontational. How would Baron proceed? What happened next on this journey, and Baron's career during the 1920s more broadly, reveal much about the ways North Americans made and understood overseas empire in the early twentieth century. First, another question: What was a fruit company employee doing so far afoot looking for white Indians, anyway?

Not surprisingly, the imperatives of US capital lay at the heart of Baron's mission. The early 1920s found the United Fruit Company in the midst of an aggressive campaign to expand its domain in Panama. Burgeoning consumer demand for bananas in the United States fueled the expansion, as did the company's need to outpace the plant fungus that had been decimating its Atlantic-side plantings for some years.[60] Field-engineering teams from Guatemala to Colombia, headed by American employees, pushed beyond where company railways and plantations ended. They cut trails through some of the most difficult terrain and environments in the hemisphere and plotted what would become the new banana frontier. Company scouts like Baron, men of confidence and experience, ranged far and wide ahead of this construction to assess the agricultural potential of lands and any human obstacles to their acquisition and development. In this regard, Baron and Marsh engaged in similar work on a vitally important tropical resource frontier: aside from his ethnographic objectives, Marsh scouted the Darién for DuPont-owned US Rubber.

In their search for white Indians, Baron and Marsh followed in a long vein of imperialist explorers and writers whose objectives revolved around understanding the evolution of humanity and, true to the time, the biological differences between races, besides traipsing in ostensibly unknown places.[61] On this and other trips into the Panamanian interior, Baron, an anthropological hobbyist, recorded his observations of indigenous and mestizo societies in ethnographically tinted travelogues. His efforts may have lacked the scientific apparatus of others, but they reached a wide readership in the company's magazine *Unifruitco*, and probably offered many employees the only accounts they would have of life outside the fruit company's enclaves. Surely Baron had read Marsh's accounts in the US press, "The Mystery of the White Indians" and "Blond Indians of the Darien Jungle," published serially in *World's Work*, complete with photographic essays.[62] There, Marsh told the tale of his voyage into "an unexplored tropical wilderness" and his "astonishment" at finding what he posited was a population descended from Norse settlers living among the Kuna Indians.[63] The implications of this claim for debates about racial difference in the Americas were plain: Marsh was attempting to explain the rise of high civilizations in the Americas as the product of nonindigenous energies. The Indians he encountered, in his view, could in no way be related to the builders of past grandeur—a standard trope of early anthropology (and still a topic of discussion in pop culture venues). The "scores" of white Indians whom he claimed to meet "have always dominated the other Indians intellectually, and have created all the real civilizations that flourished in prehistoric times in Mexico, Central America, Peru, and Brazil."[64] Besides Marsh's accounts, Baron also would have been aware of the famed Percy Fawcett's quest for a lost civilization in Amazonia, an expedition from which no word had been heard since 1925.[65] The notoriety of Marsh and Fawcett spurred Baron to invest his professional duties with the trappings of gentlemanly exploration, in particular the drive to uncover some unknown branch of humanity. But there would be no such discovery for Baron, and no completing his mission for the company, if the paddles didn't start flying up the Sucubti.

In the eight days spent at Camp Blair, some of the men's grumbling grew more adamant. They cut trails and assessed surrounding lands during the day, but had ample time to reflect on their situation at night. "The Indians there are bad," claimed some; "they kill without warning." Those who were most afraid were porters taken on at Yaviza. Baron's American assistant, C. W. Parrish, and a few "Bocas bushmen" they had brought along remained willing to follow. He responded to the protests paternalistically, chiding the frightened men and their spokesman, Castillon, for being "afraid as a child is afraid of the dark." For the time being, Baron's ridicule and bullying were enough to get the party moving upriver from Camp Blair. The next day, however, the party came upon a set of Indian ranchos (seasonal dwellings) alongside the river. Although uninhabited, the site produced "great uneasiness" and made the doubtful crew grow sullen. Parrish and Baron's unwavering insistence overcame their trepidation for the moment and the men made camp near the Indian ranchos. Rain started to pour down, soaking everything, and the fearful members of the crew must have had a hard time finding sleep. Baron and Parrish fared little better, bitterly complaining among themselves into the night, "thoroughly disgusted by their childish talk" and worried about the progress of the expedition.[66] It must have been a miserable night for all.

Dawn broke to hardened wills on both sides. Most of the Yaviza men awoke having decided not to continue, and Baron took them on in what he termed a "sweet conference," where he unleashed a bilingual stream of sarcasm and insults to their manliness, again likening them to "children afraid of the dark." Only one of the paddlers, Hipólito País, acquiesced and at least convinced the others to go along for the time being; what motivated this decision is lost in Baron's one-sided account. What is not lost is the racially coded language of paternalism so central to Western colonial discourse in a variety of contexts.[67] Baron concluded that these men must have been bewildered by being "where none of their people had ever gone before." Although two of the men absolutely refused to paddle, the party continued on, Baron and Parrish made notes of territories around another abandoned rancho, and in a few hours, they drifted back downstream to the scene of the morning confrontation. The next day, Baron set the crew about beating trails into the bush. Unbeknownst to them, some of those trails headed straight back into the territory of the feared Kunas. "The joke now was on the men," Baron cheerily recalled. "We got a kick out of that."[68]

Just how dangerous to outsiders was the territory upriver from Yaviza in the mid-1920s? In James Howe's fine study of the Kunas in the early twentieth century, black and mestizo locals, as well as the Emberá-Chocó Indians who lived around Yaviza, circulated the rumors that the *cunas bravos* (ferocious Kunas) who inhabited the upper Chucunaque watershed treated outsiders roughly. Certainly Kunas and other upstream groups had recently resisted the incursions of black and mestizo settlers, and relations between the national government and indigenous peoples deteriorated rapidly during that decade, in no small part due to the government's attempt to eradicate cultural expressions of Indianness. There was also a history of tension between local Indian groups. When Marsh reached the "wild Kuna" in 1924, they in turn claimed to be preparing for attacks from the hostile Morti and Wala peoples, who lived even farther upstream. Howe gives a nod to the truth behind such claims, gauging from his more recent knowledge of the region. In any event, Marsh's account in *World's Work* greatly inflated the dangers posed by Indians. Epidemic-stricken Indians, wary of outsiders after recent clashes with Panamanian authorities, became devious and menacing; Indian efforts to reconnoiter the expedition's camps in their territory spurred its jittery members to fire bursts from their automatic weapons into the air.

Ultimately it was Marsh's faith in the group's great technological advantages—in particular outboard motors and plenty of modern small arms—that gave him the confidence to carry on. His penetration of the interior, then, became a tale of primitive dangers faced and overcome and an object lesson in the technological prowess of modern white explorers. These narrative devices at once drew on tropes in colonial exploration accounts and gave expression to Marsh's racialist worldview, in which racial conflict propelled human evolution.[69] Hyperbole also served his penchant for self-promotion.

Baron must have shaken his head upon reading Marsh's account of the dangers of the "unexplored" Chucunaque. Before he set off from Bocas del Toro in 1927, he had already made three scouting trips for United Fruit into the Darién and considered himself something of a seasoned tropical hand. "You've got to feel the Tropics or you hate them," he wrote before the expedition, "and if you feel 'em you love 'em."[70] Clearly he considered himself at home in the wilds of Central America, and he had a stronger understanding than Marsh of the potential for trouble in the Darién. During his previous voyage in the area, he had negotiated the "protection" of Inapaquina, a San Blas Kuna chief. "While the Indians up on the divide [between the Chucunaque and the Caribbean coast] didn't receive us with open arms," he remembered, "they at least suffered our presence because Inapaquina had ordered it."[71] Although he didn't mention it, Baron was surely aware that the Kuna had a recent history of violent resistance to outsiders. In 1925 the Kunas on the Caribbean coast rebelled against the Panamanian authorities and killed a number of abusive police officials in their territories. Marsh played a key role in that rebellion, and probably authored the Kuna Declaration of Independence.[72] Baron also knew from experience that the Kunas would see his scouting work for the company "with anything but enthusiasm," and so resolved to get as much work as possible done before being discovered.[73] It is unclear whether Baron concealed his mission from the Kunas themselves with the gloss of an apparently innocent, altruistic search for white Indians.[74] More likely, he, like Marsh, shared a racially tinged confidence in modern weapons and methods of triumphing over savage frontiers, should the necessity arise.

Up the Sucubti River, one incident in particular afforded Baron the opportunity to draw a contrast between himself and his nervous crew. A couple of days after fooling the men into cutting trails back into Kuna territory, Baron and Parrish set out to scout an area miles from camp. As dusk approached, they missed a connecting trail and found themselves swallowed by thick forest. Expecting a quick return to camp, they each had packed only a machete, a Colt revolver, and a first-aid kit. Apparently unfazed, the two built a shelter and endured a night of mosquitoes and all manner of strange noises. The next morning, they found their bearings and calculated their return. Later in the morning they heard gunshots, which they rightly assumed were signals from the rest of the party, and by returning the signal they found the ever-loyal Bocas bushmen who had headed up the search. It was, claimed Baron, "a perfect example of the advisability of taking things calmly and using one's head."[75] If he or Parrish felt anxious that night, Baron later excised those emotions from his account. Upon returning to camp later that morning, the two found the Yaviza crew even more exercised about being in Indian territory. Most likely the search party's decision to arm itself to the teeth spurred them to realize that even those loyal to Baron perceived some danger. Even Hipólito País, the Yaviza man who had encouraged the others to continue upriver, refused to venture on. It would be up to Baron and the Bocas men to carry the expedition to its farthest point—a rancho the deceived Yaviza men had cut out of the forest some three miles upriver, which Baron had named Camp MacFarland.

Baron must have known that Camp MacFarland represented a real intrusion into Kuna territory, for he intentionally concealed it from the riverbank, the main thoroughfare of the river-going Indians. Despite the effort, an encounter was inevitable. It came two days after the night spent lost in the forest. En route to the upstream outpost, the crew suddenly came upon a cayuco with three supposedly hostile Sucubti Kunas, "naked except for loin cloths and painted in bands of red and black." Although Baron knew one of the men from a previous trip and was able to approach the three for a "pow-wow," the reception was cool. The Indians reluctantly agreed to allow the men passage up to the mouth of the Asnati, a tributary of the Sucubti, but insisted that the expedition not approach their nearby village. Given the recent history of epidemics and outsider intrusions in the area, this reluctance was understandable. Whether or not he understood it, Baron knew enough to stay clear of the village and keep a low profile. On their way downstream and out of Kuna territory for good, Baron's party met another group of Sucubtis, who "greeted us gruffly and were decidedly unfriendly."[76] Their welcome had worn thin.

According to Baron, it probably wore out entirely soon after their departure. Although in his telling the Sucubtis were "puzzled" by the expedition's presence and activities, he knew they would get "quite a shock when they finally discovered the amount of trail we had cut through the heart of their country." That intrusion would make a return expedition in the near future unlikely. "I don't believe it would be healthy for us to go back there," he postulated in his account, acknowledging that his deceit would seriously damage whatever relationships he had cultivated among the Kunas.[77] Indeed, the company directed its efforts at opening new plantation zones where indigenous resistance would not risk a scandal in the US press of the kind engendered by Marsh's expedition and complicity in the Kuna revolt of 1925. By the early 1930s, new fields of operations would dot the Pacific lowlands of Costa Rica and Panama, forming the new divisions of Quepos, Golfito, and Puerto Armüelles. These new enclaves, with the added advantage of lying on the coast, would soon serve the growing demand for tropical fruit in the western United States.

Upon returning to Yaviza, Baron and Parrish took part in the celebration that greeted the men who had participated so timorously in the expedition. With the fears of hostile Indians left far upstream, the returning locals enjoyed the attention of the Yaviza ladies. Baron himself slipped into ethnographic mode in his observation of the dance, as he would whenever he had occasion to observe "native" life on other expeditions. His gaze could not help but seek confirmation of his wider cultural judgment. "The music, or rather the rhythm of the continually repeated notes," he concluded, was "primitive, certainly" and lacking "harmony of motion."[78] Like Marsh, Baron tended to romanticize "authentic" or "picturesque" Indians and look down upon mestizo and black populations, like the people of Yaviza. As for the white Indians, they proved to be a chimera for both men, but in different ways. Baron didn't see any at all, and those that Marsh so fervently defended as remnants of a lost Nordic settlement turned out to be albinos. Albinism is more prevalent among the Kuna than among any other human population.

Although he didn't meet with much success ethnographically nor for the purposes of banana cultivation, Baron's expedition into the Darién produced a different sort of value. For Baron himself, it furthered his career within United Fruit. We can never know what precisely his mission in the Darién was, but in 1927 he was already a key figure in opening the Puerto Armüelles division, operated by the United Fruit subsidiary, the Chiriquí Land Company.

In 1923, he "combed over all the watersheds" in the area and apparently approved of their potential for bananas.[79] Construction there began in 1927, and by 1928 he was charged with escorting office staff recently arrived from Boston via Almirante overland to Puerto Armüelles.[80] The records' last glimpse of him is as a railway superintendent in that same division in late 1929.[81]

What fueled Baron's account of the Darién was less intellectual curiosity or desire and more a demonstration of his identity as a white American male, a company man of the best sort. Company propaganda celebrated a few different masculinities: sea captains, field engineers, and "banana cowboys"—but none so much as the highly (and upwardly) mobile field agent, busy doing the company's most sensitive work. An essential part of these idealized masculinities was the willingness and ability to domineer groups of nonwhite laborers. Baron's preoccupation with drawing a contrast between he and Parrish, on the one hand, and the Yaviza men, on the other, is particularly revealing in this regard. As the cool-headed Americans confronted the dangers of the Darién, and the terror of a night alone in the jungle, the cowardly crew nursed their "childish" fears. Baron's ability to chide and bully the black and mestizo crew into continuing, and the loyalty of the "Bocas bushmen" established his natural authority as a white man in the colonized tropics; in his account, the divide between loyal and recalcitrant colonial servants showed that those who knew best silently accepted his leadership while the fearful revealed their lack of manly fiber. Surviving the human and ecological dangers of the tropics formed another pillar of Baron's identity. Taking on those dangers as a matter of pleasure and fulfillment underlined this capability, and ties Baron most firmly to his closest cultural mentor, Theodore Roosevelt.

"On holidays I headed for the forest"

As the expansion of the banana and sugar frontiers peaked in the UFCO's domains in the 1920s, gangs of laborers chopped and sawed their way through thousands of acres of dense, highly diverse lowland forests around the Caribbean basin. In the midst of this wave, some company men were busily exploring and cataloguing what seemed to them an inexhaustible sea of tropical nature surrounding them. For these people, tropical organisms became objects of intense interest, one fueled by their excited sense of personally advancing an incomplete taxonomic project on a frontier of natural science. This leisure-oriented interest served as a key node in the company's relationship with the scientific complex in the United States. United Fruit's collaboration with forester Samuel Record provides a case in point. Record had initiated his "wholly unofficial" relationship with the UFCO in 1924 as part of a search for corporate support for the Yale School of Forestry. In his account, the banana company stood out as the only tropical company "willing to help without restricting our freedom of action."[82] UFCO tropical manager George Chittenden funded the Yale-based journal *Tropical Woods*, and later made the company's tropical divisions available as fields of study and jumping-off points of more far-ranging explorations. Even more important than the financial and logistical support was the collaboration of American employees in Central America, which Chittenden secured by asking division managers to find "any employees who might be persuaded to collect and prepare samples of various woods." Chittenden believed that the effort would be "amply repaid eventually," although he did not specify how.[83]

In Guatemala, the tropical manager's request spurred Andes district superintendent Henry Kuylen and other first-class employees to set about following the detailed collecting instructions Record forwarded to the company. A steady flow of plant specimens north on the company's steamers resulted. The quality of Kuylen's first three samples sent north to Yale were enough to interest Record in his first collecting expedition in 1927. From this first encounter, a curious scientific friendship was born in the outlying lands of the Andes District. This scientific project centered on accumulating that mass of information and imposing taxonomic order and geographical species distributions onto a diverse set of tropical microclimates, and organizing the transmission of that growing matrix to researchers. The men spent a week exploring Los Andes in February of that year, a venture that brought in specimen series on fifty plants, "several of which proved to be new to science."[84] The men's collaboration in the field must have been strong, for they coauthored an article about their discoveries in *Tropical Woods* and went on to undertake two more expeditions together.[85] Upon greeting Record in person, Kuylen was surprised and impressed by the academic's robust stature, for at forty-five he stood six feet tall and weighed two hundred pounds. The men became fast friends, united by their shared interest in exploring the little-understood botanical landscape of Central America, even though Kuylen was a hobbyist with no background or training in forestry. For months prior to Record's arrival, "without interfering in any way with my regular duties," he had explored the forests surrounding Los Andes, made his own collections, and corresponded with the Yale forester.[86] Over the next five years, Record and the man he described as his "kindred spirit" undertook three collecting expeditions in Guatemala, Honduras, and Colombia.[87] This confluence of recreational dedication and the work of a prominent figure in tropical forestry produced thousands of samples that made their way to collections in the United States, a series of shared scholarly publications (in the UFCO-funded Yale journal *Tropical Woods*, among others), and, most proudly for Kuylen, his own "discovery" canonized in the botanical record, *Vitex kuylenii*, an herbaceous plant found in Guatemala.

Even in other Central America divisions, UFCO hobbyists collected wood, sap, bark, and leaves, being careful to ensure that the samples were from the same specimen and taking "particular pains to keep everything clear and plain."[88] Upon returning to New Haven from his various expeditions, Record continued to receive specimens from UFCO hobbyists in Cuba, Honduras, and Panama. George Cooper and George Slater, both working in Almirante, sent one group of specimens that proved especially exciting. Like Kuylen, their prize for collecting unknown species was to have their names inscribed in the taxonomic record.[89] Upon making additions to his own collection at Yale, Record distributed remaining specimens to institutions and researchers around the world, beginning with the Smithsonian Institution in Washington, DC.[90] The Smithsonian's associate curator of plants, Paul C. Standley, processed and codified the finds of these collectors and offered high praise for the their "important contribution to our knowledge of the trees of the Atlantic Coast."[91]

The consolidation of the taxonomic order tightly interwove with the company's interest, even though the connection was not always apparent. Record and his UFCO collaborators reveled in their apparently disinterested quest for knowledge. Curious unknown species might attract the most public attention, Record noted, but the greatest value of their work rested in "the mass of information that is being brought together and made available for use."[92] "Such discoveries may not have much monetary value," Record wrote to Kuylen, "but they have the same attraction to a botanist that new stars have to astronomers. They at least add to the sum total of human endeavor and that means progress."[93] Such a sense of mission was not lost on Kuylen, who felt himself a part of the "world-wide investigation of woods," a "great undertaking" he was proud to contribute to.[94] He recalled that this "side-line" transformed his relationship to the landscape. "Mine is a hobby," he noted, "that makes every plant an object of observation, and creates the feeling that one is always a member of a scientific expedition."[95] Despite such sentiments, surely Kuylen understood the UFCO's interest in better understanding the composition of the tropical forests it owned—the hardwoods felled to make way for plantations, after all, were a significant part of the company's exports at the time. Although these forests were removed wholesale, the company's vast tracts of uncleared forest still covered the majority of the company's landholdings. It was in the company's best interest to understand the differences between tree species as they bore on the commercial applications and marketability of tropical woods. Chittenden's decision to offer patronage to Record helped the company's export men (among whom Kuylen counted himself) better measure and predict the value tied up in uncultivated lands. The opportunity to pursue inquiries beyond timber resources was the coin that purchased the best expertise the US scientific complex could offer. From the UFCO's point of view, publicizing its patronage of the sciences formed an important part of an effort to improve its public image and the morale of its own employees.

Like Henry Kuylen, entomologist Marston Bates threw himself into tropical landscapes with great gusto during his off hours. Unlike his plant-collecting contemporary, however, Bates brought university training and a young lifelong scientific hobby to bear on the new environment that confronted him in Central America. After graduating from the University of Florida in 1927 with a BS in biology, Bates cut his teeth as an entomologist with the United Fruit Company in Honduras and Guatemala from 1928 until 1931. While with the fruit company, Bates first worked at Lancetilla research station under Dr. Wilson Poponoe, the famed "agricultural explorer" and then the company's head of research. A few months later, Popenoe promoted him to head the corporation's new agricultural extension agency in Guatemala, the Servicio Técnico. Along the way, Bates always complemented his work with the company by rigorously tending to his private curiosity through personal field expeditions of varying length. The documentary record provides us a much more detailed picture of Bates's life in Central America than of the other characters in this chapter. That experience merits our attention, for it reveals the intimate fabric of the corporation's relationship with the broader scientific community, including the various informal ties that bound fruit enclaves to the production of knowledge.

Marston Bates came to his position with United Fruit through an intersection of professional and personal ties that already tethered him to the US scientific community. His introduction to Wilson Popenoe came at the hands of a mutual family friend, eminent botanist David Fairchild, who was in charge of the Office of Foreign Seed and Plant Introduction with the USDA. Fairchild, probably through his son Graham—a close friend of Bates—knew that the young man had been a dedicated collector of Florida insects since he was twelve years old, and surely understood that he would be seeking work after completing his degree in the spring of 1927.[96] Wilson Popenoe had once worked for Fairchild at the USDA, and after 1925 had taken his position with the UFCO.[97] He was ideally situated to place a promising student like Bates, and responded favorably to the introduction. So deep was Bates's tie to the Fairchild family that he married David Fairchild's daughter Nancy (also the granddaughter of Alexander Graham Bell) after returning from Central America. The connection proved necessary, especially after Bates, due to a heart murmur, failed a company physical exam in Havana. The Fairchilds—Marston's future mother-in-law, in his telling—personally pressured Popenoe to accept the candidate.[98] "From what I have heard of you from the Fairchilds and others," Popenoe wrote a relieved Marston, "I believe your interest in tropical work is keen, and that you would be able to do good work down here."[99] Bates's personal connection to one of the grand families of American science secured his position with the company and soon led to being entrusted with significant responsibilities for such a young man.

During his three years with United Fruit, much of Bates's work centered on the entomological dimension of experimental plant introduction, a project in which the company was assuming a prominent role in the 1920s. Plant introduction work, based on the large-scale transportation of organisms around the world, had deep roots in the same nexus of personal and professional relationships that brought Bates to Central America. Wilson Popenoe's work as an agricultural explorer with David Fairchild at the USDA centered on botanical exploration and species introduction, all with an eye to boosting agricultural productivity of US farmers by finding potentially profitable "economic plants." Fairchild was a prominent figure in this larger project going back to the late nineteenth century. In 1889, he engineered the creation of the Office of Foreign Seed and Plant Introduction within the USDA, and was personally responsible for introducing more than twenty thousand plant species to the United States, many of them common products today (mangoes, nectarines, and dates among them).[100] Popenoe himself had become an eminence in the field before his United Fruit career, having traveled the world for years, gathering seed samples. In 1920, he published the authoritative *Manual of Tropical and Subtropical Fruits*.[101] Bates played an important role in determining how different pests affected the various tropical fruits the UFCO experimented with at Lancetilla.

A few months after Popenoe's intervention on his behalf, Bates was on the ground in Honduras at the company's tropical research station at Lancetilla. His entomological work with the company centered on defining and cataloguing "economic insects," that is, insects whose life-cycles affected the profitability of tropical agribusiness. He was immediately put to work figuring out how different insects affected crops in the company's "introduction gardens," where potential tropical commodities went through all manner of experiments to determine their profitability.[102] Bates, an expert in insect life-cycle histories, proved equal to this task and a pleased Popenoe enclosed his first report within his own to Dr. John R. Johnson, the company's head of agricultural research.[103] A year into his work at Lancetilla, Bates had an insectary full of fruit flies, which he exposed to guavas, citrus, and bananas in an effort to better understand the insects' relationship with different species of fruit.[104] Popenoe also charged him with studying a species of bee that scarred bananas, and locusts, all in an effort to find vulnerabilities in their life-cycles where chemical insecticides could be effective.[105] Bates confessed that he did not "know enough about bananas" to make much of an impact, a problem compounded by the many possible vectors and five kinds of banana spotting he identified. Nonetheless, his success was measured more by his command of method than by concrete results.[106] Soon his thorough work at the research station and in the banana fields led to more autonomy and to more field work all over Honduras and Guatemala. His research into economic insects under the company's auspices led to a compendium that he thought would "clean up the taxonomic and distributional muddle" of the chief insect pests threatening agriculture in Central America, a body of work he later published in *The Florida Entomologist* after he left United Fruit for graduate work at Harvard University.[107]

After arriving in Honduras in August 1928, Bates devoted much of his off time to the rich insect life around Lancetilla and registering his work with the US entomological community. His work in the experimental plots afforded him "enough spare time for considerable collecting and life-history work on the side," and the lines between his duties and his leisure blurred. "I am having a lovely time now," he wrote to his mother, "with a table beautifully littered with jars of caterpillars and vials of scale insects."[108] While the company required Bates to compile useful data about pests, he quickly subsumed that work to a broader preoccupation with taxonomy and species distribution. His ambitions for expanding the frontiers of entomological knowledge in the region were grand—"a list of species with their distribution, both geographical and ecological, within the republic"—and transcended his mission for the UFCO.[109] He articulated his private intentions to a series of new contacts he had at the USDA's Bureau of Entomology, with whom he also routinely communicated the results of his work for the company: "My position with the Fruit Company gives me an almost unique chance to work for an extended length of time on the Central American fauna. My own systematic interests are limited to certain families of Heterocera, but I want to do as much general collecting as possible: both of economic and non-economic species."[110] Where other white-collar men experienced life on the banana frontier as a Rooseveltian testing ground for their masculinity, Bates embraced the place as a scientific frontier—a no less powerful and freighted notion.[111]

And collect he did. "On holidays," he wrote of this time years later, "I headed for the forest."[112] He ranged widely within the world of insects, and found himself especially fortunate to be assigned surveys of possible pests that were "both interesting and economic."[113] While many Anglo-American company men burnished their masculinity in strenuous sports and outdoor activities, Bates quietly cultivated his scientific identity—sometimes in the very same spaces. He turned the surroundings of Lancetilla into his own private research station. Where the Tela Railroad Company's "big guns" (a UFCO subsidiary) had built a hunting shack in the nearby mountains, Bates based his own collecting hobby (this is the cabin pictured in fig. 1.1). The

Figure 6.4. Marston Bates collecting in the "magnificent forest" near Lancetilla, Honduras, 1930. Photograph #522, Honduras folder, Box 22, Marston Bates Papers, Bentley Historical Library.

shack, "it seems to me," he noted, was "even more admirably suited for scientific operations."[114] Along the uphill trail to the cabin, Bates set markers every 100 feet, measured a range of environmental conditions, and recorded changes in insect habitation over the whole course of the trail's 1,500-foot elevation gain.[115] "The trees at the top are quite different from those near the bottom, and I imagine that the insects change the same way," he hypothesized.[116] Far from being bound only by the company's prerogatives and preoccupation with "economic insects," Bates desired to understand the workings of a complex ecosystem. This time with the UFCO shaped his intellectual future. Some thirty years later, a well-published luminary in his field, Bates wrote about the importance of understanding what he termed "biological communities"—in other words, ecosystems.[117] Working for the Rockefeller Foundation in Colombia in the 1940s, Bates continued to collect insects and create portraits of complex biological communities. In his effort to understand a strain of yellow fever and different mosquito habitats, he organized a series of platforms spanning the rainforest from floor to canopy, a better-funded iteration of his first impromptu research station in Lancetilla.[118] He later wrote that Lancetilla was "really just about as fine an environment for your entomologist as could be devised."[119]

Within just months of arriving in Honduras, Bates had pleased Popenoe enough to have earned broader responsibilities, which in their turn fed his personal projects. First, a charge as photographer added to his duties. He kept up his work on fruit spotting in the insectary, and spent three days a week behind a camera. He enjoyed a "considerably greater freedom of action" in this capacity, he wrote home to his mother.[120] Such confidence did he cultivate that management entrusted him to shepherd the constant flow of visiting writers and scientists through the Honduras division. This was a task of some import, given the potential liabilities of allowing possibly critical eyes access to company operations. He was the perfect companion for these visiting luminaries, with his sharp curiosity, professional background, and knowledge of the surroundings. He understood that his job was to protect the company's interest, and he did it well. Among those he toured through company properties in Honduras and Guatemala were a Cuban delegation of agronomists, famed Soviet botanist Nikolai Vavilov, several North American academics, travel writer Lewis Freeman, and Charles Kepner, the latter of whom authored two trenchant critiques of the UFCO that remain standards to this day.[121]

Becoming a man of confidence to his superiors led to an effervescence of Bates's entomological hobby, for hosting these visitors provided welcome inspiration and spurred him to collect even more. While with United Fruit, he became part of a network of entomologists interested in tropical life—an important part, since he was based in a major area of interest. Barely out of college, the young man found himself at the heart of a constant flow of prominent scientists at a major tropical research station. After the visit of entomologist and *Lepidoptera* expert Carl Heinrich, "a scientist who draws considerable water" in Honduras, Bates wrote contentedly that "he has got me all enthused over the fauna of [the] Lancetilla Valley again."[122] A couple of weeks later, he wrote home about his plans for a "concentrated attack on the valley leps, especially on their life histories." His goal: to accumulate a collection on which he could base publications. "I have got to make a name for myself in the scientific world," he remarked bluntly.[123] Besides this professional ambition, Bates declared that hunting down moths "should be great sport"; clearly, the man's milieu inspired him on its own merits.[124] In his off time, Bates collected and sent specimens with a widening network of entomologists and botanists, including Richard Leussler, J. A. Hyslop, and Oakes Ames.

After just a year at Tela, Popenoe moved Bates into a role as goodwill ambassador for the UFCO. He was sent on a short trips to Guatemala in late 1929 and early 1930, and the possibilities of his young career assumed exciting proportions. "I am traveling in a part of the world that few people know exists," he wrote to his mother, "and doing work that is immensely interesting, and possibly very valuable."[125] These visits boosted his confidence, a feeling only increased by rich fieldwork, always his greatest joy. "I have been having splendid success lately with insect collecting," he declared, "and have got a lot of nice stuff, mostly fruit flies and scale insects."[126] Bates saw his value to the company's interest clearly. First, the company required a detailed assessment of the pest landscape for its own operations; second, that information would be exploited as fodder for public relations.[127] At the time, United Fruit sought to consolidate its already significant hold on Guatemala by opening a Pacific division at Tiquisate. The young scientist was there to demonstrate the company's benevolence to Guatemalan growers, who stood to lose as the UFCO expanded its monopolistic control over the country's transportation infrastructure.[128] Although he had doubts about how the company's strategy would be perceived, he outlined his own input to public relations, which centered on providing Guatemalan growers with knowledge about pest distribution, and in Spanish. The effort would entail a "regional approach," he argued, based on the laboratory facilities at Lancetilla as the hub of the grand taxonomic project. The outcome of this proposal is murky—likely it fell apart due to budget retrenchments in the 1930s—but Bates made an earnest effort to popularize entomological knowledge by learning to speak Spanish and create displays for information booths at local fairs.[129]

As Popenoe groomed Bates to be the company's top North American outreach officer in Guatemala, he sent the rising star to Washington, DC; New York City; and Boston so that he could make personal connections within the UFCO and with the wider scientific community. Bates met with a number of botanists and entomologists there, affiliated with the United States National Museum, the USDA's Bureau of Entomology, and American Museum of National History, and Museum of Comparative Zoology. These contacts would help Bates expand the entomological data at the company's disposal and help him complete his regional insect survey. Such a project entailed a constant flow of insect specimens north and "determinations"—concrete information about pest species and life cycles—back south. Bates sometimes enticed entomologists to make such determinations for the company in exchange for collections of noneconomic species he knew would be of personal interest to them.[130] He also forwarded photographs, plant materials, and insects to colleagues in the north, as a matter of professional courtesy.[131] These endeavors blurred the lines between company duties and private leisure—a line that never particularly troubled Bates—and played a key role in tying the company to a wide network of scientists.

Bates astutely leveraged his UFCO duties to assure his larger professional ambitions, which involved pursuing doctoral work in zoology at Harvard University. Indeed, he likely cultivated some of his collecting relationships to connect himself more closely key natural sciences faculty at Harvard, including Thomas Barbour, Joseph Bequaert, and Oakes Ames. When Barbour, then curator of the university's Museum of Comparative Zoology, visited Tela in early 1931, his host Bates was "working on him industriously" to wrangle a fellowship.[132] A few months later, he undertook a significant collecting expedition in Honduras on behalf of botanist Ames, who was impressed by Bates's thorough, efficient work cataloguing different orchid species.[133] His years of personal entomological initiative, however, formed the keystone of his appeal to Harvard. In his application he spoke to the museum's needs. "I have already accumulated quite a bit of material, which I can bring to Cambridge for study," he promised.[134] Popenoe was behind Bates, spoke personally with Thomas Barbour, and wrote a glowing recommendation for his subordinate.[135] By the start of classes in the fall, Bates had carted his collections to Cambridge and begun doctoral studies, well on his way to a distinguished scientific career.

Conclusions

These stories about explorers and collectors reveal much about the cultural dynamics of corporate colonialism. First, their leisurely pursuit of knowledge, artifacts, and specimens played a vital role in tying the UFCO more closely to the wider enterprise of knowing Latin America. It was in no small part the personal networks and friendships between the company's hobbyists and professional, institutionally-affiliated experts that made those linkages possible. These relationships rested not only on intellectual affinity, but also on an intellectual economy of objects and information. Specimens, artifacts, and first-hand narratives drawn from tropical landscapes flowed north into private and institutional collections of various sorts, and very often print media and correspondence flowed south, engaging in a continual dialogue with company-affiliated amateurs who did the exploring and collecting. This sort of traffic echoes the extractive logic of early twentieth-century US capitalism in important ways, with the raw materials of scientific inquiry enriching the intellectual capital and productive capacity of a metropolitan power. Indeed, these hobbyists were engaged in what can be termed "imperial science," inquiry that more often than not buttressed the corporation's interest and naturalized US power in the region more broadly. Amateurs and professionals alike took advantage of the UFCO's preponderant power in the region to pursue their agendas, and it is thus little surprise that their work and leisure intertwined with its interest. (The same could be said for the relationship between North American scientists and US political and military interest in Latin America during the early twentieth century: Wilson Popenoe himself was a paid agent of the Office of Naval Intelligence.)[136] In their "self-fashioning exercises"—their ways of crafting personal identity—employee explorers often acted like agents of empire, empowered and entitled in different ways to appropriate and explore at will in a foreign land.[137] These identities shaped around an exploring hobby mediated their relationship to tropical landscapes and peoples in concrete ways, sometimes through gendered and racial constructions that construed local peoples as inferior and local landscapes as fundamentally available.

In some ways, the practice of leisurely amateur inquiry complicates this tidy picture of knowledge production in the service of US economic power. First, these stories upset a top-down, diffusionist model of knowledge in which the prime movers are institutionally affiliated professionals and the flow of scientific or archaeological narrative emanates from those metropolitan spaces. The banana frontier and its environs were sites of knowledge production themselves, not just a field for gathering data, specimens, and artifacts. The environmental and human context shaped hobbyists, and their immersion in that world was often more substantial than that of their professional peers. These experiences could also shape ambivalent perceptions and attitudes about the company in particular and Western approaches to the tropics more broadly considered. Marston Bates represents a case in point—recall his notion of "biological community," an appreciation of diversity shaped by witnessing the destruction of forests to make way for banana fields. While an employee, he privately voiced apprehension about the impact of his work with the UFCO, especially in his capacity as goodwill ambassador. Twenty years later, he published a reflection on "the characteristics of men and nature in the tropical environment," *Where Winter Never Comes*. Despite having lived on the UFCO's Anglo-Saxon frontier of empire during his formative years, Bates produced a trenchant critique of "the toplofty attitude" of Westerners toward the tropics, which he attributed to cultural ignorance and the lingering influence of racialist arguments about the inferiority of tropical peoples.[138] The experiences of these leisure scientists, ethnographers, and archaeologists help us better understand the important role of knowledge production to the culture of early-twentieth-century corporate colonialism, both as an adjunct to that project and as a potential site of ambivalence.

Conclusion

Looking back over the company's first quarter-century at a Swampscott, Massachusetts, shareholder conference in 1926, UFCO Director Bradley Palmer lauded the company's success in making the tropics habitable for white American workers. He recalled the past difficulties of recruiting "anybody, let alone white men, to go to and live on the banana plantations in the jungles of the Tropics."[1] Palmer attributed the negative image of the tropics to Minor Cooper Keith's late nineteenth-century railroad-building project in Costa Rica, which cost the lives of about four thousand workers, including Keith's brothers. Typical to the language of such public addresses, he identified the company's genius and vision as the solution to this problem. By the mid-1920s, Palmer claimed, US employees in tropical divisions enjoyed living standards at least as healthy and comfortable as those in the United States itself.[2] Surely, in its first twenty-five years United Fruit had made significant strides in infrastructure and sanitation in its tropical divisions. But Palmer's message, produced for the consumption of stockholders, belied a serious personnel problem for United Fruit in the 1920s—lengthy stints in company enclaves remained unattractive for the white, Anglo-Saxon managers, technicians, and staff who faced such a possibility.

President Victor M. Cutter offered a more critical assessment. He claimed that sanitation had made disease rare in tropical divisions, but turnover of personnel remained as high as 60 percent in some departments. For Cutter, high attrition among North American employees in the tropical divisions resulted from "hiring people without proper physical and mental qualifications."[3] As we have seen, his perspective was deeply rooted in his sense of white masculinity. Aside from remunerative issues of job stability and fairness in pay and benefits, other speakers pointed to several social factors behind the personnel problem. R. H. Davis, Superintendent of Agriculture at Truxillo, Honduras, attributed discontent to strange environments, the lack of entertainment, and the absence of stable family life. He proposed several measures to improve life in tropical divisions, among them "using more American girls in various capacities in the Tropics" and establishing entertainment committees "to get people's minds off their work."[4] L. E. Weaver, United Fruit's superintendent of agriculture, argued that the company should take more care in selecting tropical employees, making sure they had "a true picture of life and work in the tropics before they go there."[5] He proposed that new employees be greeted upon arrival in their tropical divisions by executives—a touch of corporate intimacy that would solidify a new employee's sense of belonging to a community. Like Davis, he recognized the importance of family life and advocated sufficient housing for married employees. Underneath the veneer of Bradley Palmer's sunny message, these comments revealed the limitations of corporate colonialism in the tropics.

To be sure, the UFCO's effort to make its white labor force content and compliant—both as formal policy and as less tangible corporate culture—enjoyed a measure of success. The individual stories in this book reveal their subjects' ambivalence, but also a variety of ways they made fulfilling careers and lives in the UFCO tropics, even if some were very short. The glimmers of widespread discontent that ripple through the comments made at Swampscott in 1926 point to a set of unresolved tensions in the company's effort to discipline its white American employees by transforming the tropical milieu around them. These tensions were already merging with other factors to undermine the UFCO's white, Anglo-Saxon colonies protected behind electrified chicken fences. Even as the UFCO's corporate welfare campaign and imperial forms of experiencing and understanding the tropics hit high gear in the late 1920s, the racialized division of labor that undergirded it all was starting to break down. The heyday of the banana cowboy, when one had to be a white Anglo-Saxon to hold most technical and supervisory positions, would soon fade.

A brief consideration of labor conditions in the UFCO's Northern Railway Company in Costa Rica will show how this process worked on the ground. The breakdown of the white color bar occurred in the context of a much broader Latinization of the company's labor force and its general retreat from investing in direct ownership of production. This process began in the early 1910s as a strategy to segment laborers racially and culturally and thereby diffuse their potential for organization, a process Colby and Bourgois have documented well in the company's tropical divisions.[6] Pressure from nationalist political interests around the Caribbean Basin in the 1920s led the company to curtail even further its recruitment of black West Indian laborers.[7] The records of the NRC bear out these changes. In 1921, the engineering department at Siquirres reported that 22 percent of its labor force was "native" (the rest being "colored"); by 1930, natives comprised almost 56 percent of laborers in the same department. The NRC's Maintenance of Way Department, which tracked a similar demographic breakdown in the early 1930s, reported that natives made up 72 percent of laborers by 1940.[8]

Percentages of Anglo-American labor are elusive, but the decisions of management reveal that the white color bar was receding steadily in the 1920s. Restive and troublesome white Americans helped drive this process. In 1923, UFCO Superintendent M. M. Marsh reported to Boston that he was "gradually weeding out" the "undesirable class" of white employee. Part of that effort involved replacing these men with locals: "A number of native overseers have been employed during the year and are making very satisfactory progress. Prospects are being closely watched and given an opportunity to obtain as varied a training as possible."[9] Company records show that a steady trickle of complaints about drunk or belligerent American employees crossed management desks into the 1930s, although these showed no evidence of involving the tropical travelers—left-leaning labor organizers—of previous decades. In 1927, several locals from the town of Pejibaye wrote to the NRC superintendent protesting the behavior of the white American conductor based in nearby Turrialba. "He treats all us passengers from Pejivaye [sic] like dogs," they wrote, and had been physically abusive, kicking and pushing some of the locals. What was more, they claimed, he did not speak Spanish and "todo el tiempo anda sacado" (he is drunk all the time). The protest then took a darker turn: "Le pedimos a su ecselencia [sic] que nos ponga un conductor que nos estime porque no respondemos á ese macho lo que le pueda suseder [sic] si sigue en Turrialba." (We beg your excellency to give us a conductor who respects us, because we cannot answer for what might happen to this fellow if he stays in Turrialba.)[10]

Within a few days, management placed a Costa Rican on this line and the troubles apparently stopped.[11] Complaints from the same locality two years later centered on the inability of other American conductors to communicate in Spanish, which made cargo transfers tense and difficult.[12] Although subordinate whites could be haughty, insensitive, and downright abusive in their treatment of nonwhites, management usually tried to resolve such tensions by removing problematic individuals.

The Central American and Caribbean labor market also put pressure on the UFCO's color bar. In short, white supremacy eventually ran aground on the hard rocks of labor costs. As detailed in chapter 2, management's concern over high wages in the Panama Canal Zone and the United States went back to the first decade of the century, and apparently led the company and its subsidiaries to admit nonwhites to skilled positions as early as 1917. That year, manager George Chittenden reported that a dearth of white American mechanics in Limón had led him to recruit and train local apprentices. "Much work formerly performed by white mechanics is now being done by them and there is not the same necessity for bringing high-priced men from abroad," he wrote to tropical divisions manager Victor Cutter.[13] A decade later, master mechanic Randall Ferris reiterated these worries. High railroad salaries in the United States made it "practically impossible to obtain any more men from that source." As far as hiring from the United Kingdom, Ferris noted that different norms of railway operation there meant that very few such men could meet the company's technical requirements. "Our only alternative is to use native help," he wrote to his higher-ups, "picking out suitable boys, training them in the shops for awhile [sic] and working them through firemen to enginemen."[14] The payoff of such an effort was real, and economy started to eclipse race as the governing logic of managers. It was no wonder, given that nonwhite railroad conductors earned about half of what their white counterparts did: $80 monthly, as opposed to $170 in 1929.[15] This labor pool produced proficient replacements for white Americans, and when presented with such a clear choice in hiring managers were happy to hire locally—as a series of such decisions laid out in their internal records make clear.[16]

By the late 1930s, natives predominated in the staffing of the NRC, except for high-level supervisory positions.[17] A final example from those years shows that wages and the lifestyle demands of American employees placed them at a serious disadvantage as racial criteria evaporated. In July 1939, NRC manager Frank Sheehy faced a decision when choosing a construction department foreman. He opted to promote a Costa Rican, Fermín González, over white American engineer Carl Riggs, "for economical reasons." Riggs presented no disciplinary problems, but he did carry serious costs: "We will have to pay Riggs not less than $225.00 a month, furnish him with a house to accommodate his family with the perquisites allowed and, in addition, first class camp service equipment with cook when on line, where he will be the majority of the time. He will, undoubtedly, want a foreman whereas Gonzalez would act as foreman and would not have to be paid over $90.00 per month, living in the same equipment with the gang."[18]

This glimpse into the decisions made in one UFCO division suggests that the generalized trend toward cutting labor costs by "Latinizing" was underway around the tropical divisions and on both farms and railways, although the process was surely varied and uneven. The ubiquitous company town with its American zones behind electrical chicken fences was far from disappearing from Latin America. But the heady days when thousands of white-collar banana cowboys undertook a racialized "conquest of the tropics" were fast fading, as was the need for a paternalistic disciplinary project to shape their behavior. Weighed down by external political pressures, the costs of corporate welfare, persistently poor retention, and the realities of the regional labor market, the UFCO's Anglo-Saxon colonial project was forced to transform. The company remained a powerful presence in the region for years, but a wave of retrenchments during the economic difficulties of the Depression, the disruption of marine traffic during World War II, antitrust actions by the US government, and the ascendancy of serious nationalist challenges within Latin America all led to the UFCO's divestment from banana production by the 1950s.[19] According to business historian Marcelo Bucheli, "the 'octopus' of the 'Banana Empire' in the early twentieth century consciously dismantled itself in later years."[20] By that time, Anglo-American communities had become a shadow of their former selves, and the cultural boundaries of UFCO enclaves had become much more porous that in the early part of the century.[21] The present study roots this transformation in the company's challenges many decades before.

In a sweeping, seminal treatment of US territorial expansion, distinguished historian Walter Nugent has situated a "habit of empire" at the center of American identity and experience.[22] In this book, I have used a storied case of US economic expansion to tell a story of this habit at work around the Caribbean Basin in the early twentieth century. The UFCO's most expansive period depended on a series of imperial practices that at once reinforced its power and tied it to a broader set of US engagements with Latin America. Far from comprising monolithic colonial communities, white Anglo-Saxon enclaves could seethe with discontent and internal tension. These tensions spurred management to undertake a massive effort to transform its field of operations and to govern all levels of its workforce. The most salient aspects of the banana frontier—orderly, segregated company towns, social clubs, sporting venues, hospitals, and the like—existed primarily to retain and control a large population of expatriate employees, termed at various times "white Anglo-Saxons," "temperates," or "first-class." The practice of corporate welfare translated into a tropical milieu amounted to a system of corporate colonial governance. The project depended in good measure on shaping expatriates' relationship to unfamiliar, dangerous surroundings. This book has documented various ways in which the company enlisted the hearts and minds of restive American employees into the its mission of uplift and rational exploitation of the lowland tropics of the Caribbean Basin. The spirit of adventure and masculine swagger that many sought on the banana frontier found fertile soil in this context. "Structures of attitude and reference," as one eminent scholar of empire has posited, mattered a great deal in imperial encounters.[23]

Colonialism can be defined as a series of claims made over other territories and peoples, claims that may not necessarily involve formal territorial acquisition but that do involve the aspirational or real control over resources. We could add conceptual control to this description. Human, natural, and medical science provided a language for such an "imperial sense of epistemic superiority"; in other words, a sense of entitlement over a foreign space driven by a purportedly altruistic quest for knowledge.[24] Company leadership understood well the link between the generation of knowledge and the exercise of power; scientists both professional and amateur, on the other hand, understood that the company offered them a vital space in which to undertake their various projects. Fueled by such a partnership, the company's purview thus became a far-flung set of nodes within a much larger fabric of US scientific interest in Latin America. Medical science, agronomy, archaeology, ethnology, and biology—already deeply invested in European and North American expansion—came to the UFCO's sphere conditioned to such an exercise. The systems of meaning developed there most often undergirded the company's interest, if not directly, then more obliquely as a set of conceptual claims that contributed to the enterprise as a whole. Whether centered on the etiology of malaria, the discovery and rescue of neglected ancient ruins, the search for white Indians, or the expansion of taxonomic frontiers, experts and hobbyists alike were pondering a series of questions that were often much more closely related to corporate expansion and US empire than they thought. The effort to catalog and understand "economic" diseases, insects, and plants related quite directly to company interest, and the everyday practices essential to these fields leveraged the UFCO over tropical laborers and landscapes. The search for white Indians or Mayan potsherds was, in fundamental ways, tied to and fueled by the corporation's interest. Studying the eclipse of ancient primitives and comparing them to their backwards modern descendants in the context of a triumphant, racialized culture of corporate colonialism provided deep historical resonance to the company's power over laborers and landscapes. For white American men raised on tales of the recent conquest of the North American West, the redolence of such narratives was obvious. All of these fields of inquiry laid the company's tropical milieu open as an object of possession.

These webs of imperial power, however, were laced with ambivalence. Looked at closely, the edifice of the corporation was riven with internal tensions, contradictions, and unintended consequences. Those hired based on their Anglo-Saxon blood to dominate nonwhite laborers could become rebellious themselves and their restiveness was an important reason behind the shape of tropical colonies and the company's massive investment in them. Managers often took a callous attitude toward subordinate whites and their feelings of homesickness and isolation, and then puzzled over why they left in such great numbers. Company indoctrination could sweep up some banana cowboys in its sense of mission and adventure, but the specter of white male failure always haunted the fringes. UFCO doctors and management labored mightily to mitigate the impact of economic diseases on productivity, but failed to provide living conditions that did so. Twentieth-century tropical agribusiness, like every plantation-based regime before it in the Americas, remade human societies and landscapes in ways that propagated the organisms responsible for such diseases. Company scientists made great strides in cataloguing and understanding the organisms and environments in which they worked, but their efforts only enhanced an industrially-driven monoculture that steadily erased biological diversity and made bananas yet more susceptible to plant pathogens. Seeking out these fissures has become essential to the study of grand colonial projects.

The clearest window I have found onto the complicated position a UFCO employee from these years can be found in the writing of Marston Bates. Unlike many of his contemporaries with the fruit company, he found himself quite at home in the tropics. He relished his times alone in the forests near Lancetilla, Honduras, and approached the people he encountered with curiosity and respect. His "happy three years in the forests and banana plantations of the Honduras coast" from 1928 to 1931 served as a spring-board for a long, prestigious career as a zoologist, science writer, and public intellectual.[25] Although in private he was frequently critical of the compa-ny's management and of its effort to generate goodwill among Central Amer-ican growers, he threw himself into the company's business, cataloguing economic insect pests, building scientific networks, and organizing regional outreach to bolster the UFCO's public image. The ability to pursue his own interests on the side, tied as they were to a broader, altruistic enterprise of knowledge, surely reconciled him to these duties. But in his later books, especially *Where Winter Never Comes* (1952) and *The Forest and the Sea* (1960), we have seen Bates express his ambivalence and caution readers against the "toplofty attitude that the Western world is apt to take of the tropics."[26] Most tellingly, he lamented the destruction of forests for rationalized agri-culture and dismantled climatological arguments for racial hierarchy—the two interlocking pillars of the UFCO's early twentieth-century enterprise. Such a critical perspective reveals that the Anglo-Saxon banana frontier could cast a long, complicated shadow over its former denizens.

In the end, the extractive, profit-driven thrust of the company's project was a business success. The world created by the corporation between 1899 and 1930 generated enormous wealth for stockholders. Thousands of white American employees earned their livelihood from it (sometimes barely), and, as the stories of Marston Bates and Everett Brown show, a stint in the UFCO's tropics often served as an important touchstone within much longer career trajectories. The story of this white-collar empire helps us better understand that such a large-scale, capitalist intervention into a distant, difficult environment faced serious challenges from within but ultimately fostered various ways its most important agents could connect with their surroundings. In some respects deeply insular, UFCO enclaves also served as springboards to a set of far-reaching interventions and explorations that helped individuals make sense of themselves as tropical Americans. These ways of living and knowing the tropics were essential to the operation of the most iconic US corporation in Latin America.

NOTES

Introduction

1. Gabriel García Márquez, *Cien años de soledad*.

2. For literary depictions of the banana invasion, see in particular Guatemalan Nobel laureate Miguel Ángel Asturias's "banana trilogy": *Viento fuerte, El papa verde*, and *Los ojos de los enterrados*. See also Honduran P. Amaya Amador's *Prisión verde*; Costa Ricans Carlos Luis Fallas, *Mamita Yunai*, and Quince Duncan, *Dos novelas: Los cuatro espejos y La Paz del pueblo*; and Chilean poet Pablo Neruda's *Canto general*. Paeans to United Fruit's enterprise include Frederick Upham Adams, *Conquest of the Tropics*; Charles Morrow Wilson, *Empire in Green and Gold*; Stacy May and Galo Plaza, *The United Fruit Company in Latin America*. A critical analysis is Charles Kepner and Jay Soothill, *The Banana Empire*.

3. For an account of the company's corporate consolidation and its expansion, see Marcelo Bucheli, *Bananas and Business*, 44–85. On the "managerial revolution" and vertical integration in US business more broadly, see Alfred Chandler, *The Visible Hand*; on how those structural changes in US corporate culture affected Latin America, see Thomas F. O'Brien, *The Revolutionary Mission*, especially parts I and II; and César Ayala, *American Sugar Kingdom*.

4. I borrow this term from Gilbert Joseph, Catherine C. LeGrand, and Ricardo Salvatore, *Close Encounters of Empire*.

5. For an analysis of the UFCO in Panama, see Philippe Bourgois, *Ethnicity at Work*. Jason M. Colby considers Costa Rica and Guatemala in *The Business of Empire*. For other enclave-focused studies that examine the company's political, economic, and social impact, see Oscar Zanetti and Alejandro García, *United Fruit Company: Un caso del dominio imperialista en Cuba*; Darío Euraque, *Reinterpreting the Banana Republic*; Steve Striffler, *In the Shadows of State and Capital*; Catherine C. LeGrand, "Living in Macondo: Economy and Culture in a United Fruit Company Banana Enclave in Colombia," in Joseph, LeGrand, and Salvatore, *Close Encounters of Empire*, 333–68; John Soluri, *Banana Cultures*; Bucheli, *Bananas and Business*; Lara Putnam, *The Company They Kept*; Trevor Purcell, *Banana Fallout*; Mark Moberg, "Responsible Men and Sharp Yankees: The United Fruit Company, Resident Elites, and Colonial State in British Honduras," in Striffler and Moberg, *Banana Wars*, 145–70; and Cindy Forster, "'The Macondo of Guatemala': Banana Workers and National Revolutions in Tiquisate, 1944–1954," in Striffler and Moberg, *Banana Wars*, 191–228.

6. On the banana in US consumer culture, see Soluri, *Banana Cultures*; Bucheli, *Bananas and Business*; and Virginia S. Jenkins, *Bananas: An American History*.

7. O'Brien, *The Revolutionary Mission*.

8. Aviva Chomsky, *West Indian Workers and the United Fruit Company in Costa Rica, 1870–1940*; and Ronald Harpelle, *The West Indians of Costa Rica*.

9. For research charting the UFCO's political influence, see Euraque, *Reinterpreting the Banana Republic*; Bucheli, *Bananas and Business*; Piero Gleijeses, *Shattered Hope*; and Steven Kinzer and Steven Schlesinger, *Bitter Fruit*.

10. Colby, *The Business of Empire*; Ronald Harpelle, "White Women on the Frontier," 6–34; Ronald Harpelle, "White Zones: American Enclave Communities of Central America," in Lowell Gudmundson and Justin Wolfe, *Blacks and Blackness in Central America*, 307–33; Atalia Shragai, "Do Bananas Have a Culture?" 65–82.

11. For valuable state-driven histories of US expansion, see for example Emily S. Rosenberg, *Spreading the American Dream*; Walter Nugent, *Habits of Empire*; John Lindsay-Poland, *Emperors of the Jungle*; Brian Loveman, *No Higher Law*; Richard Immerman, *Empire for Liberty*; and Peter H. Smith, *Talons of the Eagle*. Thomas F. O'Brien offers an approach that considers both state and economic agents of expansion in *The Revolutionary Mission*. For a case study of the interplay of economic influence and diplomacy, see Linda B. Hall, *Oil, Banks, and Politics*. For economically oriented studies of US expansion, see Steven C. Topik and Allen Wells, *The Second Conquest of Latin America*.

12. Three recent works that focus on state-driven US tropical colonies in this period are Julie Green, *The Canal Builders*; Mary Renda, *Taking Haiti*; and Warwick Anderson, *Colonial Pathologies*.

13. Philippe Bourgois has observed this dynamic in the company's management of labor and political foes. See "One Hundred Years of United Fruit Company Letters," in Striffler and Moberg, *Banana Wars*, 104.

14. Cindy Aron, *Working at Play*.

15. See Jason Colby's recent study of the racial and labor politics behind United Fruit's division of labor in *The Business of Empire*, 79–100. On the structure of UFCO's workforce in different divisions, see also Bourgois, *Ethnicity at Work*; Chomsky, *West Indian Workers*; Striffler, *In the Shadows of State and Capital*; LeGrand, "Living in Macondo"; and Soluri, *Banana Cultures*.

16. Peter Chapman, *Bananas*, 77.

17. See the classic study on the necessity of unpacking "traditions," Eric Hobsbawm and Terence Ranger, *The Invention of Tradition*.

18. My understanding of cultural conscription has been shaped by Mary Renda's examination of the US occupation of Haiti in *Taking Haiti*.

19. On corporate welfare in the early twentieth century, see Roland Marchand, *Creating the Corporate Soul*; Andrea Tone, *The Business of Benevolence*; Stuart D.

Brandes, *American Welfare Capitalism, 1880–1940*; and Neil J. Mitchell, *The Generous Corporation*.

20. Colby, *The Business of Empire*.

21. On banana company relations with nonwhite laborers in the early twentieth century, see O'Brien, *The Revolutionary Mission*, 80–108; Colby, *The Business of Empire*; Striffler, *In the Shadows of State and Capital*; LeGrand, "Living in Macondo"; Soluri, *Banana Cultures*; and Bucheli, *Bananas and Business*.

22. On the close relationship between knowledge production and the constitution of colonized spaces, see, for instance, Edward Said, *Orientalism*; Bernard S. Cohn, *Colonialism and Its Forms of Knowledge*; John Gillis, *Islands of the Mind*; David Spurr, *The Rhetoric of Empire*; and Ricardo Salvatore, *Imágenes de un imperio*. United Fruit was part of a much wider culture of collecting and display that scholars have established as vital to the functioning of imperial power. See Robert Aguirre, *Informal Empire*; Robert Rydell, *All the World's A Fair*; and Steven Conn, *Museums in American Life*. On the production of particularly tropical spaces, see David Arnold, *The Problem of Nature*; Felix Driver and Luciana Martins, *Tropical Visions in an Age of Empire*; Nancy Leys Stepan, *Picturing Tropical Nature*; and Warwick Anderson, *Colonial Pathologies*.

23. On the relationship of tropical medicine to US power overseas, see Mariola Espinosa, *Epidemic Invasions*; Anderson, *Colonial Pathologies*; Diego Armus, *Disease in the History of Modern Latin America*; Laura Briggs, *Reproducing Empire*; and Stepan, *Picturing Tropical Nature*.

24. On the UFCO's paternalist medical narrative, see David Aliano, "Curing the Ills of Central America: The United Fruit Company's Medical Department and Corporate America's Mission to Civilize,1900–1940." For an account of resistance to the same, see Aviva Chomsky, "Afro-Jamaican Tradition and Labour Organizing on United Fruit Company Plantations in Costa Rica, 1910."

25. On scientific networks in imperial contexts, see Thierry Hoquet, "Botanical Authority: Benjamin Delessert's Collections between Travelers and Candolle's Natural Method (1803–1847)"; Jim Endersby, *Imperial Nature*; Daniel Goldstein, "Outposts of Science: The Knowledge Trade and the Expansion of Scientific Community in Post–Civil War America"; Felix Driver and Luciana Martins, *Tropical Visions in an Age of Empire*.

26. Colby considers the gendered performativity of white superiority in the company's world in *The Business of Empire*, 79–82; Nicholas Thomas has termed such actions "self-fashioning exercises" in *Colonialism's Culture*, 5. For studies that center North American gendered masculinities within the making of US overseas empire, see Amy Kaplan, *The Anarchy of Empire in the Making of U.S. Culture*; Renda, *The Taking of Haiti*; and Kristen Hogansen, *Fighting for American Manhood*.

27. Renda, *Taking Haiti*, 17.

28. I draw the concept of "contact zone" from Mary Louise Pratt, *Imperial Eyes*,

4. On the notion of contact zones and US–Latin American relations in particular, see Gilbert Joseph, "Close Encounters: Toward a New Cultural History of U.S.–Latin American Relations," in Joseph, LeGrand, and Salvatore, *Close Encounters of Empire*, 3–46.

29. For a superb microhistory of a company division, see Putnam, *The Company They Kept*. For recent works that situate the generation of Americanness at peripheries of empire, see James T. Campbell, Matthew P. Guterl, and Robert G. Lee, *Race, Nation, and Empire in American History*; Robert Campbell, *In Darkest Alaska*; Ann Stoler, *Haunted by Empire: Geographies of Intimacy in North American History*; and Kaplan, *The Anarchy of Empire*.

30. Joseph, "Close Encounters," 4.

31. Philippe Bourgois, "One Hundred Years of United Fruit Company Letters," in Striffler and Moberg, *Banana Wars*, 103–44.

32. Greg Grandin, *Fordlandia*.

33. Ricardo Salvatore, "The Enterprise of Knowledge: Representational Machines of Informal Empire," in Joseph, LeGrand, and Salvatore, *Close Encounters of Empire*, 85.

34. Harpelle, "White Women on the Frontier."

35. On UFCO enclaves as contact zones, see Shragai, "Do Bananas Have a Culture?"

36. See Bourgois, *Ethnicity at Work*; and Colby, *The Business of Empire*.

37. Bucheli details this process of divestment in *Bananas and Business*, 58–85.

38. See Shragai, "Do Bananas Have a Culture?"

39. Bourgois lays out the continuity in such cultural blinders in "One Hundred Years of United Fruit Company Letters," in Striffler and Moberg, *Banana Wars*.

40. Ann Stoler, *Carnal Knowledge and Imperial Power*.

Chapter One

1. For literary depictions of the banana invasion, see in particular Guatemalan Nobel laureate Miguel Ángel Asturias's "banana trilogy": *Viento fuerte*, *El papa verde*, and *Los ojos de los enterrados*. See also Honduran P. Amaya Amador's *Prisión verde*; Costa Ricans Carlos Luis Fallas, *Mamita Yunai*, and Quince Duncan, *Dos novelas: Los cuatro espejos y La Paz del pueblo*; and Chilean poet Pablo Neruda's *Canto general*.

2. O. Henry, *Cabbages and Kings*.

3. Gabriel García Márquez, *Cien años de soledad*.

4. Frederick Upham Adams, *Conquest of the Tropics*, 306, 356. A series of articles in the employee newsmagazine *Unifruitco* during the 1920s propagated the message internally, as did Charles Morrow Wilson, *Empire in Green and Gold*. For an

analysis of racialist approaches to Latin American uplift and economic development in the early twentieth century, see Thomas F. O'Brien, *Making the Americas:
The United States and Latin America from the Age of Revolutions to the Era of Globalization*. On the roots of racial Anglo-Saxonism, see Reginald Horsman, *Race and Manifest Destiny*.

5. Watt Stewart, *Keith and Costa Rica*, 97.

6. Adams, *Conquest of the Tropics*, 55. See also Stewart, *Keith and Costa Rica*.

7. Lorenzo Dow Baker Sr. to Lorenzo Dow Baker Jr., 10 October 1885, p. 2,
Box 1, Lorenzo Dow Baker Papers, Cape Cod Community College Library, West
Barnstable, MA (hereafter LDBP).

8. Baker Sr. to Baker Jr., 23 November 1886, p. 3, Box 1, LDBP.

9. Ibid.

10. Andrew Preston to Baker Jr., 19 December 1891, p. 1, Box 5, LDBP.

11. For the development of banana grading standards and varieties on US markets in the early twentieth century, see John Soluri, *Banana Cultures*, 66–70.

12. Preston to Baker Jr., 23 July 1892, p. 4, Box 5, LDBP.

13. Baker Sr. to Baker Jr., 13 August 1887, p. 3, Box 1, LDBP. Bartlett documents Capt. Baker's attachment to Jamaica and his enduring belief that the island
should remain the main supply point for bananas, even after the formation of
United Fruit. W. Randolph Bartlett, "Lorenzo Dow Baker and the Development of
the Banana Trade between Jamaica and the United States, 1881–1890," 227.

14. Baker Sr. to Baker Jr., 16 January 1888, p. 2, Box 1, LDBP.

15. On vertical integration, see Alfred Chandler Jr., *Scale and Scope*, 37–38.

16. Baker Sr. to Baker Jr., 5 September 1885, p. 4, Box 1, LDBP.

17. Preston to Baker Jr., 28 June 1890, p. 3, Box 6, LDBP.

18. Preston to Baker Jr., 23 July 1892, p. 4, Box 5, LDBP.

19. Preston to Baker Jr., 16 October 1890, p. 2, Box 6, LDBP.

20. Preston to Baker Jr., 10 July 1891, p. 2, Box 5, LDBP.

21. For United Fruit's attempts to undermine competing fruit companies, see
Charles D. Kepner and Jay H. Soothill, *The Banana Empire*, 43–76, 286–314.

22. Preston to Baker Jr., 28 June 1890, p. 2, Box 6, LDBP.

23. W. J. Stover to Baker Jr., 27 August 1897, p. 2, Box 6, LDBP.

24. Wilson estimated that the hurricanes damaged five times more bananas
than the company exported, but his source is unclear. Charles Morrow Wilson,
Empire in Green and Gold, 103.

25. Stephen Hislop to Baker Jr., 22 August 1899, p. 6, Box 5, LDBP.

26. Hislop to Baker Jr., 27 December 1899, p. 3, Box 5, LDBP.

27. *Annual Report to Stockholders of the United Fruit Company* (hereafter
ARSUFC), 1900, 5.

28. *ARSUFC*, 1903, 5.

29. *ARFUFC*, 1904, 6–7.

30. See Kepner and Soothill, *The Banana Empire*, and Luis Montes and William Siegel, *Bananas*.

31. Soluri, *Banana Cultures*, 54. This is the definitive study of the environmental impact of banana production in the Caribbean.

32. For a study of these transformations, see Chandler, *Scale and Scope*. Recent scholarship emphasizes the role of vertically integrated corporations in creating far-flung, capital-intensive extractive geographies. See, for example, David Igler, *Industrial Cowboys*; César J. Ayala, *American Sugar Kingdom*; and Bucheli, *Bananas and Business*.

33. René de la Pedraja argues that United Fruit's proprietary fleet strategy was successful because the company could guarantee a stable flow of its own commodities through its routes. See his *The Rise and Decline of U.S. Merchant Shipping in the Twentieth Century*, 38–44.

34. Baker Sr. to Baker Jr., 13 August 1887, p. 3, Box 1, LDBP.

35. Baker Sr. to Baker Jr., 23 June 1886, p. 2, Box 1, LDBP.

36. Preston to Baker Jr., 13 June 1890, p. 3, Box 6, LDBP.

37. William Cronon details the effect of steam power on regional economies in *Nature's Metropolis*, 80–81.

38. Readers desiring a comprehensive survey of company shipping should consult Mark H. Goldberg's indispensable *"Going Bananas": 100 Years of American Fruit Ships in the Caribbean*.

39. I draw most of the technical data on banana shipping from Goldberg, *"Going Bananas,"* 528–95.

40. For the admiral class, see Goldberg, *"Going Bananas,"* 301, 305–7, and 529.

41. For the "mail boats" of the early 1930s, see Goldberg, *"Going Bananas,"* 437–43.

42. Pedraja, *The Rise and Decline of U.S. Merchant Shipping*, 39.

43. For tonnage figures, see *ARSUFC*, various years.

44. H. Harris Robson, "Going Down!" *Unifruitco*, July 1928, 711.

45. Hislop to Baker Jr., 13 December 1898, p. 2, Box 5, LDBP.

46. *ARSUFC*, 1902, 7.

47. Quoted in "Tales of the Great White Fleet: Refrigeration and the S. S. *Venus*," *Unifruitco*, April 1929, 528.

48. "Tales of the Great White Fleet: Refrigeration and the S. S. *Venus*," 530–32.

49. *ARSUFC*, 1904, 7.

50. United Fruit Company Steamship Service, *Cruising the Spanish Main*, 11.

51. Cecil Langlois to Baker Jr., 5 October 1891, p. 4, Box 6, LDBP.

52. Hislop to Baker Jr., 4 October 1898, p. 5, Box 5, LDBP.

53. Cronon, *Nature's Metropolis*, 79–80.

54. J. Mace Andress and Julia E. Dickson, *Radio Bound for Banana Land*, 24.

55. The impact of railroads on banana production echoes the dynamics of the

sugar complex in nineteenth-century Cuba. Sugar cane's susceptibility to drying after harvest set spatial limits to the island's plantation economy before the advent of steam. After the 1830s, steam power in railroads and sugar mills permitted the dramatic expansion of sugar cane cultivations into previously inaccessible areas. Oscar Zanetti and Alejandro García, *Sugar and Railroads: A Cuban History, 1837–1959*, trans. Franklin Knight and Mary Todd (Chapel Hill: University of North Carolina Press, 1998), and Martín Moreno Fraginals, *El ingenio*. Some United Fruit railroad infrastructure remains in use today. In Costa Rica, some of the company's trestles are still used to bridge canals and rivers. The small-gauge banana-train rails, cut into crosspieces, provide a bed for the asphalt of more recent highway construction.

56. *ARSUFC*, 1904, 10.

57. *ARSUFC*, 1913, 7.

58. *ARSUFC*, 1924, 8.

59. See Bucheli, *Bananas and Business*, 24–33; Soluri, *Banana Cultures*; and Virginia Scott Jenkins, *Bananas: An American History*.

60. Soluri, *Banana Cultures*, 68.

61. Alfred D. Chandler, *The Visible Hand*, 207–39.

Chapter Two

1. On the roots of Anglo-Saxonism as an ideological undergirding of US expansion, see Reginald Horsman, *Race and Manifest Destiny* and Paul A. Kramer, "Empires, Exceptions, and Anglo-Saxons."

2. Jason M. Colby, *The Business of Empire*, 6.

3. For discussion of the color bar as it functioned in Costa Rica, see Colby, *The Business of Empire*, 91–100; Philippe Bourgois also roots the company's racialized labor management "in the upper-class context of Boston's white Anglo-Saxon Protestant society" (*Ethnicity at Work*, 85). On the racial divisions within the North American workforce more broadly, see David R. Roediger, *The Wages of Whiteness*.

4. W. E. Mullins to James Coleman, 11 November 1908, folio 191, Instituto Costarricense del Ferrocarril #4965, Archivo Nacional de Costa Rica, San José (hereafter cited as INCOFER).

5. W. E. Mullins to H. S. Kennerly, 31 July 1913, folio 207, INCOFER #4855.

6. John Keith to Andrew Preston, 1 July 1904, folio 384, INCOFER #4973.

7. W. E. Mullins to James Coleman, 28 January 1907, folio 11, INCOFER #4965.

8. W. E. Mullins to James Coleman, 16 July 1907, folio 106, INCOFER #4965.

9. Harry Bestor, United Fruit Company Engineering Department, "Instructions for Field Engineers and Draftsmen," 1920, INCOFER #4959.

10. Victor Macomber Cutter Early Life Chronology and Description of United Fruit Company Employment, page 6, folder 8, box 1, Victor Macomber Cutter Papers, Rauner Special Collections Library, Dartmouth College, Hanover, NH (hereafter cited as VMCP).

11. Colby discusses Cutter's masculine prowess in *The Business of Empire*, 79–82.

12. Everett Brown to Ethel Brown, 8 May 1920, p. 3, Costa Rica Folder, Everett C. Brown Collection, Department of Special and Area Collections, Smathers Library, University of Florida, Gainesville (hereafter ECBC).

13. Ibid.

14. Prospero Alger, "Some Traits of Anglo-Saxon Character," *Unifruitco*, October 1925, 143.

15. John Stuart Erskine, "Jones," *Unifruitco*, August 1926, 27.

16. "The Effects of Tropical Light on White Men," unattributed editorial, *Journal of the American Medical Association* XLIV:21 (May 27, 1905), 1687; see also Dane Kennedy, "The Perils of the Midday Sun: Climatic Anxieties in the Colonial Tropics," in MacKenzie, ed., *Imperialism and the Natural World*, 118–40.

17. John M. Keith to Minor Cooper Keith, 25 May 1901, folio 905, INCOFER #4909, ANCR.

18. John M. Keith to Minor Cooper Keith, 5 December 1911, INCOFER #4915.

19. W. E. Mullins to Dr. R. Swigart, 19 August 1912, folio 57, INCOFER #4857.

20. For an analysis of the paternalistic aspects of the UFCO's medical department, see David Aliano, "Curing the Ills of Central America: The United Fruit Company's Medical Department and Corporate America's Mission to Civilize, 1900–1940."

21. William C. Gorgas, "The Conquest of the Tropics for the White Race."

22. Warwick Anderson, *Colonial Pathologies*, 103.

23. *Annual Report of the Medical Department of the United Fruit Company* (hereafter cited as *ARUFCMD*), 1922, 81.

24. See, for instance, *ARUFCMD*, 1922, 75–76, 80.

25. *ARUFCMD*, 1924, 46.

26. W. E. Mullins to E. McMurphy, 16 February 1907, folio 22, INCOFER #4965.

27. William E. Deeks, in *ARUFCMD*, 1923, 23, 24.

28. "Form 2536: United Fruit Company Health Certificate," *ARUFCMD*, 1916, 100–101.

29. William E. Deeks, "Letter of Transmittal," *ARUFCMD*, 1918, 10.

30. See, for example, "Comments on Some of the More Important Diseases Occurring in the Tropical Divisions," *ARUFCMD*, 1931, 4.

31. Company president Victor Cutter claimed that annual turnover among

salaried tropical employees stood around 60 percent in some divisions. "Introductory Address Delivered by Victor M. Cutter, President," *Unifruitco*, October 1927, 135.

32. "The Response of Different Races to Hot Climates," unattributed editorial, *Journal of the American Medical Association* LXV:7 (August 14, 1915), 627.

33. *ARUFCMD*, 1912, 53.

34. Frederick L. Hoffman, "The Problems of Morality and Acclimatization in the Central American Tropics," in United Fruit Company, *Proceedings of the International Conference on Health Problems in Tropical America*, 673.

35. John Keith to A. D. Rather, 26 August 1904, folio 161, INCOFER #4832.

36. W. E. Mullins to Chittenden, 30 July 1913, folio 191, INCOFER #4855.

37. W. E. Mullins to Minor Cooper Keith, 26 September 1906, folio 382, INCOFER #4986.

38. W. E. Mullins to C. Strasburger, 12 September 1906, folio 150, INCOFER #4986.

39. W. E. Mullins to C. J. Stevens, 25 September 1906, folio 327, INCOFER #4986.

40. W. E. Mullins to R. J. Schweppe, 25 September 1906, folio 368, INCOFER #4986.

41. Mullins to Keith, 26 September 1906.

42. W. E. Mullins to Charles Hubbard, 27 January 1907, folio 474, INCOFER #4823.

43. Mullins laid out these improvements in a lengthy letter to NRC traffic manager G. A. Norson, 26 September 1906, folio 375–381, INCOFER #4986.

44. W. E. Mullins to R. J. Schweppe, 29 September 1906, folio 434, INCOFER #4986.

45. W. E. Mullins to A. J. Shepherd, 27 April 1907, folio 30, INCOFER #4839.

46. Green, *The Canal Builders*, chapter 2.

47. W. E. Mullins to John Keefe, 21 May 1907, folio 464, INCOFER #4839.

48. W. E. Mullins to Robert Ford, 8 April 1907, folio 54, INCOFER #4965.

49. W. E. Mullins to John Keefe, 14 April 1907, folio 60, INCOFER #4965.

50. Colby, *The Business of Empire*.

51. W. E. Mullins to James Coleman, 9 August 1910, folio 350, INCOFER #4965.

52. Colby, *The Business of Empire*, 102–5.

53. E. Hitchcock to Minor Cooper Keith, 2 August 1910, folio 432, INCOFER # 4953.

54. W. E. Mullins to US Consul Samuel Lee, 3 August 1910, folio 438, INCOFER #4954.

55. W. E. Mullins to Minor Cooper Keith, 6 August 1910, folio 497, INCOFER #4953.

56. W. E. Mullins to E. D. Nash, 12 August 1910, folio 355, INCOFER #4965.

57. Mullins to Coleman, 9 August 1910.

58. W. E. Mullins to C. E. Soule, 29 August 1910, folio 18, INCOFER #4897.

59. Mullins to Nash, 12 August 1910.

60. Ibid.

61. Mullins to Soule, 29 August 1910.

62. Mullins to Coleman, 9 August 1910.

63. Salary figures for the farms are from E. Hitchcock to P. K. Reynolds, folio 183, 18 September 1911, INCOFER #4869; for the railroad, they are from Northern Railway Company General Manager's Report, 1919, folio 3, INCOFER #937.

64. Colby, *The Business of Empire*.

65. E. Hitchcock to Charles Hubbard, 22 July 1910, folio 282, INCOFER #4953.

66. E. Hitchcock to Charles Hubbard, 3 September 1909, folio 476, INCOFER #4833.

67. E. Hitchcock to Charles Hubbard, 1 August 1910, folio 417, INCOFER #4953.

68. Hitchcock to Hubbard, 22 July 1910.

69. Ibid.

70. Hitchcock to Hubbard, 1 August 1910.

71. Northern Railway Company General Manager's Report, 1919, p. 3, INCOFER #937.

72. Ibid., p. 41.

73. Ibid., pp. 3 and 41.

74. Northern Railway Company, Annual Report Year 1921, p. 4, INCOFER #2875.

75. M. M. Marsh, NRC Annual Report for 1923, folio 4, INCOFER #2969.

76. Everett Brown to Ethel Brown, 9 November 1919, p. 2, Cuba Folder, ECBC.

77. Everett Brown to Ethel Brown, 6 October 1919, p. 3–4, Cuba Folder, ECBC.

78. Everett Brown to Ethel Brown, 21 August 1919, p. 2, Cuba Folder, ECBC.

79. Everett Brown to Ethel Brown, 31 December 1919, p. 2, Cuba Folder, ECBC.

80. Everett Brown to Ethel Brown, 6 October 1919, p. 2–3, Cuba Folder, ECBC.

81. Everett Brown to Ethel Brown, 29 September 1919, p. 4, Cuba Folder, ECBC.

82. Brown to Brown, 6 November 1919, p. 7.

83. Brown to Brown, 9 November 1919, p. 2.

84. Everett Brown to Ethel Brown, 28 August 1919, p. 4, Cuba Folder, ECBC.

85. Everett Brown to Ethel Brown, 23 November 1919, p. 6, Cuba Folder, ECBC.

86. Everett Brown to Ethel Brown, 25 March 1920, p. 5., Panama 1 Folder, ECBC; Everett Brown to Ethel Brown to Ethel Brown, April 1920, p. 1., Panama 1 Folder, ECBC.

87. Everett Brown to Ethel Brown, 20 October 1919, p. 7, Cuba Folder, ECBC.

88. Everett Brown to Ethel Brown, 23 November 1919, p. 4, Cuba Folder, ECBC.

89. Everett Brown to Ethel Brown, 17 December 1919, p. 1, Cuba Folder, ECBC; Everett Brown to Ethel Brown, 5 February 1920, p. 3, Cuba Folder, ECBC.

90. Everett Brown to Ethel Brown, 31 December 1919, p. 1, Cuba Folder, ECBC.

91. Everett Brown to Ethel Brown, 12 January 1920, p. 2, Cuba Folder, ECBC.

92. Brown to Brown, 6 October 1919, p. 5.

93. W. E. Mullins to J. M. Kyes, 23 August 1912, folio 90, INCOFER #4857.

94. Everett Brown to Ethel Brown, 25 July 1920, p. 2, Panama 2 Folder, ECBC.

95. Ibid.

96. Everett Brown to Ethel Brown, 8 August 1920, p. 5, Panama 2 Folder, ECBC.

97. Marsh, "Annual Report for 1923," folio 5.

98. M. M. Marsh, "Annual Report, Year 1927," folio 23–24, INCOFER #2966; Victor M. Cutter, "Introductory Address Delivered by Victor M. Cutter, President," *Unifruitco*, October 1927, 135.

Chapter Three

1. Crowther, *Romance and Rise of the American Tropics*, 228.

2. Ibid., 197–98.

3. Ibid.

4. Ibid., 199.

5. See John S. Garner, *The Model Company Town* and Richard M. Candee, "Early New England Mill Towns of the Piscataqua River Valley," in Garner, *The Company Town*, 111–38.

6. On the rise of corporate welfarism, see Stuart Brandes, *American Welfare Capitalism, 1880–1940*; Roland Marchand, *Creating the Corporate Soul*; and Andrea Tone, *The Business of Benevolence*.

7. Garner, *The Model Company Town*, 43.

8. For the Illinois towns, see John S. Garner, "Leclaire Illinois: A Model Company Town"; and Stanley Buder, *Pullman*. Milton Hershey publicized his benevolence in *The Story of Hershey: The Chocolate and Cocoa Town and Central Hershey: The Sugar Town* (Hershey, Penn.: Hershey Chocolate Company, ca. 1920). For Hershey's Cuban operations, see Michael D'Antonio, *Hershey: Milton S. Hershey's Extraordinary Life of Wealth, Empire, and Utopian Dreams* (New York: Simon & Schuster, 2006), 160–68. On American company towns in Chile, see Thomas M. Klubock, *Contested Communities: Class, Gender, and Politics in Chile's El Teniente Copper Mine*.

9. Margaret Crawford, "The 'New' Company Town," *Perspecta* 30 (1999): 48–57.

10. From the early twentieth century into the 1960s, US and European

companies built similar infrastructure in remote southern-cone mining and sugar-cane areas. Olga Paterlini de Koch, "Company Towns of Chile and Argentina," in Garner, *The Company Town*, 207–32.

11. Ricardo D. Salvatore, "The Enterprise of Knowledge: Representational Machines of Informal Empire," in Joseph, LeGrand, and Salvatore, *Close Encounters of Empire*, 85.

12. David E. Nye, *American Technological Sublime*, xiii.

13. Nye, *American Technological Sublime*, 282–83.

14. Ibid., 43. Michael Adas concurs with this conclusion, and has documented how "technological imperatives" in US expansionism were solidly middle-class projects. See *Dominance by Design: Technological Imperatives and America's Civilizing Mission* (Cambridge: Belknap Press, 2006), 26.

15. On the Indian origins of terms like *verandah* and *bungalow* and their adoption by the British, see Anthony King, *Colonial Urban Development*, 90–91.

16. On ventilation and fears of stagnant interior spaces, see Philip, 60–61.

17. Curtin, *Death by Migration*, 138.

18. According to Adams, the company mandated that vegetation be cleared for 150 yards around all structures. Frederick Upham Adams, *Conquest of the Tropics*, 274.

19. Adams, *Conquest of the Tropics*, 272, 274.

20. W. E. Deeks, "Address of Welcome," in United Fruit Company, *Proceedings of the International Conference on Health Problems in Tropical America*, 1–5.

21. Deeks, "Address of Welcome," 3.

22. See Ron Harpelle, "White Women on the Frontier" and Ronald Harpelle, "White Zones: American Enclave Communities of Central America," in Gudmundson and Wolfe, *Blacks and Blackness in Central America*, 307–33. Two recent studies show that these divisions persisted into the 1950s. See Steve Striffler, "The Logic of the Enclave: United Fruit, Popular Struggle, and Capitalist Transformation in Ecuador," in Striffler and Moberg, *Banana Wars*, 171–90; and Cindy Forster, "'The Macondo of Guatemala': Banana Workers and National Revolutions in Tiquisate, 1944–1954," in Striffler and Moberg, *Banana Wars*, 191–228.

23. Crandall A. Shifflett, *Coal Towns*, 60–66; Paterlini de Koch, "Company Towns of Chile and Argentina," 210, 225; Margaret Crawford, "Earl S. Draper and the Company Town in the American South," in Garner, *The Company Town*, 146, 148, and 164; Leland M. Roth, "Company Towns in the Western United States," in Garner, *The Company Town*, 183–84; Thomas O'Brien, *The Revolutionary Mission*, 88–90; and John D. Porteous, "Social Class in Atacama Company Towns."

24. Porteous, "Social Class in Atacama Company Towns" and Striffler, "The Logic of the Enclave," 184.

25. Everett Brown to Ethel Brown, 20 October 1919, p. 7, Cuba Folder,

Everett C. Brown Collection, Department of Special and Area Collections, Smathers Library, University of Florida, Gainesville (hereafter ECBC).

26. Everett Brown to Ethel Brown, 6 November 1919, p. 3–4, Cuba Folder, ECBC.

27. Everett Brown to Ethel Brown, 9 December 1919, p. 6, Cuba Folder, ECBC.

28. See Luis Montes and William Seigel, *Bananas – The Fruit Empire* (New York: International Pamphlets, 1933), 6–7, 14, and Charles D. Kepner and Jay H. Soothill, *The Banana Empire*, 29–31.

29. O'Brien, *The Revolutionary Mission*, 89.

30. Verson W. Gooch, "Guatemala Has Another Good Year," *Unifruitco*, April 1927, 537.

31. Arthur J. Ruhl, *The Central Americans: Adventures and Impressions between Mexico and Panama* (New York: Charles Scribner's Sons, 1928), 270.

32. King, *Colonial Urban Development*, 142.

33. The policy of fostering unity and community among white employees stood in contrast with the company's approach to nonwhite labor. In the well-documented case of Costa Rica, the company exploited the racial and linguistic fault lines of its diverse work force in order to weaken organized labor. See Trevor W. Purcell, *Banana Fallout*.

34. Verson W. Gooch, "Una quincena en Almirante," *Unifruitco*, November 1926, 232.

35. Atalia Shragai, "Do Bananas Have a Culture?"

36. See evidence in Box 49 (Cuba-3), United Fruit Company Photograph Collection, Mss: 1 (1891–1962), U860, Baker Library, Harvard Business School (hereafter UFCPC).

37. On the softening of industrial landscapes with parks, see Garner, "LeClaire, Illinois," 223–24, and Margaret Crawford, *Building the Workingman's Paradise*, 64–65.

38. Brown to Brown, 19 March 1920, p. 7.

39. See James M. Mayo, *The American Country Club*.

40. King, *Colonial Urban Development*, 173.

41. Gooch, "Una quincena en Almirante," 231.

42. Everett Brown to Ethel Brown, n.d. [April 1920], p. 2, Panama Folder, ECBC.

43. Crawford, "Earl S. Draper and the Company Town," 146.

44. "Tropical Divisions: Castilla," *Unifruitco*, August 1926, 32.

45. Everett Brown to Ethel Brown, 19 March 1920, p. 6.

46. King, *Colonial Urban Development*, 141. On the display of social status in American country clubs, see Mayo, *The American Country Club*, 2–3.

47. Brown to Brown, 19 March 1920, p. 3.

48. Verson W. Gooch, "My Two Weeks in Colombia," *Unifruitco*, October 1926, 190.

49. Edmund Whitman, "Notes on Tropical Travel," *Unifruitco*, January–February 1927, 379.

50. "Listen to Dem Tela Tambourines," *Unifruitco*, January, 1926, 312.

51. For the origins of the Boy Scouts in an imperial context, see Allen Warren, "Citizens of the Empire: Baden-Powell, Scouts and Guides, and an Imperial Ideal," in *Imperialism and Popular Culture*, ed. John M. MacKenzie (Manchester: Manchester University Press, 1986), 232–56.

52. "Tela B.S.," *Unifruitco*, January 1926, 383.

53. Hubert Davis, "Scoutcraft in the Tropics," *Unifruitco*, July 1926, 775.

54. See for instance Gooch, "My Two Weeks in Colombia," 188–95; "Limón," *Unifruitco*, November 1926, 252–53; "Guatemala: Readin', Ritin', 'n' 'Rithmetic as expounded in Virginia," *Unifruitco*, August 1928, 35.

55. For the abusive practices of company stores, see Montes and Siegel, *Bananas* and Kepner and Soothill, *The Banana Empire*, 319–22.

56. Mack, "A New Resident's Impressions," 554. Typical of *Unifruitco* contributors, Mack omitted any mention of the notorious massacre of United Fruit laborers in Santa Marta in 1928.

57. See "Refrigerated Cargo," *Unifruitco*, December 1928, 294.

58. Herman Wacker, "A Caribbean Cruise: A Vacation on the *S. S. Santa Marta* with many interesting experiences at ports of call," *Unifruitco*, August 1927, 19.

59. Everett Brown to Ethel Brown, 17 December 1919, p. 2, Cuba Folder, ECBC.

60. Everett Brown to Ethel Brown, 31 December 1919, p. 2, Cuba Folder, ECBC.

61. Everett Brown to Ethel Brown, 24 September 1919, p. 4, Cuba Folder, ECBC.

62. Everett Brown to Ethel Brown, 20 October 1919, p. 4, Cuba Folder, ECBC.

63. Everett Brown to Ethel Brown, 4 July 1920, p. 6, Panama 2 Folder, ECBC.

64. Everett Brown to Ethel Brown, 29 October 1919, p. 4, Cuba Folder, ECBC.

65. "New York or the Tropics? Which Would You Select to Live in, If You Had Your Choice?" *Unifruitco*, June 1930, 651.

66. For insightful analyses of racial domination in UFCO enclaves, see Harpelle, "White Women on the Frontier" and Harpelle, "White Zones"; on domesticity in other US imperial contexts, see Amy Kaplan, *The Anarchy of Empire in the Making of U.S. Culture*, 33–34.

67. Verson W. Gooch, "Una quincena en Almirante," *Unifruitco*, November 1926, 236.

68. See, for example, "An Eventful Day for Puerto Castilla," *Unifruitco*, January–February 1927, 387.

69. "Second Annual Conference of the United Fruit Company and Subsidiary

Companies at Swampscott, Mass., October 5–6–7, 1927," *Unifruitco*, November 1927, 200.

70. How the company induced these women into tropical employment is unclear.

71. "The Castilla Sphinx," *Unifruitco*, September 1925, 92.

72. "Santa Marta," *Unifruitco*, December 1925, 303.

73. "Limon," *Unifruitco*, May 1926, 602.

74. *Unifruitco*, March 1928, 509.

75. Theodore A. Walters, "The Fairy Godmother, or – Godfather of the Unifruitco Club of New Orleans," *Unifruitco*, March 1929, 511.

76. Ibid.

77. Ibid.

78. *Unifruitco*, October 1926, 199.

79. "Barrios," *Unifruitco*, April 1926, 524.

80. For American social clubs in United Fruit divisions, see photographic evidence in Box 76 (Recreation [Welfare, Schools]), United Fruit Company Photograph Collection, Mss: 1 (1891–1962), U860, Baker Library, Harvard Business School.

81. "Truxillo," *Unifruitco*, April 1926, 528.

82. "Preston," *Unifruitco*, May 1926, 606.

83. William H. Fagen, "A Trip to Black River, Honduras," *Unifruitco*, May 1926, 580–81.

84. "Guatemala," *Unifruitco*, October 1925, 158–59.

85. "Tela," *Unifruitco*, February–March 1926, 468.

86. Mayo, *The American Country Club*, 87.

87. Adams, *Conquest of the Tropics*, 262.

88. Adams, *Conquest of the Tropics*, 250.

89. T. B. Wall, "The Importance of Physical Fitness," *Unifruitco*, June 1929, 690.

90. *Unifruitco*, September 1928, 96.

91. "Soccer Players of 1905," *Unifruitco*, January–February 1927, 394.

92. Cutter Early Life Chronology, Sheet 7, VMCP.

93. On the place of sport in US corporate welfare campaigns in the early twentieth century, see Marchand, *Creating the Corporate Soul*, 115–16; Stuart D. Brandes, *American Welfare Capitalism, 1880–1940*, 78–82; and Mitchell, *The Generous Corporation*, 24. For analyses of sport in company- or region-specific cases, see Margaret Crawford, "Earl S. Draper and the Company Town in the American South," in Garner, *The Company Town*, 153; Buder, *Pullman*, 124–25; and Clark Davis, *Company Men*, 190.

94. *Unifruitco*, September 1926, 105.

95. "Jamaica," *Unifruitco*, October 1926, 185.

96. "Preston," *Unifruitco*, June 1926, 689.

97. "Report on Baseball Game at Limon between Married and Single Men, May 20," *Unifruitco*, July 1928, 732.

98. Earle F. Currier, "How to Keep Fit in the Tropics," *Unifruitco*, April 1929, 557.

99. Currier, "How to Keep Fit," 558.

100. Everett Brown to Ethel Brown, 11 October 1919, p. 3, Cuba Folder, ECBC.

101. Brown's experience confirms Davis's argument that masculine "physical cultures" outside the workplace helped white-collar employees reconcile themselves to work in large corporations. Davis, *Company Men*, 145.

102. A. Garsaud, "Old Timer Talks," *Unifruitco*, July 1926, 760–64.

103. Since the late nineteenth century, US soldiers had carried baseball with them to occupations of the western frontier and the US overseas empire, although Pérez shows that Cubans had embraced the sport since the 1860s. See Louis A. Pérez, "Between Baseball and Bullfighting" and Rob Ruck, *The Tropic of Baseball: Baseball in the Dominican Republic* (Westport, CT: Meckler Publishing, 1991), 24.

104. Steven M. Gelber, "Working at Playing", 3.

105. Donald J. Mrozek, *Sport and American Mentality*, 173–75; Steven A. Riess, *Touching Base: Professional Baseball and American Culture in the Progressive Era*, rev. ed. (Urbana: University of Illinois Press, 1999), 24.

106. Mrozek, *Sport and American Mentality*, 174; Riess, *Touching Base*, 23.

107. Mrozek has discussed the arguments of sport commentators, who held that baseball helped nurture healthy civic values and national character—a cohesive effect that corporate leaders surely sought to harness in corporate welfare campaigns. *Sport and American Mentality*, 173–82.

108. For such matchups, see for example *Unifruitco*, January–February 1927, 386, and "Tela Baseball Team," *Unifruitco*, November 1926, 249.

109. *Unifruitco*, November 1926, 246.

110. Everett Brown to Ethel Brown, 1 September 1919, p. 4, Cuba Folder, ECBC; Everett Brown to Ethel Brown, 3 September 1919, p. 1, Cuba Folder, ECBC; and Everett Brown to Ethel Brown, 25 March 1920, p. 4, Panama Folder, ECBC.

111. Gooch, "Una quincena en Almirante," 235.

112. For a typical Fourth of July visit, see "Tela Visits Castilla," *Unifruitco*, September 1928, 89.

113. Quoted in *Unifruitco*, April 1929, 560.

114. Verson W. Gooch, "Three Weeks at Tela," *Unifruitco*, January–February 1927, 403.

115. Gooch, "My Two Weeks in Colombia," 193.

116. Allen Wells, "Conclusion: Dialectical Bananas," in Stiffler and Moberg, *Banana Wars*, 317.

117. My conclusions echo those of other researchers of the UFCO's white

communities. See Shragai, "Do Bananas Have a Culture?," 65–82; Harpelle, "White Women"; Harpelle, "White Zones," 307–33.

Chapter Four

1. The terms of the company's invitation to the conference were spelled out in the "Circular Letter to Guests Attending the International Conference on Health Problems in Tropical America To Be Held in Kingston, Jamaica," Box 34, Richard Pearson Strong Papers, Francis A. Countway Library of Medicine, Center for the History of Medicine, Harvard University. (Hereafter Strong Papers.)

2. William E. Deeks, "Activities of the Medical Department of the United Fruit Company," in United Fruit Company, *Proceedings of the International Conference on Health Problems in Tropical America*, 1006.

3. Deeks, "Activities of the Medical Department," 1008.

4. Ibid., 3, 1008.

5. On the topic of fugitive landscapes and populations in the face of modern practices of governance, see James Scott, *Seeing Like a State*; Raymond Craib, *Cartographic Mexico*; and Samuel Truett, *Fugitive Landscapes*.

6. Examples most relevant to the US experience with overseas empire include Mariola Espinosa, *Epidemic Invasions*; Warwick Anderson, *Colonial Pathologies*; Diego Armus, ed., *Disease in the History of Modern Latin America*; and Nancy Leys Stepan, *Picturing Tropical Nature*.

7. See David Aliano, "Curing the Ills of Central America." For a history of one company hospital in particular, see Clyde Stevens, *A History of Punta Hospital* (Leesburg, Flor.: Leesburg Printing Company, 1997).

8. Alexander Butchart, *The Anatomy of Power*, ix.

9. Deeks, "Activities of the Medical Department," 1007.

10. Annual Report of the United Fruit Company Medical Department (hereafter cited as ARUFCOMD), 1924, 17–20.

11. Deeks, "Activities of the Medical Department," 1008.

12. ARUFCOMD, 1922, 84.

13. ARUFCOMD, 1925, 170.

14. Michael Worboys, "Germs, Malaria, and the Invention of Mansonian Tropical Medicine: From 'Diseases in the Tropics' to 'Tropical Diseases,'" in Arnold, *Warm Climates and Western Medicine*, 193.

15. Charles C. Mann, *1493: Uncovering the World Columbus Created*, 131, 143–44; and Randall M. Packard, *The Making of a Tropical Disease*, 84–88.

16. John Soluri has shown that the company's expansion in response to plant disease placed workers in closer contact with malaria-prone environments. *Banana Cultures*, 141.

17. Packard, *The Making of a Tropical Disease*, 84.

18. For an examination of such human and insect "hybrid causation," see Brett Walker, *Toxic Archipelago*, 22–44. On the interconnection between patterns of consumption in the United States and changing geographies of production in Central America, see Soluri, *Banana Cultures*.

19. ARUFCOMD, 1912, 34, 16.

20. ARUFCOMD, 1921, 11.

21. ARUFCOMD, 1922, 85.

22. Packard, *The Making of a Tropical Disease*, 118–19.

23. N. P. McPhail, "Plasmochin as an Aid in Malaria Prevention in Guatemala," ARUFCOMD, 1930, 29–32; W. Thonnard-Neumann, "The Treatment of Malaria with Erion (Atebrin), a New Synthetic Drug–Report of 75 Cases," ARUFCOMD, 1931, 57–69. For a discussion of synthetic antimalarials, see Steven R. Meshnick and Mary J. Dobson, "The History of Antimalarial Drugs," in Rosenthal, *Antimalarial Chemotherapy: Mechanisms of Action, Resistance, and New Directions in Drug Discovery*, 20.

24. P. S. Malaret, "The Control of Malaria in Preston," ARUFCOMD, 1928, 83.

25. William E. Deeks, in ARUFCOMD, 1925, 185.

26. William E. Deeks, "Program of Malaria Control," ARUFCOMD, 1928, 98.

27. J. R. Maltsberger, "Malarial Preventive Measures as Applied in the Chiriqui Land Company," ARUFCOMD, 1929, 84.

28. For the Medical Department's recapitulation of the campaign in the last annual report, see "Comments on Some of the More Important Diseases Occurring in the Tropical Divisions," ARUFCOMD, 1931, 18.

29. "Comments on Some of the More Important Diseases Occurring in the Tropical Divisions," ARUFCOMD, 1931, 21–23.

30. H. C. Clark, "Laboratory Report of Tela Hospital," ARUFCOMD, 1924, 173.

31. Scott, *Seeing Like a State*, 2.

32. ARUFCOMD, 1920, 12.

33. S. B. Strong, in ARUFCOMD, 1915, 108.

34. ARUFCOMD, 1922, 136.

35. W. M. James, "A Survey for Amoebiasis at Santa Marta, Colombia," ARUFCOMD, 1925, 162.

36. Deeks, in ARUFCOMD, 1922, 8.

37. Butchart, *The Anatomy of Power*, 95; for a discussion of the American laboratory as a technology of colonial power, see also Anderson, *Colonial Pathologies*, 111–14.

38. ARUFCOMD, 1924, 28.

39. Warwick Anderson, "'Where Every Prospect Pleases and Only Man Is Vile': Laboratory Medicine as Colonial Discourse," *Critical Inquiry* 18:3 (Spring 1992): 519; and Alexandra Minna Stern, "The Public Health Service in the Panama Canal:

A Forgotten Chapter of US Public Health," *Public Health Reports* 120:6 (November/December 2005): 677.

40. Anderson, "'Where Every Prospect Pleases and Only Man Is Vile,'" 521.

41. ARUFCOMD, 1926, 17

42. ARUFCOMD, 1922, 84.

43. On transnational networks of knowledge production in Latin America, see Ricardo Salvatore, *Los lugares del saber.*

44. William C. Gorgas, *Sanitation in Panama*, 238; W. E. Deeks and W. M. James, *A Report on Hemoglobinuric Fever in the Canal Zone, A Study of Its Etiology and Treatment* (Mount Hope, Panama: Isthmian Canal Commission Department of Sanitation, 1911).

45. For a hagiographic treatment of Deeks's life and career, see Charles Morrow Wilson, *Ambassadors in White.*

46. William C. Gorgas, *Sanitation in Panama*, 209–14.

47. William E. Deeks to Victor M. Cutter, in ARUFCOMD, 1925, 9.

48. Richard P. Strong, "Report to the Faculty," p. 3, Box 33, Strong Papers.

49. Kristine A. Campbell, "Knots in the Fabric."

50. See, for instance, ARUFCOMD, 1928, 297–98.

51. Anderson, *Colonial Pathologies*, 75.

52. William E. Deeks, "Address of Welcome," in United Fruit Company, *Proceedings of the International Conference on Health Problems in Tropical America*, 2.

53. Deeks, "Problems of Preventive Medicine in the Tropics," 298.

54. Otto Brosius, "Functional Disorders Attributable to Tropical Sunlight," ARUFCOMD, 1925, 280–85.

55. On the melding of public health and US interest in the Caribbean, see Espinosa, *Epidemic Invasions.*

56. Deeks, "Problems of Preventive Medicine in the Tropics," 298.

57. For a penetrating analysis of the role of representations in US constructions of Latin America, see Ricardo D. Salvatore, *Imágenes de un imperio.*

58. Mark Carey, "Inventing Caribbean Climates," 135; David Arnold, *Colonizing the Body*, 42–43; and David Livingston, "Tropical Climate and Moral Hygiene," 104–8.

59. Paul Sutter, "Nature's Agents or Agents of Empire?" 733.

60. Anderson, *Colonial Pathologies*, 96–97.

61. For a superb examination of how medicine intertwined with forms of cultural expression to rearticulate "tropicality," see Nancy Leys Stepan, *Picturing Tropical Nature*, 149–79.

62. ARUFCMD, 1912, 34–35.

63. Scott, *Seeing Like a State.*

64. ARUFCMD, 1924, 47–51.

65. ARUFCMD, 1924, 101.

66. On this transition in the Philippines, see Anderson, *Colonial Pathologies*, 103.

67. Deeks, "Problems of Preventive Medicine in the Tropics," 312.

68. William E. Deeks, ARUFCOMD, 1925, 18.

69. On the challenges of labor recruitment in tropical agriculture in the postemancipation Caribbean, see Barry Carr, "'Omnipotent and Omnipresent'?: Labour Shortages, Worker Mobility, and Employer Control in the Cuban Sugar Industry," in Chomsky and Lauria-Santiago, *Identity and Struggle at the Margins of the Nation-State*, 260–91; and Philippe Bourgois, "Ethnic Diversity on a Corporate Plantation: The United Fruit Company in Bocas del Toro, Panama and Talamanca, Costa Rica" (PhD diss., Stanford University, 1985).

70. On the company's effort to maintain a racially segmented workforce and its response to various nationalist pressures to exclude black labor, see Bourgois, "Ethnic Diversity," and Jason Colby, *The Business of Empire*.

71. ARUFCOMD, 1920, 6.

72. ARUFCOMD, 1922, 74.

73. ARUFCOMD, 1923, 45.

74. See Frederick Pike, *The United States and Latin America*; and John Johnson, *Latin America in Caricature* (Austin: University of Texas Press, 1980).

75. Alfred Gage, "The Machete Versus the Microbe in Central America," ARUFCOMD, 1926, 205.

76. Gage, "The Machete Versus the Microbe," 209.

77. W. A. Hutchinson, "Review of Machete Wounds Treated during 1927," ARUFCOMD; and Ricardo Aguilar, "The Surgical Treatment of Machete Wounds," ARUFCOMD, 1928, 232.

78. Gage, "The Machete Versus the Microbe," 205, 206.

79. José A. López, "The Lower Class of Tropical American Patients," ARUFCOMD, 1930, 163–68.

80. Anderson, *Colonial Pathologies*, 92.

81. William E. Deeks, in ARUFCOMD, 1922, 9.

82. Charles A. Kofoid, Olive Swezy, and Luther M. Boyers, "A Report on an Investigation of Intestinal Protozoan Infections at Santa Marta, Colombia, in the Hospital of the United Fruit Company, with Special Reference to the Incidence of Amoebiasis," ARUFCOMD, 1925, 151, 152.

83. Kofoid, et al., "A Report on an Investigation of Intestinal Protozoan Infections," 148–49.

84. "Amoebic Dysentery," ARUFCOMD, 1925, 115.

85. Kofoid, et al., "A Report on an Investigation of Intestinal Protozoan Infections," 151.

86. R. B. Nutter, in ARUFCOMD, 1930, 10.

87. ARUFCOMD, 1922, 95; Deeks, "Problems of Preventive Medicine in the Tropics," 301.

88. ARUFCOMD, 1916, 79; "Venereal Diseases," ARUFCOMD, 1925, 30.

89. William E. Deeks, in ARUFCOMD, 1925, 18.

90. William E. Deeks, in ARUFCOMD, 1923, 12.

91. Deeks, "Problems of Preventive Medicine in the Tropics," 301.

92. "Comments on Some of the Chief Tropical Diseases and Their Treatment," ARUFCOMD, 1922, 47.

93. For these anxieties in particular, see ARUFCOMD, 1930, 11 and ARUF-COMD, 1928, 28.

94. J. R. Ariza, report cited in "Typhoid Fever," ARUFCOMD, 1928, 27.

95. T. de la Torre, "A District Medical Officer's Annual Report," ARUFCOMD, 1930, 60.

96. J. R. Maltsberger, "Malarial Preventive Measures as Applied in the Chiriqui Land Company," ARUFCOMD, 1929, 81.

97. Marcelo Bucheli, *Bananas and Business*, 123, 126.

98. Two researchers from the US Public Health Service, working with company doctors in Honduras, identified nocturnal worker socialization as a serious obstacle to preventing malaria. M. A. Barber and W. H. W. Komp, "Report on Some Malaria Work Done in the Tela and Guatemala Divisions, January–February 1925," ARUF-COMD, 1924, 218.

99. Aviva Chomsky, "Afro-Jamaican Tradition and Labour Organizing on United Fruit Company Plantations in Costa Rica."

100. For one example of multivalent imaging practices, see Howard Fox, "Carate (Pinta) as Observed in Colombia, South America," ARUFCOMD, 1928, 156–71.

101. Deeks, "Problems of Preventive Medicine in the Tropics," 312.

102. For the construction of the tropical/temperate distinction through medical representations, see Stepan, *Picturing Tropical Nature*, 149–79. The circulation of medical representations formed part of a burgeoning apparatus of display in the United States encompassing exhibitions, museums, films, and popular literature. See Robert Rydell, *All the World's a Fair*; Steven Conn, *Museums in American Life*; Gilbert Joseph, Catherine LeGrand, and Ricardo Salvatore, *Close Encounters of Empire*.

103. Randall Packard, "The Invention of the 'Tropical Worker.'"

104. See Anderson, *Colonial Pathologies*; and Espinosa, *Epidemic Invasions*.

105. Deeks, "Address of Welcome," 5.

Chapter Five

1. Everett Brown to Ethel Brown, 17 August 1919, pp. 3–4, Cuba File,

Everett C. Brown Collection, Department of Special and Area Collections, Smathers
Library, University of Florida, Gainesville (hereafter cited as ECBC).

2. Several recent studies situate the formation of masculine identities at the
center of US imperial projects in the tropics. See, for instance, Amy Kaplan, *The
Anarchy of Empire in the Making of US Culture*; Kristin Hogansen, *Fighting for American Manhood*; Mary Renda, *Taking Haiti*; and Warwick Anderson, *Colonial
Pathologies*.

3. Colby, *The Business of Empire*, p. 3.

4. For studies of American colonies in extractive enclaves, see Thomas
O'Brien, *The Revolutionary Mission*, and Greg Grandin, *Fordlandia*. Demographic
information is drawn from the United Fruit Company Medical Department Annual
Report, published from 1912 to 1931 (hereafter UFCMDAR). The numbers are
approximate, due to the company's shifting definitions of whiteness. (In 1924,
Medical Department doctors jettisoned a white/colored division in favor of the
temperate/other binary, which better enabled them to statistically isolate white
persons born in temperate zones from those born in the tropics.) For remarks on
poor retention, see "Introductory Address Delivered by Victor M. Cutter, President," *Unifruitco*, October 1927, p. 135.

5. "Introductory Address Delivered by Victor M. Cutter," 134.

6. On early twentieth-century middle-class masculinities, see Gail Bederman,
Manliness and Civilization, and Anthony Rotundo, *American Manhood*. For discussion
of anxieties about white-collar work and overcivilization, see T. J. Jackson Lears,
No Place of Grace, 3–58.

7. Richard Slotkin, *Gunfighter Nation*, 38.

8. For a portrayal of United Fruit as a triumph of white racial energies, see
Frederick Upham Adams, *Conquest of the Tropics*, and Colby, *The Business of Empire*,
2–3. On the western frontier in US popular culture at home, see Richard Slotkin,
Gunfighter Nation, 38. On the overseas career of the frontier, see Robert Rydell and
Rob Kroes, *Buffalo Bill in Bologna*. For an examination of frontier engineer heroes in
popular literature, see Ruth Oldenziel, *Making Technology Masculine*, 119–47. On
"barbarian virtues," see Matthew Frye Jacobson, *Barbarian Virtues*.

9. Everett Brown to Ethel Brown, 24 September 1919, p. 3, Cuba File, ECBC.

10. Ibid.; Everett Brown to Ethel Brown, 10 October 1919, p. 4, Cuba File,
ECBC; Everett Brown to Ethel Brown, 24 September 1919, p. 4; Everett Brown to
Ethel Brown, 13 June 1920, p. 3, Panama File no. 2, ECBC.

11. Everett Brown to Ethel Brown, 8 May 1920, p. 3, Costa Rica File, ECBC. In
the early twentieth-century United States, some white male university students
took up strikebreaking as an extracurricular activity; like Brown, they constructed
their masculine selves in part through confrontation with working-class others.
Stephen Norwood, "The Student as Strikebreaker: College Youth and the Crisis of

Masculinity in the Early Twentieth Century." Everett Brown to Ethel Brown, June 27, 1920, p. 3, Panama File, ECBC; Brown to Brown, 8 May 1920, p. 3.

12. Ruth Oldenziel, *Making Technology Masculine*, 119–47; Everett Brown to Ethel Brown, 26 December 1919, p. 4–5, Cuba File, ECBC; Everett Brown to Ethel Brown, March, 1920, p. 4, Miscellaneous File no. 2, ECBC.

13. Everett Brown to Ethel Brown, 27 April 1920, p. 3, Panama File no. 1, ECBC; Everett Brown to Ethel Brown, 1 May 1920, p. 1, Costa Rica File, ECBC.

14. On the culture of white-collar work in the United States, see Clark Davis, *Company Men*.

15. Everett Brown to Ethel Brown, 14 October 1919, p. 3–4, Cuba File, ECBC; Everett Brown to Ethel Brown, 9 December 1919, p. 3, 7; Everett Brown to Ethel Brown, 17 August 1919, p. 4; Everett Brown to Ethel Brown, 19 June 1920, p. 4, Panama File no. 2, ECBC.

16. Everett Brown to Ethel Brown, 17 August 1919, p. 4; Everett Brown to Ethel Brown, 9 December 1919, p. 3, Cuba File, ECBC.

17. See Adams, *Conquest of the Tropics* and Victor M. Cutter, "Caribbean Tropics in Commercial Transition"; Everett Brown to Ethel Brown, 9 December 1919, p. 1; Everett Brown to Ethel Brown, 15 April 1920, p. 2, Panama File no. 1, ECBC; Everett Brown to Ethel Brown, 1 May 1920, p. 1; and Everett Brown to Ethel Brown, May 1920, p. 1, Costa Rica File, ECBC; Everett Brown to Ethel Brown, 8 May 1920, p. 4, Costa Rica File, ECBC; Everett Brown to Ethel Brown, 27 June 1920, p. 3, Panama File no. 2, ECBC.

18. Ethel Brown to Everett Brown, 6 June 1920, pp. 9, 11, 2–3, Miscellaneous File no. 2, ECBC.

19. Everett Brown to Ethel Brown, 8 August 1920, p. 1, Panama File no. 2, ECBC; Everett Brown to Ethel Brown, 4 August 1920, p. 2, Panama File no. 2, ECBC; Everett Brown to Ethel Brown, 5 September 1920, p. 4, Panama File no. 2, ECBC; Everett Brown to Ethel Brown, 12 August 1920, pp. 3–4, Panama File no. 2, ECBC.

20. Victor Macomber Cutter Early Life Chronology and Description of United Fruit Company Employment, Sheet 2, Folder 8, Box 1, Victor Macomber Cutter Papers, MS 63, Rauner Special Collections Library, Dartmouth College; Roland Marchand, *Creating the Corporate Soul*, 15–17.

21. "Early Days," *Unifruitco*, December 1928, 269; Victor Macomber Cutter Early Life Chronology; "Address at Third Annual Dinner by Victor M. Cutter, President, United Fruit Company at Swampscott, Massachusetts, October 7, 1927," *Unifruitco*, November 1927, 137.

22. R. V. Howley, "Snapping out of a Grouch," *Unifruitco*, August 1925, 12; G. C. Noble, "Facts and Fiction: Extracts from a Newcomer"s First Letter Home," *Unifruitco*, October 1925, 155.

23. Howley, "Snapping out of a Grouch," 12.

24. Reproduction of *The Banana Herders Gazook*, in *Unifruitco*, April 1926, 521.

25. Joseph W. Cole, "Porthole Observations of the Banana Cowboy," *Unifruitco*, April 1926, 553; George H. Cox, "Shall I Go to the Tropics?: Part 4," *Unifruitco*, April 1926, 505.

26. "The Race Meet at Puerto Castilla," *Unifruitco*, January 1926, 381; Verson W. Gooch, "Una quincena en Almirante," *Unifruitco*, November 1926, 236.

27. Tina Loo, "Of Moose and Men: Hunting for Masculinities in British Columbia, 1880–1939," 302.

28. Ibid., 296.

29. R. B. Nutter to Richard P. Strong, 21 December 1923, p. 2, United Fruit–Nutter Folder, Box 34, Richard Pearson Strong Papers, Countway Library of Medicine, Cambridge, MA.

30. *Unifruitco*, April 1928, 548.

31. "Fishing in and around Almirante Bay," *Unifruitco*, January–February 1927, 408.

32. Ibid.

33. Alanson D. Morehouse, "Egrets and Aigrettes," *Unifruitco*, July 1927, 706.

34. Ibid.

35. "Like Father—Like Son," *Unifruitco*, August 1930, 31.

36. For an exposition of the tropical tramp culture, see Harry L. Foster, *The Adventures of a Tropical Tramp*, and Buckner Beasley, "The Tropical Tramps," *Unifruitco*, November 1927, 239. Renato Rosaldo, "Imperialist Nostalgia," 108. On the feminization of landscape in imperial discourses, see David Spurr, *The Rhetoric of Empire*, 170–83; and Anne McClintock, *Imperial Leather*.

37. Eric Hobsbawm and Terence Ranger, eds., *The Invention of Tradition*, 1; Beasley, "The Tropical Tramps," 239; "On the Road to Rincon Bay," *Unifruitco*, October 1926, 181.

38. On the emergence of homesickness as a potentially debilitating medical condition in the early twentieth-century United States, see Susan J. Matt, "You Can't Go Home Again"; Howley, "Snapping out of a Grouch," 13; Cox, "Shall I Go to the Tropics? Part 4," 505.

39. Victor Cutter, quoted in Bruce Barton, "A Big Human Fellow Named Cutter," *Unifruitco*, September 1925, 66; UFCMDAR, 1921, 109; Howley, "Snapping out of a Grouch," 12; Cox, "Shall I Go to the Tropics?: Part 4," 505; Cox, "Shall I Go to the Tropics?: Part 1," *Unifruitco*, December 1925, 270. H. M. Walker, "Lobar Pneumonia," UFCMDAR, 1925, 206.

40. Cox, "Shall I Go to the Tropics?: Part 1," 270; Cox, "Shall I Go to the Tropics?: Part 4," 505.

41. V. E. Fewell, "An Indoor Overseer who came to the tropics to seek an Outdoor Life," *Unifruitco*, August 1926, 45.

42. Ethel Brown to Everett Brown, June 6, 1920, pp. 9, 11, Miscellaneous File no. 2, ECBC.

43. Bryce Traister, "Academic Viagra," 299.

Chapter Six

1. Diane Stanley, *For the Record*, 146.

2. F. L. S., "A Visit to Some American Antiquities," p. 103, article manuscript in Box 3, Victor Macomber Cutter Papers, Rauner Special Collections Library, Dartmouth College (hereafter VMCP).

3. On the Archaeological Institute of America's excavations during the 1910s, see Neil M. Judd, "The Use of Glue Molds in Reproducing Aboriginal Monuments at Quirigua, Guatemala"; Stanley, *For the Record*, 146–47.

4. Judd, "The Use of Glue Molds," 128.

5. On scientific networks in imperial contexts, see John MacKenzie, *Imperialism and the Natural World*; Thierry Hoquet, "Botanical Authority"; Jim Endersby, *Imperial Nature*; Daniel Goldstein, "Outposts of Science"; Felix Driver and Luciana Martins, *Tropical Visions in an Age of Empire*.

6. On the importance of amateur networks, see for instance Bernard Lightman and Gowan Dawson, *Victorian Scientific Naturalism*; Azadeh Achbari, "Building Networks for Science"; Regina Horta Duarte, "Between the National and the Universal"; Deborah J. Neill, *Networks in Tropical Medicine*; and Karita Philips, "Imperial Science Rescues a Tree." Megan Raby's recent work on the history of tropical biology in the Americas does much to clarify the institutional networks of the which the UFCO was part. See "Making Biology Tropical."

7. Foundational research linking the production of Western knowledge and colonialism can be found in Edward Said, *Orientalism*; and Mary Louise Pratt, *Imperial Eyes*. See also Roy MacLeod, ed. *Nature and Empire: Science and the Colonial Enterprise*, Osiris, 2nd ser, 15 (Chicago: University of Chicago Press, 2000); Paolo Palladino and Michael Worboys, "Science and Imperialism"; and Michael Reidy and Helen Rozwadowski, "The Spaces in Between." For works that place science at the heart of Latin America's relationship with Europe and North America, see Paula de Vos, "Natural History and the Pursuit of Empire in Eighteenth-Century Spain"; Jorge Cañizares-Esguerra, *Nature, Empire, and Nation*; Camilo Quintero Toro, *Birds of Empire, Birds of Nation*; Laura Briggs, *Race, Sex, Science, and U.S. Imperialism in Puerto Rico*; Robert Aguirre, *Informal Empire*. For an analysis of US archaeological institutions in the early twentieth century, see Thomas Patterson, *Toward a Social History of Archaeology in the United States*, especially chapter 3.

8. Salvatore borrows the notion of "representational machine" from Stephen Greenblatt, himself keenly interested in the relationship between representational

cultures and European expansion; see Stephen Greenblatt, *Marvelous Possessions*. On the influence of US academics in the region, see Ricardo Salvatore, *Disciplinary Conquest*.

9. Robert Rydell, *All the World's A Fair*.

10. Ricardo Salvatore, *Imágenes de un imperio*, 101–19; Helen Delpar, *Looking South*; Helen Delpar, *The Enormous Vogue of Things Mexican*.

11. For works that decenter scientific inquiry and incorporate the role of amateur practitioners, see for instance Henrika Kuklick and Robert Kohler, *Science in the Field*, Osiris, 2nd series, 11 (Chicago: University of Chicago Press, 1996); and Daniel Goldstein, "Outposts of Science."

12. Victor Macomber Cutter Early Life Chronology and Description of United Fruit Company Employment, p. 6, folder 8, box 1, VMCP.

13. Ibid.

14. Ibid.

15. Ibid., p. 7, folder 8, box 1, VMCP.

16. Sylvanus G. Morley, *Guide Book to the Ruins of Quirigua*.

17. Morley, *Guide Book to the Ruins of Quirigua*, 12; Stanley, *For the Record*, 146–47.

18. Morley, *Guide Book to the Ruins of Quirigua*, 3.

19. For research examining international networks and the generation of knowledge, see Ricardo Salvatore, *Los lugares del saber*.

20. Salvatore, *Los lugares del saber*, 12. For details about the glue-mold process of reproducing stelae, see Neil M. Judd, "The Use of Glue Molds in Reproducing Aboriginal Monuments at Quirigua, Guatemala."

21. Molly Lee, "Tourism and Taste Cultures: Collecting Native Art in Alaska at the Turn of the Twentieth Century," in Phillips and Steiner, *Unpacking Culture*, 267–81; on collecting and colonial practice, see Bernard S. Cohn, *Colonialism and Its Forms of Knowledge*; especially chapter 4.

22. Cutter Early Life Chronology, p. 7.

23. Deborah T. Haynes, e-mail message to author, April 1, 2015.

24. On "authenticity" and its central role in modern mass tourism, see Dean MacCannell, *The Tourist: A New Theory of the Leisure Class*, 91–105.

25. The indifference of locals to the ruins and artifact in their midst was a trope in US anthropological thought at the time. See Delpar, *Looking South*, 52–72.

26. Watt Stewart, *Keith and Costa Rica*, 168.

27. M. Carrington, "The Aborigines of Banes," *Unifruitco*, February–March 1926, 418–19.

28. Ibid., 419.

29. Ibid., 421, 423.

30. Wilson Popenoe, "Regional Differences in the Guatemalan Huipil," *Annaes do XX Congreso Internacional de Americanistas, 20 a 30 de agosto de 1922*, 217–20.

31. Dorothy Popenoe, "The Ulua River," *Unifruitco*, January–February 1927, 368–70; Wilson and Dorothy Popenoe, "Quiriguá: An Ancient City of the Mayas," *Unifruitco*, May 1927, 564–73; Wilson and Dorothy Popenoe, "The Human Background of Lancetilla," *Unifruitco*, August 1931, 19–25.

32. Frederick Rosengarden, *Wilson Popenoe*, 105–9.

33. Popenoe and Popenoe, "The Human Background of Lancetilla," 19–25.

34. Rosemary A. Joyce, "Dorothy Hughes Popenoe: Eve in an Archaeological Garden," in Cheryl Claassen, *Women in Archaeology*, 64.

35. Daniel Schávelzon, "Dorothy Hugues Popenoe (1899–1932) en la arqueología de América Central," *Cuadernos de arquitectura mesoamericana* 14 (1991): 93–95.

36. Dorothy Popenoe, *Santiago de los Caballeros de Guatemala*.

37. Christina Luke, "Diplomats, Banana Cowboys, and Archaeologists in Western Honduras," 39.

38. For an in-depth discussion of the role of the UFCO in Honduran archaeology in the 1920s and 1930s, see Luke, "Diplomats, Banana Cowboys, and Archaeologists," 39–45; and Darío Euraque, "Antropólogos, arqueólogos, imperialismo, y la mayanización de Honduras, 1890–1940."

39. Popenoe, "The Ulua River," 370.

40. "The Ulua Society," *Unifruitco*, February–March 1926, 470.

41. Ibid.

42. By the mid-1930s, the once-robust research station at Lancetilla had been reduced to three scientists on the orders of Samuel Zemurray, who "thought little of professional scientists." John Soluri, *Banana Cultures*, 106.

43. "The Ulua Society," 471.

44. Ibid., 472.

45. Ibid., 471.

46. Ibid.

47. Marston Bates Journal, 2 Oct 1930, 90, Marston Bates Papers, Bentley Historical Library, University of Michigan, Ann Arbor (hereafter MBP).

48. Marston Bates Journal, 2 October 30, 90.

49. Bates Journal, 30 September 1930, 89.

50. Brunkard-Bates Expedition Journal, October 1930, p. 97, MBP.

51. Ibid.

52. Brunkard-Bates Expedition Journal, October 1930, pp. 95–96, MBP.

53. Brunkard-Bates Expedition Journal, October 1930, p. 100, MBP.

54. See Bates Journal, 1 January–10 March 1931, pp. 117–66, Box 15, MBP.

55. Leah Dilworth, *Imagining Indians in the Southwest*, 3.

56. Brunkard-Bates Expedition Journal, October 1930, p. 92, MBP.

57. Brunkard-Bates Expedition Journal, October 1930, p. 99, MBP.

58. Brunkard-Bates Expedition Journal, October 1930, p. 97, MBP.

59. F. H. Baron, "A Journey in the Jungle," *Unifruitco*, May 1927, 575.

60. Marcelo Bucheli, *Bananas and Business*, 24–43; and Soluri, *Banana Cultures*, 52–55.

61. For a fine survey of the Victorian tradition of colonial exploration, see Peter Raby, *Bright Paradise*. Robert D. Aguirre focuses more tightly on Latin America in *Informal Empire*. For early twentieth-century expeditions in Latin America, see Candace Millard, *River of Doubt*; and David Grann, *The Lost City of Z*. For other expeditions into the Isthmus of Panama, see Stanley Heckadon-Moreno, *Selvas entre dos mares*.

62. Marsh, "Blond Indians of the Darien Jungle," and "The Mystery of the White Indians."

63. Marsh, "Blond Indians of the Darien Jungle," 483. For an excellent analysis of Marsh's expeditions and his role in an indigenous uprising in 1925, see James Howe, *A People Who Would Not Kneel*, 199–300.

64. Marsh, "Blond Indians of the Darien Jungle," 489.

65. Grann, *The Lost City of Z*.

66. Baron, "A Journey in the Jungle," 578.

67. For a useful analysis of paternalism in the context of US overseas empire, see Mary Renda, *Taking Haiti*, 13–18.

68. Baron, "A Journey in the Jungle," 580.

69. On Marsh's expeditions and subsequent US tour with the white Indians, see Howe, *A People Who Would Not Kneel*, 200–253.

70. F. H. Baron, "Just People – On a Trip," *Unifruitco*, December 1926, 308.

71. Baron, "A Journey in the Jungle," 577.

72. Howe, *A People Who Would Not Kneel*, 262.

73. Baron, "A Journey in the Jungle," 576.

74. Pratt refers to such logical legerdemain as a discourse of anticonquest in *Imperial Eyes*, 56.

75. Baron, "A Journey in the Jungle," 582.

76. Ibid.

77. Ibid.

78. Baron, "A Journey in the Jungle," 583.

79. Verson Gooch, "Chiriqui, Most Southern Development," *Unifruitco*, December 1929, 261.

80. F. H. Baron, "The Traveling Auditor on the Road to Chiriqui," *Unifruitco*, February 1928, 426–29. On the opening of Chiriqui, see F. H. Baron, "Pioneering for the Chiriqui Land Company," *Unifruitco*, July 1928, 706–8, 718.

81. Gooch, "Chiriqui," 261.

82. Samuel J. Record, "A Word of Appreciation," *Unifruitco*, June 1927, 637.

83. George Chittenden to G. Bennett, quoted in Henry Kuylen, "Serving Science on the Side," *Unifruitco*, May 1931, 472.

84. Kuylen, Serving Science on the Side," 474. On the transoceanic traffic of specimens—"a science of things in motion"—see Christopher Parsons and Kathleen Murphy, "Ecosystems under Sail: Specimen Transport in the Nineteenth-Century French and British Atlantics," *Early American Studies* 10 (Fall 2012): 539.

85. Samuel J. Record and Henry Kuylen, "Trees of the Lower Motagua Valley, Guatemala."

86. Kuylen, "Serving Science on the Side," 472.

87. Record, "A Word of Appreciation," 638.

88. Kuylen, "Serving Science on the Side," 473.

89. Record, "A Word of Appreciation," 639.

90. Today the 55,000-specimen collection resides with the USDA's Forest Products Laboratory in Madison, Wisconsin. http://www.fpl.fs.fed.us/research/centers/woodanatomy/sjrw_collection.php (accessed 16 March 2015).

91. Paul C. Standley to Samuel J. Record, 19 April 1927, reproduced in *Unifruitco*, June 1927, 636.

92. Record, "A Word of Appreciation," 639.

93. Record to Kuylen, cited in Kuylen, "Serving Science on the Side," 474.

94. Kuylen, "Serving Science on the Side," 475.

95. Kuylen, "Serving Science on the Side," 472–75.

96. Marston Bates, "Application for Fellowship, to Chairman, Dept. of Zoology, Harvard," 14 March 1931, Box 1, MBP.

97. "Noted Agriculturalist Enters Our Service," *Unifruitco*, December 1925, 271.

98. Marston Bates, *Where Winter Never Comes*, 2.

99. Wilson Popenoe to Marston Bates, 30 May 1928, Box 1, MBP.

100. Robert R. Alvarez, "The March of Empire: Mangos, Avocados, and the Politics of Transfer," 28. For an overview of USDA plant exploration, see Howard L. Hyland, "History of US Plant Introduction." For a broader consideration of empire and botanical exploration, see Londa Schiebinger, *Plants and Empire*; and Philip, "Imperial Science Rescues a Tree."

101. Wilson Popenoe, *Manual of Tropical and Subtropical Plants, Excluding the Banana, Coconut, Pineapple, Citrus Fruits, Olive, and Fig.*

102. Marston Bates to Amy Mabel and Glenn Bates, 30 September 1928, p. 3, Box 1, MBP.

103. Wilson Popenoe to John R. Johnson, 8 November 1928, p. 6, Box 1, MBP.

104. Marston Bates to Amy Mabel Bates, 25 November 1929, Box 1, MBP.

105. Marston Bates to Mabel and Glenn Bates, 1 September 1929, p. 2, Box 1, MBP; Wilson Popenoe to Marston Bates, 19 February 1929, Box 1, MBP.

106. Marston Bates to Glenn Bates, 12 November 1928, Box 1, MBP.

107. Marston Bates, "The Mediterranean Fruit Fly in Florida," memorandum written for the UFCO, 6 June 1930, Box 1, MBP; Marston Bates, "Insect Parasites

of Citrus in Central America," published in two parts in *The Florida Entomologist* 17:2 (August 1933): 29–32 and 17:3 (October 1933): 45–47.

108. Marston Bates to Amy Mabel Bates, 7 October 1928, p. 2, Box 1, MBP.

109. Marston Bates to R. A. Leussler, 27 October 1928, p. 1, Box 1, MBP.

110. Marston Bates to P. W. Mason, 12 February 1929, Box 1, MBP.

111. On the frontier metaphor in US science, see Leah Ceccarelli, *On the Frontier of Science*.

112. Bates, *Where Winter Never Comes*, 194.

113. Bates Journal, 16 November 1929, p. 61, Box 15, MBP.

114. Marston Bates to T. H. Hubbell, 18 February 1929, Box 1, MBP.

115. Ibid.

116. Marston Bates to Amy Mabel Bates, 26 May 1929, Box 1, MBP.

117. Marston Bates, *The Forest and the Sea* (New York: Time Incorporated, 1960), 138.

118. Marston Bates, *The Forest and the Sea*, 17–18.

119. Marston Bates to Amy Mabel Bates, 7 September 1931, Box 1, MBP.

120. Marston Bates to Amy Mabel Bates, 6 January 1929, p. 2, MBP.

121. Lewis R. Freeman, *Afloat and Aflight in the Caribbean* (New York: Dodd, Mead and Company, 1932); Charles Kepner and Jay Soothill, *The Banana Empire*; Charles Kepner, *Social Aspects of the Banana Industry*.

122. Marston Bates to Amy Mabel Bates, 1 June 1929, Box 1, MBP.

123. Marston Bates to Amy Mabel Bates, 14 June 1929, Box 1, MBP.

124. Marston Bates to Amy Mabel Bates, 26 May 1929, Box 1, MBP.

125. Marston Bates to Amy Mabel Bates, 2 February 1930, Box 1, MBP.

126. Marston Bates to Amy Mabel Bates, 20 February 1930, Box 1, MBP.

127. Marston Bates, "Report on trip to Guatemala, Sept. 25 to Oct. 16, 1929," p. 1, Box 1, MBP.

128. On the UFCO's control of Guatemala, see Jason M. Colby, *The Business of Empire*, especially chapter 4.

129. Marston Bates, Memorandum to Mr. Popenoe, The Exposition of the Servicio Tecnico at the Feria de Agosto, August 1930, Box 1, MBP.

130. Marston Bates to Herbert Osborn, 18 August 1930, Box 1, MBP.

131. Such relationships are detailed in several sources: Marston Bates to F. M. Gaige, 9 May 1930, Box 1, MBP; Marston Bates to Richard Leussler, 9 May 1930, Box 1, MBP; Foster H. Benjamin to Marston Bates, 19 March 1931, Box 1, MBP; Marston Bates to Oakes Ames, 5 May 1931, Box 1, MBP.

132. Marston Bates to T. H. Hubbell, 11 March 1931, Box 1, MBP.

133. Marston Bates, Report for Professor Oakes Ames on The West Coast of Honduras, May 1931, Box 1, MBP.

134. Marston Bates to Chairman of Department of Zoology (Harvard University), Application for Fellowship, 14 March 1931, Box 1, MBP.

135. Wilson Popenoe to Chair of Department of Zoology (Harvard University), 14 March 1931, Box 1, MBP.

136. Charles H. Harris III and Louis R. Sadler, *The Archaeologist Was a Spy*, 301–2.

137. Nicholas Thomas, *Colonialism's Culture*, 5.

138. Bates, *Where Winter Never Comes*, 3.

Conclusion

1. Bradley W. Palmer, "Swampscott Conference, 1926: Address of Bradley W. Palmer," *Unifruitco*, December 1926, 297.

2. Ibid.

3. Victor M. Cutter, "Introductory Address Delivered by Victor M. Cutter, President," *Unifruitco*, October 1927, 135.

4. "Second Annual Conference of the United Fruit Company and Subsidiary Companies at Swampscott, Mass., October 5–6–7, 1927," *Unifruitco*, November 1927, 200.

5. Ibid.

6. Jason Colby, *The Business of Empire*, and Philippe Bourgois, *Ethnicity at Work*.

7. Colby details this process in *The Business of Empire*, chap. 5.

8. Engineering Department, Siquirres, Annual Report – Year 1930, p. 1, INCOFER #217; Maintenance of Way Department, Annual Report – Year 1940, p. 1, INCOFER #758.

9. M. M. Marsh, Annual Report for 1923, p. 12, INCOFER #2969.

10. Algunos vesinos [*sic*] del Pejivaye to F. Sheehy, 20 September 1927, INCOFER #1259.

11. John Dolan to F. Sheehy, 25 September 1927, INCOFER #1259.

12. Benjamín Ovando et al. to F. Sheehy, 6 July 1929, INCOFER #1259.

13. George Chittenden to Victor M. Cutter, 22 September 1917, p. 34, INCOFER #937.

14. R. Ferris to F. Sheehy, 7 March 1927, INCOFER # 1251; see various apprenticeship contracts with Costa Rican workers dating from the mid-1920s in INCOFER #3029.

15. A. E. Payton to F. Sheehy, List of Transportation Department Employees and Salaries, 25 November 1929, sheet 1, INCOFER #790.

16. See, for instance, the case of US engineer J. W. Hickman, in F. Sheehy to Crawford Ellis, 8 April 1927, INCOFER #1251.

17. Northern Railway Company, Regular Assigned Crews, 1937, INCOFER #1261.

18. F. Sheehy to B. E. Bookout, 22 July 1939, INCOFER #229.

19. Marcelo Bucheli lays out this process of divestment in *Bananas and Business*.

20. Bucheli, *Bananas and Business*, 69.

21. Atalia Shragai, "Do Bananas Have a Culture?"

22. Walter Nugent, *Habits of Empire*.

23. Edward Said, *Culture and Imperialism*, 52.

24. Nicholas Thomas, *Colonialism's Culture*, 7.

25. Bates, *Where Winter Never Comes*, 2.

26. Ibid., 3.

Archival Collections

Lorenzo Dow Baker Papers, Cape Cod Community College Library, West Barnstable, MA.

Everett C. Brown Collection, Department of Special and Area Collections, Smathers Library, University of Florida, Gainesville.

Marston Bates Papers, Bentley Historical Library, University of Michigan, Ann Arbor.

Victor Macomber Cutter Papers, MS 63, Rauner Special Collections Library, Dartmouth College.

United Fruit Company Photograph Collection, Mss: 1 (1891–1962), U860, Baker Library, Harvard Business School.

Richard Pearson Strong Papers, GA82, Harvard Medical Library in the Francis A. Countway Library of Medicine, Boston.

Instituto Costarricense del Ferrocarril, Archivo Nacional de Costa Rica, San José.

United Fruit Company Publications

Annual Reports to Stockholders of the United Fruit Company, 1900–1969.

Annual Reports of the Medical Department of the United Fruit Company, 1912–1931.

Middle American Information Bureau (United Fruit Company). *Zaculeu. Restoration by the United Fruit Company*. New York: United Fruit Company, 1947.

Popenoe, Wilson and Dorothy. *A Guide to Quirigua, an Ancient Maya City*. Boston: United Fruit Company, ca. 1950.

Unifruitco, 1925–1931.

United Fruit Company. *Proceedings of the International Conference on Health Problems in Tropical America Held at Kingston, Jamaica, B. W. I. July 22 to August 1, 1924*. Boston: United Fruit Company, 1924.

United Fruit Company Steamship Service (UFCSS). *Cruising the Spanish Main*. Boston: United Fruit Company, 1912.

Books and Articles

Achbari, Azadeh. "Building Networks for Science: Conflict and Cooperation in Nineteenth-Century Global Maritime Studies." *Isis* 106:2 (June 2015), 257–82.

Adas, Michael. *Machines as the Measure of Men: Science, Technology, and Ideologies of Western Dominance*. Ithaca, NY: Cornell University Press, 1989.

Adams, Frederick Upham. *Conquest of the Tropics: The Story of the Creative Enterprises Conducted by the United Fruit Company*. Garden City, NY: Doubleday, Page, 1914.

Aguirre, Robert D. *Informal Empire: Mexico and Central America in Victorian Culture*. Minneapolis: University of Minnesota Press, 2005.

Aliano, David. "Curing the Ills of Central America: The United Fruit Company's Medical Department and Corporate America's Mission to Civilize, 1900–1940." *Estudios interdisciplinarios de América Latina y el Caribe* 17:2 (2006), 35–59.

Allen, James. *The Company Town in the American West*. Norman: University of Oklahoma Press, 1966.

Alvarez, Robert R. "The March of Empire: Mangos, Avocados, and the Politics of Transfer." *Gastronomica* 7:3 (Summer 2007), 28–33.

Amaya Amador, P. *Prisión verde*. Buenos Aires: AGEPE, 1957.

Anderson, Warwick. *Colonial Pathologies: American Tropical Medicine, Race, and Hygiene in the Philippines*. Durham, NC: Duke University Press, 2006.

Andress, J. Mace, and Julia E. Dickerson. *Radio Bound for Banana Land*. Boston: United Fruit Company Education Department, 1932.

Andrews, Malcolm. *The Search for the Picturesque: Landscape Aesthetics and Tourism in Britain, 1760–1800*. Stanford: Stanford University Press, 1989.

Andrews, Thomas G. "'Made by Toile'?: Tourism, Labor, and the Construction of the Colorado Landscape, 1858–1917." *Journal of American History* 92:4 (December 2005), 837–63.

Arango Z., Carlos. *Sobrevivientes de las bananeras*. Bogotá: Editorial Colombia Nueva, 1981.

Aron, Cindy. *Working at Play: A History of Vacations in the United States*. Oxford: Oxford University Press, 2001.

Arbena, Joseph L., and David G. LaFrance. *Sport in Latin American and the Caribbean*. Wilmington, DE: Scholarly Resources, 2002.

Armus, Diego, ed. *Disease in the History of Modern Latin America: From Malaria to AIDS*. Durham: Duke University Press, 2003.

Arnold, David. *Colonizing the Body: State Medicine and Epidemic Disease in Nineteenth-Century India*. Berkeley: University of California Press, 1993.

————. *The Problem of Nature: Environment, Culture, and European Expansion*. Oxford: Blackford Publishers, 1996.

————, ed. *Warm Climates and Western Medicine*. Atlanta: Rodopi, 1996.

Asturias, Miguel Ángel. *Los ojos de los enterrados*. Buenos Aires: Editorial Losada, 1979.

————. *El papa verde*. Buenos Aires: Editorial Losada, 1954.

————. *Viento Fuerte*. Buenos Aires: Editorial Losada, 1950.

Ayala, César J. *American Sugar Kingdom: The Plantation Economy of the Spanish Caribbean, 1898–1934*. Chapel Hill: University of North Carolina Press, 1999.

Bartlett, W. Randolph, Jr. "Lorenzo Dow Baker and the Development of the Banana Trade between Jamaica and the United States, 1881–1890." PhD diss., The American University, 1977.

Bates, Marston. *Where Winter Never Comes: A Study of Man and Nature in the Tropics*. New York: Charles Scribner's Sons, 1952.

Bederman, Gail. *Manliness and Civilization: A Cultural History of Gender and Race in the United States, 1880–1917*. Chicago: University of Chicago Press, 1995.

Bell, David, and Gill Valentine, eds. *Mapping Desire: Geographies of Sexualities*. London: Routledge, 1995.

Berghoff, Harmut, Barbara Korte, Ralf Schneider, and Christopher Harvie, eds. *The Making of Modern Tourism: The Cultural History of the British Experience, 1600–2000*. Hampshire, GB: Palgrave, 2002.

Black, Jeremy. *Maps and History: Constructing Images of the Past*. New Haven: Yale University Press, 1997.

Bloom, Nicholas D., ed. *Adventures into Mexico: American Tourism beyond the Border*. Lanham, MD: Rowman & Littlefield, 2006.

Blythe, Robert. "Unraveling the Threads of Community Life: Work, Play, and Place in Alabama Mill Villages of the West Point Manufacturing Company." *Perspectives in Vernacular Architecture* 9 (2003), 135–50.

Bourgois, Philippe. *Ethnicity at Work: Divided Labor on a Central American Banana Plantation*. Baltimore: Johns Hopkins University Press, 1989.

Brandes, Stuart D. *American Welfare Capitalism, 1880–1940*. Chicago: University of Chicago Press, 1970.

Briggs, Laura. *Reproducing Empire: Race, Sex, Science, and U.S. Imperialism in Puerto Rico*. Berkeley: University of California Press, 2002.

Bucheli, Marcelo. *Bananas and Business: The United Fruit Company in Columbia, 1899–2000*. New York: New York University Press, 2005.

Buckley, James M. "A Factory without a Roof: The Company Town in the Redwood Lumber Industry." *Perspectives in Vernacular Architecture* 7 (1997), 75–92.

Buder, Stanley. *Pullman: An Experiment in Industrial Order and Community Planning, 1880–1930*. New York: Oxford University Press, 1967.

———. *Visionaries and Planners: The Garden City Movement and the Modern Community*. New York: Oxford University Press, 1990.

Butchart, Alexander. *The Anatomy of Power: European Constructions of the African Body*. London: Zed Books, 1998.

Campbell, Robert. *In Darkest Alaska: Travel and Empire along the Inside Passage*. Philadelphia: University of Pennsylvania Press, 2007.

Campbell, James T., Matthew Guterl, and Robert Lee, eds. *Race, Nation, and Empire in American History*. Chapel Hill: University of North Carolina Press, 2007.

Campbell, Kristine A. "Knots in the Fabric: Richard Pearson Strong and the Bilibid Prison Vaccine Trials, 1905–1906." *Bulletin of the History of Medicine* 68 (January 1994), 600.

Cañizares-Esguerra, Jorge. *Nature, Empire, and Nation: Explorations of the History of Science in the Iberian World*. Stanford: Stanford University Press, 2006.

Carey, Mark. "Inventing Caribbean Climates: How Science, Medicine, and

Tourism Changed Tropical Weather from Deadly to Healthy." *Osiris* 26:1 (2011), 129–41.

Carlson, Linda. *Company Towns of the Pacific Northwest*. Seattle: University of Washington Press, 2003.

Ceccarelli, Leah. *On the Frontier of Science: An American Rhetoric of Exploration and Exploitation*. East Lansing: Michigan State University Press, 2013.

Chandler, Aldred D. *The Visible Hand: The Managerial Revolution in American Business*. Cambridge: Belknap Press, 1977.

———. *Scale and Scope: The Dynamics of Industrial Capitalism*. Cambridge: Belknap Press, 1977.

Chapman, Peter. *Bananas: How the United Fruit Company Shaped the World*. Edinburgh: Canongate, 2007.

Chomsky, Aviva. *West Indian Workers and the United Fruit Company, 1870–1940*. Baton Rouge: Louisiana State University Press, 1996.

———. "Afro-Jamaican Tradition and Labour Organizing on United Fruit Company Plantations in Costa Rica, 1910." *Journal of Social History* 28:4 (Summer 1995), 837–55.

Chomsky, Aviva, and Aldo Lauria-Santiago, eds. *Identity and Struggle at the Margins of the Nation-State: The Laboring Peoples of Central America and the Hispanic Caribbean*. Durham: Duke University Press, 1998.

Claassen, Cheryl, ed. *Women in Archaeology*. Philadelphia: University of Pennsylvania Press, 1994.

Clark, Steve. *Travel Writing and Empire: Postcolonial Theory in Transit*. London: Zed Books, 1999.

Cohn, Bernard S. *Colonialism and Its Forms of Knowledge: The British in India*. Princeton: Princeton University Press, 1996.

Colby, Jason M. *The Business of Empire: United Fruit, Race, and U.S. Expansion in Central America*. Ithaca: Cornell University Press, 2011.

Conn, Steven. *Museums in American Life, 1876–1926*. Chicago: University of Chicago Press, 2000.

Craib, Raymond B. *Cartographic Mexico: A History of State Fixations and Fugitive Landscapes*. Durham: Duke University Press, 2004.

Craib, Raymond B., and D. Graham Burnett. "Insular Visions: Cartographic Imagery and the Spanish-American War." *The Historian* 61:1 (1998), 101–18.

Crawford, Margaret. "Designing the Company Town, 1910–1930." PhD diss., University of Southern California, 1991.

———. *Building the Workingman's Paradise: The Design of American Company Towns*. London: Verso, 1995.

Cronon, William. *Nature's Metropolis: Chicago and the Great West*. New York: W. W. Norton, 1991.

Crowther, Samuel. *Romance and Rise of the American Tropics*. Garden City, NY: Doubley, Doran & Company, 1929.

Curtin, Philip. *Death by Migration: Europe's Encounter with the Tropics in the Nineteenth Century*. Cambridge: Cambridge University Press, 1989.

———. *Disease and Empire: The Health of European Troops in the Conquest of Africa*. Cambridge: Cambridge University Press, 1998.

Cutter, Victor M. "Caribbean Tropics in Commercial Transition." *Economic Geography* 2:4 (October 1926), 494–507.

Davis, Clark. "'You are the Company': The Demands of Employment in the Emerging Corporate Culture, Los Angeles, 1900–1930." *The Business History Review* 70:3 (Autumn 1996): 328–62.

———. *Company Men: White-Collar Life and Corporate Cultures in Los Angeles, 1892–1941*. Baltimore: Johns Hopkins Press, 2000.

De Vos, Paula. "Natural History and the Pursuit of Empire in Eighteenth-Century Spain." *Eighteenth-Century Studies* 40:2 (Winter 2007), 2009–39.

Deeks, William, and W. M. James. *A Report on Hemoglobunuric Fever in the Canal Zone, A Study of Its Etiology and Treatment*. Mount Hope, Panama: Isthmian Canal Commission Department of Sanitation, 1911.

Delpar, Helen. *The Enormous Vogue of Things Mexican: Cultural Relations between the United States and Mexico, 1920–1935*. Tuscaloosa, University of Alabama Press, 1992.

———. *Looking South: The Evolution of Latin Americanist Scholarship in the United States, 1850–1975*. Tuscaloosa: University of Alabama Press, 2008.

Dilworth, Leah. *Imagining Indians in the Southwest: Persistent Visions of a Primitive Past*. Washington, DC: Smithsonian Institution Press, 1996.

Driver, Felix, and Luciana Martins, eds. *Tropical Visions in an Age of Empire*. Chicago: University of Chicago Press, 2005.

Dosal, Paul. *Doing Business with the Dictators: A Political History of United Fruit in Guatemala, 1899–1944.* Wilmington, DE: Scholarly Resources, 1993.

Duarte, Regina Horta. "Between the National and the Universal: Natural History Networks in Latin America in the Nineteenth and Twentieth Centuries." *Isis* 104:4 (December 2013), 777–87.

Duncan, Quince. *Dos novelas: Los cuatro espejos y La paz del pueblo.* Bloomington, IN: Editorial Palibrio, 2013.

Endersby, Jim. *Imperial Nature: Joseph Hooker and the Practices of Victorian Science.* Chicago: University of Chicago Press, 2008.

Espinosa, Mariola. *Epidemic Invasions: Yellow Fever and the Limits of Cuban Independence, 1878–1930.* Chicago: University of Chicago Press, 2009.

Euraque, Darío. *Reinterpreting the Banana Republic: Region and State in Honduras, 1870–1972.* Chapel Hill: University of North Carolina Press, 1996.

———. "Antropólogos, arqueólogos, imperialismo, y la mayanización de Honduras, 1890–1940." *Revista de Historia* 45 (January–June 2002), 73–103.

Ewen, Stuart. *Captains of Consciousness: Advertising and the Social Roots of Commercial Culture.* New York: McGraw-Hill, 1975.

Ewen, Stuart, and Elizabeth Stuart. *Channels of Desire: Mass Images and the Shaping of American Consciousness.* New York: McGraw-Hill, 1982.

Fallas, Carlos Luis. *Mamita Yunai.* San José: Editorial Costa Rica, 2006.

Foster, Harry L. *The Adventures of a Tropical Tramp.* New York: A. L. Burt Company, 1922.

Freeman, Lewis R. *Afloat and Aflight in the Caribbean.* New York: Dodd, Mead, 1932.

García Márquez, Gabriel. *Cien años de soledad.* Madrid: Cátedra, 1987.

Garner, John S. "Leclaire Illinois: A Model Company Town (1890–1934)." *Journal of the Society of Architectural Historians* 30:3 (October 1971), 219–27.

———. *The Model Company Town: Urban Design through Private Enterprise in Nineteenth-Century New England.* Amherst: University of Massachusetts Press, 1984.

————, ed. *The Company Town: Architecture and Society in the Early Industrial Age*. New York: Oxford University Press, 1992.

Gaspar, Jeffrey Casey. *Limón, 1880–1940: Un estudio de la industria bananera en Costa Rica*. San José: Editorial Costa Rica, 1979.

Gelber, Steven M. "Working at Playing: The Culture of the Workplace and the Rise of Baseball." *Journal of Social History* 16:4 (Summer 1983), 3–22.

Gilderhus, Mark T. *Pan American Visions: Woodrow Wilson in the Western Hemisphere, 1913–1921*. Tucson: University of Arizona Press, 1986.

Gillis, John. *Islands of the Mind: How the Human Imagination Created the Atlantic World*. New York: Palgrave MacMillan, 2004.

Gleijeses, Piero. *Shattered Hope: The Guatemalan Revolution and the United States, 1944–1954*. Princeton: Princeton University Press, 1992.

Goldberg, Mark H. *"Going Bananas": 100 Years of American Fruit Ships in the Caribbean*. Kings Point, NY: The American Merchant Marine Museum Foundation, 1993.

Goldstein, Daniel. "Outposts of Science: The Knowledge Trade and the Expansion of Scientific Community in Post-Civil War America." *Isis* 99:3 (September 2008), 519–46.

Gorgas, William C. "The Conquest of the Tropics for the White Race." President's Address at the Sixtieth Annual Session of the American Medical Association at Atlantic City, June 9, 1909. *Journal of the American Medical Association* 52:25 (June 19, 1909), 1969.

————. *Sanitation in Panama*. New York: D. Appleton and Company, 1915.

Grandin, Greg. *Fordlandia: The Rise and Fall of Henry Ford's Forgotten Jungle City*. New York: Metropolitan Books, 2009.

Grann, David. *The Lost City of Z: A Tale of Deadly Obsession in the Amazon*. New York: Vintage Books, 2005.

Green, Julie. *The Canal Builders: Making America's Empire at the Panama Canal*. New York: Penguin, 2009.

Greenblatt, Stephen. *Marvelous Possessions: The Wonder of the New World*. Chicago: University of Chicago Press, 1991.

Gudmundson, Lowell and Justin Wolfe, eds. *Blacks and Blackness in Central America: Between Race and Place*. Durham: Duke University Press, 2010.

Guttmann, Allen. *Games and Empires: Modern Sports and Cultural Imperialism*. New York: Columbia University Press, 1994.

Hall, Linda B. *Oil, Banks, and Politics: The United States and Postrevolution-
ary Mexico, 1917–1924*. Austin: University of Texas Press, 1995.

Harpelle, Ronald N. "Racism and Nationalism in the Creation of Costa
Rica's Pacific Coast Banana Enclave." *The Americas* 56:3 (January
2000): 29–51.

———. *The West Indians of Costa Rica: Race, Class, and the Integration of an
Ethnic Minority*. Montreal: McGill-Queen's University Press, 2002.

———. "White Women on the Frontier: American Enclave Communities on
the Caribbean Coast of Central America." *Wadabagei* 8:2 (2005):
6–34.

Harris, Charles H. III, and Louis Sadler. *The Archaeologist Was a Spy: Sylvanus G. Morley and the Office of Naval Intelligence*. Albuquerque: University of New Mexico Press, 2003.

Harrison, Mark. *Climates and Constitutions: Health, Race, Environment and
British Imperialism in India, 1600–1850*. Oxford: Oxford University
Press, 1999.

Heckadon-Moreno, Stanley. *Selvas entre dos mares: Expediciones científicas al
Istmo de Panamá, siglos XVII–XX*. Panama City: Instituto Smithsonian de Investigaciones Tropicales, 2006.

Henry, O. *Cabbages and Kings*. Minneapolis: Amaranth Press, 1985.

Hobsbawm, Eric, and Terence Ranger, eds. *The Invention of Tradition*. Cambridge: Canto Classics, 2012.

Hogansen, Kristin. *Fighting for American Manhood: How Gender Politics Pro-
voked the Spanish-American and Philippine-American Wars*. New
Haven: Yale University Press, 1998.

Hoquet, Thierry. "Botanical Authority: Benjamin Delessert's Collections
between Tracelers and Candolle's Natural Method (1803–1847)."
Isis 105:3 (September 2014), 508–39.

Horsman, Reginald. *Race and Manifest Destiny: The Origins of American
Racial Anglo-Saxonism*. Cambridge: Harvard University Press, 1981.

Howe, James. *A People Who Would Not Kneel: Panama, the United States, and
the San Blas Kuna*. Washington, DC: Smithsonian Institution Press,
1998.

Hyland, Howard L. "History of U. S. Plant Introduction." *Environmental Review* 2:4 (1977), 26–33.

Igler, David. *Industrial Cowboys: Miller & Lux and the Transformation of the Far West, 1850–1920*. Berkeley: University of California Press, 2001.

Immerman, Richard. *Empire for Liberty: A History of American Imperialism from Benjamin Franklin to Paul Wolfowitz*. Princeton: Princeton University Press, 2010.

Jacobson, Matthew Frye. *Barbarian Virtues: The United States Encounters Foreign Peoples at Home and Abroad*. New York: Hill and Wang, 2000.

Jenkins, Virginia S. *Bananas: An American History*. Washington, DC: Smithsonian Institution Press, 2000.

Johnson, John J. *Latin America in Caricature*. Austin: University of Texas Press, 1980.

Joseph, Gilbert, Catherine C. LeGrand, and Ricardo Salvatore, eds. *Close Encounters of Empire: Writing the Cultural History of U.S.-Latin American Relations*. Durham: Duke University Press, 1998.

Judd, Neil M. "The Use of Glue Molds in Reproducing Aboriginal Monuments at Quirigua, Guatemala." *American Anthropologist* 17:1 (January–March 1915), 128–38.

Kaplan, Amy. *The Anarchy of Empire in the Making of U.S. Culture*. Cambridge: Harvard University Press, 2002.

Kaplan, Amy, and Donald Pease, eds. *Cultures of United States Imperialism*. Durham: Duke University Press, 1993.

Kepner, Charles. *Social Aspects of the Banana Industry*. New York: Columbia University Press, 1936.

Kepner, Charles D., and Jay H. Soothill. *The Banana Empire: A Case Study of Economic Imperialism*. New York: Russell & Russell, 1963.

King, Anthony D. *Colonial Urban Development: Culture, Social Power, and Environment*. London: Routledge & Kegan Paul, 1976.

Kinzer, Steven, and Steven Schlesinger, *Bitter Fruit: The Story of the American Coup in Guatemala*. New York, Anchor Books, 1983.

Kirshenblatt-Gimblett, Barbara. *Destination Culture: Tourism, Museums, and Heritage*. Berkeley: University of California Press, 1998.

Klubock, Thomas M. *Contested Communities: Class, Gender, and Politics in*

Chile's El Teniente Copper Mine, 1904–1951. Durham: Duke University Press, 1998.

Kramer, Paul. "Empires, Exceptions, and Anglo-Saxons: Race and Rule between the British and United States Empires, 1880–1910." *Journal of American History* 88:4 (March 2002), 1315–53.

Kuklick, Henrika and Robert Kohler, eds. *Science in the Field*. Osiris 2nd ser, 11 (1996).

LaBarge, Richard. "A Study of United Fruit Company Operations in Isthmian America, 1946–1956." PhD diss., Duke University, 1959.

Langley, Lester, and Thomas Schoonover. *The Banana Men: American Mercenaries and Entrepreneurs in Central America, 1880–1930*. Lexington: University Press of Kentucky, 1995.

Lears, T. J. Jackson. *No Place of Grace: Antimodernism and the Transformation of American Culture, 1880–1920*. Chicago: University of Chicago Press, 1981.

Lightman, Bernard, and Gowan Dawson, eds. *Victorian Scientific Naturalism: Community, Identity, Continuity*. Chicago: University of Chicago Press, 2014.

Lindsay-Poland, John. *Emperors of the Jungle: The Hidden History of the U.S. in Panama*. Durham: Duke University Press, 2003.

Livingston, David. "Tropical Climate and Moral Hygiene: The Anatomy of a Victorian Debate." *British Journal for the History of Science* 32:1 (March 1999), 104–8.

Lloyd, David Wharton. *Battlefield Tourism: Pilgrimage and the Commemoration of the Great War in Britain, Australia and Canada, 1919–1939*. Oxford: Berg (Oxford International), 1998.

Loo, Tina. "Of Moose and Men: Hunting for Masculinities in British Columbia, 1880–1939." *Western Historical Quarterly* 32:3 (Autumn 2001), 296–319.

Loveman, Brian. *No Higher Law: American Foreign Policy and the Western Hemisphere since 1776*. Chapel Hill: University of North Carolina Press, 2010.

Luke, Christina. "Diplomats, Banana Cowboys, and Archaeologists in Western Honduras: A History of the Trade in Pre-Columbian Materials." *International Journal of Cultural Property* 13 (2006), 25–57.

MacCannell, Dean, and Lucy R. Lippard. *The Tourist: A New Theory of the Leisure Class*. Berkeley: University of California Press, 1999.

MacKenzie, John, ed. *Imperialism and the Natural World*. Manchester: Manchester University Press, 1990.

McCann, Thomas P. *An American Company: The Tragedy of United Fruit*. New York: Crown Publishers, 1976.

Mandell, Nikki. *The Corporation as Family: The Gendering of Corporate Welfare, 1890–1930*. Chapel Hill: University of North Carolina Press, 2002.

Mann, Charles C. *1493: Uncovering the World Columbus Created*. New York: Vintage, 2012.

Marchand, Roland. *Advertising the American Dream: Making Way for Modernity, 1920–1940*. Berkeley: University of California Press, 1985.

———. *Creating the Corporate Soul: The Rise of Public Relations and Corporate Imagery in American Big Business*. Berkeley: University of California Press, 2001.

Marsh, Richard O. "Blond Indians of the Darien Jungle." *The World's Work* (March 1925), 483–97.

———. "The Mystery of the White Indians." *The World's Work* (April 1925), 633–45.

Marx, Leo. *The Machine in the Garden: Technology and the Pastoral Ideal in America*. Oxford: Oxford University Press, 1964.

Matt, Susan J. "You Can't Go Home Again: Homesickness and Nostalgia in U. S. History." *Journal of American History* 94:2 (September 2007), 469–97.

May, Stacy, and Galo Plaza. *The United Fruit Company in Latin America*. Washington, DC: National Planning Association, 1958.

Mayo, James M. *The American Country Club: Its Origins and Development*. New Brunswick, NJ: Rutgers University Press, 1998.

McClintock, Anne. *Imperial Leather: Race, Gender and Sexuality in the Colonial Contest*. New York: Routledge, 1995.

Melville, John H. *The Great White Fleet*. New York: Vantage Press, 1976.

Millard, Candace. *River of Doubt: Theodore Roosevelt's Darkest Journey*. New York: Broadway Books, 2006.

Miller, David, and Peter Reill, eds. *Visions of Empire: Voyages, Botany and*

Representations of Nature. Cambridge: Cambridge University Press, 1996.

Mitchell, Neil J. *The Generous Corporation: A Political Analysis of Economic Power*. New Haven: Yale University Press, 1989.

Montes, Luis, and William Siegel. *Bananas*. New York: International Pamphlets, 1933.

Moreno Fraginals, Martín. *El ingenio: Complejo económico social cubano del azúcar*. Barcelona: Crítica, 2001.

Morley, Sylvanus G. *Guide Book to the Ruins of Quirigua*. Washington, DC: Carnegie Institution, 1935.

Mrozek, Donald J. *Sport and American Mentality, 1880–1910*. Knoxville: University of Tennessee Press, 1983.

Neill, Deborah J. *Networks in Tropical Medicine: Internationalism, Colonialism, and the Rise of a Medical Specialty*. Stanford: Stanford University Press, 2012.

Neruda, Pablo. *Canto general*. Mexico City: Talleres Gráficos de la Nación, 1950.

Norbeck, Edward. *Pineapple Town: Hawaii*. Berkeley: University of California Press, 1959.

Norwood, Stephen H. "The Student as Strikebreaker: College Youth and the Crisis of Masculinity in the Early Twentieth Century." *Journal of Social History* 28:2 (Winter 1994), 331–49.

Nugent, Walter. *Habits of Empire: A History of American Expansion*. New York: Vintage, 2008.

Nye, David E. *American Technological Sublime*. Cambridge: MIT Press, 1994.

O'Brien, Thomas F. *The Revolutionary Mission: American Enterprise in Latin America, 1900–1945*. Cambridge: Cambridge University Press, 1996.

———. *The Century of US Capitalism in Latin America*. Albuquerque: University of New Mexico Press, 1999.

———. *Making the Americas: The United States and Latin America from the Age of Revolutions to the Era of Globalization*. Albuquerque: University of New Mexico Press, 2007.

Oldenziel, Ruth. *Making Technology Masculine: Men, Women, and Modern Machines in America, 1870–1945*. Amsterdam: Amsterdam University Press, 1999.

Packard, Randall. "The Invention of the 'Tropical Worker': Medical Research and the Quest for Central African Labour in the South African Gold Mines, 1903–36." *Journal of African History* 34:2 (1993), 271–92.

———. *The Making of a Tropical Disease: A Short History of Malaria*. Baltimore: Johns Hopkins University Press, 2007.

Palladino, Paolo, and Michael Worboys. "Science and Imperialism." *Isis* 84:1 (March 1993), 91–102.

Parsons, Christopher, and Kathleen Murphy. "Ecosystems under Sail: Specimen Transport in the Nineteenth-Century French and British Atlantics." *Early American Studies* 10 (Fall 2012), 503–39.

Patterson, Thomas. *Toward a Social History of Archaeology in the United States*. New York: Harcourt Brace College, 1994.

Pedraja, René de la. *The Rise and Decline of U.S. Merchant Shipping in the Twentieth Century*. New York: Twayne, 1992.

Pérez, Louis A. "Between Baseball and Bullfighting: The Quest for Nationality in Cuba, 1868–1898." *Journal of American History* 81:2 (September 1994), 493–517.

———. *On Becoming Cuban: Identity, Nationality, and Culture*. Chapel Hill: University of North Carolina Press, 1999.

Philips, Karita. "Imperial Science Rescues a Tree: Global Botanical Networks, Local Knowledge, and the Transcontinental Transplantation of Cinchona." *Environment and History* 1:2 (June 1995), 173–200.

Phillips, Ruth B., and Christopher B. Steiner, eds. *Unpacking Culture: Art and Commodity in Colonial and Postcolonial Worlds*. Berkeley: University of California Press, 1999.

Pike, Frederick. *The United States and Latin America: Myths and Stereotypes of Civilization and Nature*. Austin: University of Texas Press, 1992.

Popenoe, Dorothy. *Santiago de los Caballeros de Guatemala*. Cambridge: Harvard University Press, 1933.

Popenoe, Wilson. *Manual of Tropical and Subtropical Plants, Excluding the Banana, Coconut, Pineapple, Citrus Fruits, Olive, and Fig*. New York: MacMillan, 1920.

———. "Regional Differences in the Guatemalan Huipil." *Annaes do XX*

Congresso Internacional de Americanistas, 20 a 30 de agosto de 1922. Rio de Janeiro: Imprensa Nacional, 1924, 217–20.

Porteous, J. Douglas. "The Nature of the Company Town." *Transactions of the Institute Of British Geographers* 51 (November 1970), 127–42.

———. "Urban Transplantation in Chile." *Geography Review* 62:4 (October 1972), 455–78.

———. "Social Class in Atacama Company Towns." *Annals of the Association of American Geographers* 64:3 (September 1974), 409–17.

Pratt, Mary Louise. *Imperial Eyes: Travel Writing and Transculturation.* New York: Routledge, 1992.

Pred, Allan. "Place as Historically Contingent Process: Structuration and the Time-Geography of Becoming Places." *Annals of the Association of American Geographers* 74 (1984): 79–97.

Purcell, Trevor. *Banana Fallout: Class, Color, and Culture among West Indians in Costa Rica.* Los Angeles: University of California Press, 1993.

Putnam, Lara. *The Company They Kept: Migrants and the Policy of Gender in Caribbean Costa Rica, 1870–1960.* Chapel Hill: University of North Carolina Press, 2002.

Quintero Toro, Camilo. *Birds of Empire, Birds of a Nation: A History of Science, Economy, and Conservation in United States–Colombia Relations.* Bogotá: Universidad de los Andes, 2012.

Raby, Megan. "Making Biology Tropical: American Science in the Caribbean, 1898–1963." PhD diss., University of Wisconsin, Madison, 2013.

Raby, Peter. *Bright Paradise: Victorian Scientific Travellers.* Princeton: Princeton University Press, 1996.

Raucher, Alan R. *Public Relations and Business, 1900–1920.* Baltimore: Johns Hopkins University Press, 1968.

Record, Samuel J., and Henry Kuylen. "Trees of the Lower Motagua Valley, Guatemala." *Tropical Woods* no. 7 (September 1926): 10–29.

Reidy, Michael, and Helen Rozwadowski. "The Spaces in Between: Science, Ocean, Empire." *Isis* 105:2 (June 2014), 338–51.

Renda, Mary. *Taking Haiti: Military Occupation and the Culture of U.S. Imperialism, 1915–1940.* Chapel Hill: University of North Carolina Press, 2001.

Roediger, David. *The Wages of Whiteness: Race and the Making of the American Working Class*. New York: Verso, 2007.

Rojek, Chris, and John Urry, eds. *Touring Cultures: Transformations of Travel and Theory*. London: Routledge, 1997.

Rosaldo, Renato. "Imperialist Nostalgia." *Representations* 26 (Spring 1989), 107–22.

Rosenberg, Emily. *Spreading the American Dream: American Economic and Cultural Expansion, 1890–1945*. New York: Hill and Wang, 1982.

Rosengarden, Frederick. *Wilson Popenoe: Agricultural Explorer, Educator, and Friend of Latin America*. Lawaii, HI: National Tropical Botanical Garden, 1991.

Rosenthal, P. J., ed. *Antimalarial Chemotherapy: Mechanisms of Action, Resistance, and New Directions in Drug Discovery*. Totowa, NJ: Humana Press, 2001.

Rothman, Hal K. *Devil's Bargains: Tourism in the Twentieth-Century American West*. Lawrence: University Press of Kansas, 1998.

Rotundo, Anthony. *American Manhood: Transformations in Masculinity from the Revolution to the Modern Age*. New York: Basic Books, 1993.

Ruhl, Arthur. *The Central Americans: Adventures and Impressions between Mexico and Panama*. New York: Charles Scribner's Sons, 1928.

Rydell, Robert. *All the World's a Fair: Visions of Empire at American International Expositions, 1876–1916*. Chicago: University of Chicago Press, 1984.

Rydell, Robert, and Rob Kroes. *Buffalo Bill in Bologna: The Americanization of the World, 1869–1922*. Chicago: University of Chicago Press, 2012.

Said, Edward. *Orientalism*. New York: Vintage Books, 1979.

Salazar Navarrete, José Manuel. *La gran serpiente verde: Novela de la región atlántica caribeña*. San José, Costa Rica: Editorial Universidad Estatal a Distancia, 1996.

Salvatore, Ricardo. *Imágenes de un imperio: Estados Unidos y las formas de representación de América Latina*. Buenos Aires: Editorial Sudamericana, 2006.

———. *Disciplinary Conquest: U.S. Scholars in South America, 1900–1945*. Durham: Duke University Press, 2016.

———, ed. *Los lugares del saber: Contextos locales y redes transnacionales en la formación del conocimiento moderno*. Buenos Aires: Beatriz Viterbo Editora, 2007.

Schaffer, Marguerite S. *See America First: Tourism and National Identity, 1880–1940*. Washington, DC: Smithsonian Institution Press, 2001.

Schávelzon, Daniel. "Dorothy Hughes Popenoe (1899–1932) en la arqueología de América Central." *Cuadernos de Arquitectura Mesoamericana* 14 (1991), 93–95.

Schiebinger, Londa. *Plants and Empire: Colonial Bioprospecting in the Atlantic World*. Cambridge: Harvard University Press, 2004.

Scott, James. *Seeing Like a State: How Certain Schemes to Improve the Human Condition Have Failed*. New Haven: Yale University Press, 1998.

Sheller, Mimi. *Consuming the Caribbean: From Arawaks to Zombies*. London: Routledge, 2003.

Shifflett, Crandall A. *Coal Towns: Life, Work, and Culture in Company Towns of Southern Appalachia, 1880–1960*. Knoxville: University of Tennessee Press, 1991.

Shragai, Atalia. "Do Bananas Have a Culture?: United Fruit Company Colonies in Central America, 1900–1960." *Iberoamericana* 11:42 (June 2011): 65–82.

Slotkin, Richard. *Gunfighter Nation: The Myth of the Frontier in Twentieth-Century America*. Norman: University of Oklahoma Press, 1998.

Smith, Peter. *Talons of the Eagle: Dynamics of U.S.–Latin American Relations*. New York: Oxford University Press, 2000.

Soluri, John. *Banana Cultures: Agriculture, Consumption, and Environmental Change in Honduras and the United States*. Austin: University of Texas Press, 2006.

Spurr, David. *The Rhetoric of Empire: Colonial Discourse in Journalism, Travel Writing, and Imperial Administration*. Durham: Duke University Press, 1993.

Stanley, Diane. *For the Record: The United Fruit Company's Sixty-Six Years in Guatemala*. Guatemala City: Centro Impresor Piedra Santa, 1994.

Stepan, Nancy Leys. *Picturing Tropical Nature*. Ithaca: Cornell University Press, 2001.

Stephens, Clyde. *Bosquejo histórico del cultivo del banano en la provincia de Bocas del Toro, 1880–1980*. Edición de Stanley Heckadon Moreno, [1987].

Stern, Alexandra Minna. "The Public Health Service in the Panama Canal: A Forgotten Chapter of U. S. Public Health." *Public Health Reports* 120:6 (November/December 2005), 677.

Stewart, Watt. *Keith and Costa Rica: A Biographical Study of Minor Cooper Keith*. Albuquerque: University of New Mexico Press, 1964.

Stoler, Ann, ed. *Haunted by Empire: Geographies of Intimacy in North American History*. Durham: Duke University Press, 2006.

———. *Carnal Knowledge and Imperial Power: Race and the Intimate in Colonial Rule*. Berkeley: University of California Press, 2010.

Striffler, Steve. *In the Shadows of State and Capital: The United Fruit Company, Popular Struggle, and Agrarian Restructuring in Ecuador, 1900–1995*. Durham: Duke University Press, 2002.

Striffler, Steve, and Mark Moberg, eds. *Banana Wars: Power, Production and History in the Americas*. Durham: Duke University Press, 2003.

Sutter, Paul. "Nature's Agents or Agents of Empire?: Entomological Workers and Environmental Change during the Construction of the Panama Canal." *Isis* 98:4 (December 2007), 724–54.

Thomas, Nicholas. *Colonialism's Culture: Anthropology, Travel and Government*. Princeton: Princeton University Press, 1994.

Tone, Andrea. *The Business of Benevolence: Industrial Paternalism in Progressive America*. Ithaca: Cornell University Press, 1997.

Topik, Steven, and Allen Wells, eds. *The Second Conquest of Latin America: Coffee, Henequen, and Oil during the Export Boom*. Austin: University of Texas Press, 1998.

Traister, Bryce. "Academic Viagra: The Rise of American Masculinity Studies." *American Quarterly* 52 (June 2000), 274–304.

Truett, Samuel. *Fugitive Landscapes: The Forgotten History of the U.S.-Mexico Borderlands*. New Haven: Yale University Press, 2008.

Walker, Brett. *Toxic Archipelago: A History of Industrial Disease in Japan*. Seattle: University of Washington Press, 2010.

White, Trumbull. *Our New Possessions: A Graphic Account, Descriptive and Historical, of the Tropic Islands of the Sea Which Have Fallen under Our Sway*. Chicago: Henry Publishing Company, 1901.

Wilkins, Mira. *The Emergence of Multinational Enterprise: American Business Abroad from the Colonial Era to 1914*. Cambridge: Harvard University Press, 1970.

————. *The Maturing of Multinational Enterprise: American Business Abroad from 1914 to 1970*. Cambridge: Harvard University Press, 1974.

Wilson, Charles Morrow. *Ambassadors in White: The Story of American Tropical Medicine*. New York: Henry Holt, 1942.

————. *Empire in Green and Gold: The Story of the American Banana Trade*. New York: Henry Holt, 1947.

Withey, Lynn. *Grand Tours and Cook's Tours: A History of Leisure Travel, 1750–1915*. New York: Morrow, 1997.

Zahavi, Gerald. "Negotiated Loyalty: Welfare Capitalism and the Shoeworkers of Johnson, 1920–1940." *Journal of American History* 70:3 (December 1983), 602–20.

Zanetti, Oscar, and Alejandro García, eds. *United Fruit Company: Un caso del dominio imperialista en Cuba*. La Habana: Editorial de Ciencias Sociales, 1976.

Zanetti, Oscar, and Alejandro García. *Sugar and Railroads: A Cuban History, 1837–1959*. Translated by Franklin Knight and Mary Todd. Chapel Hill: University of North Carolina Press, 1998.

Printed in the USA
CPSIA information can be obtained
at www.ICGtesting.com
CBHW031931311024
16729CB00007B/551